Digital Signal Processing
Part B: Applications

Volume 9 Scientist and Science Series

Enders Anthony Robinson
Professor Emeritus of Applied Geophysics
Department of Earth and Environment Engineering
Columbia University in the City of New York
and
Manuel T. Silvia
Naval Underwater Systems Center (Retired)
Newport, Rhode Island

Goose Pond Press

Available from Amazon.com and other retail outlets

Front cover: An image of underground sedimentary earth layers as created by digital signal processing

Copyright © 2019

All Rights Reserved Worldwide

Goose Pond Press

> He that is thy friend indeed,
> He will help thee in thy need:
> If thou sorrow, he will weep;
> If thou wake, he cannot sleep;
> Thus of every grief in heart
> He with thee doth bear a part.

From *The Passionate Pilgrim*
(A book first published by William Jaggard in 1599,
it is a collection of poems commonly attributed to Shakespeare.
However, it is likely that this poem was written by someone else.)

Contents

PREFACE

1. **COMPLEX VARIABLES AND PHASORS** 1

    1.1 The real and complex number system 1
    1.2 The complex plane 7
    1.3 The vector representation of complex numbers 13
    1.4 Phasors 17
    1.5 Applications: The amplitude and Phase pattern of an array .. 21
    1.6 Taylor series 30
    1.7 Laurent series 40

2. **DIGITAL SIGNALS AND SYSTEMS** 49

    2.1 Finite differences 49
    2.2 Difference equations 58
    2.3 Digital signals 66
    2.4 Classification of digital systems 81
    2.5 Impulse response and convolution 89

3. **THE TRANSFER FUNCTION** 99

    3.1 Causal filters and Taylor series 99
    3.2 Noncausal filters and Laurent series 121
    3.3 The Laplace z-transform and the engineering z-transform ... 124
    3.4 Properties of the Laplace z-transform 133
    3.5 The inverse Laplace z-transform 144
    3.6 Invertibility and minimum-delay 153
    3.7 Recursive (ARMA) systems 163

4. **THE FOURIER TRANSFORM OF DIGITAL SIGNALS** 170

    4.1 Frequency domain representation of digital signals and systems. 170
    4.2 Fourier transform of discrete-time signals 183
    4.3 Specialization of the Fourier transform to the case of
        real sequences 197
    4.4 Minimum-delay and minimum-phase-lag 201
    4.5 All-pass systems 210
    4.6 The finite Fourier transform 217
    4.7 The fast Fourier transform, an algorithm for the
        computation of the finite Fourier transform 224
    4.8 Development of the fast Fourier transform 229

5. THE RELATIONSHIP BETWEEN ANALOG AND DIGITAL SYSTEMS 232

   5.1 Mathematical description of the uniform-rate sampling process 232
   5.2 The sampling theorem 239

6. DESIGN OF DIGITAL FILTERS 244

   6.1 Design of moving average (MA) filters 244
   6.2 Design of recursive (ARMA) filters 259
   6.3 Least-squares design of moving average (MA) filters 268

7. THE KEPSTRUM 276

   7.1 Even-odd and real-imaginary relationships for causal systems .. 276
   7.2 Relationship between gain and phase-lag 283
   7.3 The kepstrum 292
   7.4 Removal of an echo 298

8. RANDOM PROCESSES 300

   8.1 Stationary random processes 300
   8.2 Signal enhancement and prediction 308
   8.3 Spectral factorization 314

9. SPECTRAL ESTIMATION 316

   9.1 Harmonic analysis 316
   9.2 The periodogram 318
   9.3 Specialization for real-valued signals 319
   9.4 White noise sample 322
   9.5 The Gaussian and chi-square distributions 324
   9.6 Distribution of the periodogram for a white Gaussian process .. 326
   9.7 Distribution of the periodogram for a Gaussian process 329
   9.8 An example of spectral estimation by transforming the autocorrelation 333

10. SEISMIC DECONVOLUTION 336

    10.1 Exploration for oil and natural gas 336
    10.2 Sedimentary model of the earth's crust 342
    10.3 Random reflection model 354

Preface

Manuel T. Silvia
by Enders A. Robinson

I first met Manuel T. Silvia in 1975. He was a leading scientist at The Naval Undersea Warfare Center in Newport, Rhode Island. He was engaged in efforts ranging from participation in fundamental research to the support of evolving operational capabilities in the U.S. Navy. At that time he was completing work on his PhD degree in electrical engineering at Northeastern University. The University allowed me to be his thesis advisor. His thesis, an important contribution to the field of digital signal processing, attracted much scientific attention. Dr. Silvia is an exceptional person, warm and kind. He has a passion for hard work. His perseverance blends well with his scientific acumen. It might be said that Dr. Silvia is an embodiment of Thomas Edison, who was described as "indeed a pleasant man who goes ardently to his work, which averaged eighteen hours a day."

In those past days, I worked extensively with Dr. Silvia while he was the Seismic Research Manager at Cities Service Oil Company (now Citgo Petroleum Corporation), and professor of electrical engineering at the University of Tulsa.. Dr. Silvia was experienced and successful, known for his leadership skills. He was always devoted to excellence. His services were in demand. Everybody liked him and wanted to work with him. Together we wrote four books. One was *Deconvolution of Geophysical Time Series in the Exploration for Oil and Natural Gas* by M. T. Silvia and E. A. Robinson. It was published in 1979 by Elsevier and it was used as a textbook at leading universities including MIT.

We were separated when Dr. Silvia moved to California. Dr. Silvia used his extensive experience in mathematics, physics, systems engineering, and project management in consulting for educational, business, and government organizations. He taught and created curricula for academic institutions, and performed research in sonar, radar, and missile defense for business and government organizations. He was recognized for his dedication, leadership and excellence in technical and business achievements. He became President and Chief Executive Officer of SITTEL CORPORATION.

Recently, Dr. Silvia retired and returned to the east coast. We finally got together again in person. It was a heart-warming and nostalgic experience. Dr. Silvia and I wrote a manuscript more than forty years ago. As a memento of the golden days of old, I put the manuscript in the form of **Part A Theory** in the accompanying volume and **Part B Applications** in this volume. Our manuscript is written in the form of a standard mathematics textbook in the following sense. The manuscript is self-contained and all concepts are defined in mathematical terms as they are introduced. The chapters are divided into articles, and approximately ten problems are given at the end of each article. The inclusion of the introductory material and the problems make the contents accessible to students without prior knowledge of electrical engineering. In this way, Parts A and B provide an opportunity for a cross-fertilization of ideas between the digital signal processing methods and traditional methods.

This work is written for people interested in obtaining a working knowledge of digital signal processing. It is aimed at easing the entrance into this field so that these methods can be incorporated into areas of research. The emphasis is on the development of an understanding of the concepts involved and an appreciation of the problems faced in applications. The material is presented with sufficient depth to provide the reader with the background necessary to understand the details of the methods. These methods are used in such diverse areas as acoustics, biomedical engineering, data communication and telephony, economics and business analysis, geophysics, picture and image enhancement, nuclear science, oceanography, sonar, and speech communication and recognition.

Dr. Silvia and I want to express our sincere thanks to Professor George B. Thomas of the Mathematics Department of Massachusetts Institute of Technology for many valuable insights in the writing of this book. George B. Thomas was known for his ability to communicate mathematical concepts. He wrote a widely used calculus textbook which had a significant impact on the teaching of mathematics.

We want to thank Mrs. Gardiner W. White for her excellent work in the typing of the manuscript.

Comments by Dean Clark on the Geophysical Analysis Group

Dean Clark writes: The right man, the right time, and the right place (which, believe it or not, was in the vicinity of Boston). In 1950, two professors at MIT, a mathematician and a geologist, used to ride to work together. During one of these commutes, one happened to mention that traces on a seismogram looked vaguely like various lines on weather maps and wondered aloud if the recent developments in the mathematics of time series, pioneered by MIT's resident genius Norbert Wiener and which were being used to assist weather forecasting, could be adapted to "clean up" the notoriously dirty seismic data of that era. As a result, Enders Robinson, who had just received his bachelor's degree in mathematics from MIT and was looking for a master's research project, was given the job. Robinson seemed an unlikely choice. He had grown up only a few miles from the MIT campus (about as far away, then and now, geographically and culturally as you can get from the oil patch) and had never heard the word geophysics. But this was a classic case of the "blank slate" providing the perfect working conditions. The concept of predictive deconvolution was proved within a year (and without the aid of computers) and the famous Geophysical Analysis Group was quickly established. It is a remarkable story in which all the elements (this is a scientific meeting so I can't say stars) arranged themselves in perfect alignment and, as a result, exploration geophysics got a jump start on the digital revolution of the 1960s and the benefit of an innovative thinker who has made major contributions over a period now exceeding a half century.

Preface
Story of the MIT Geophysical Analysis Group (GAG)

By Enders A. Robinson in GEOPHYSICS, Vol. 70, July-August, 2005

Abstract

The beginning of digital signal processing (DSP) took place in the years 1950 to 1954. Using an econometric model, E. A. Robinson in 1951 came up with the method of deconvolution which he tested on 32 seismic traces. Professors Norbert Wiener, George Wadsworth, Paul Samuelson, and Robert Solow were the advisors. On the basis of this work, the MIT president's office in 1952 set up and sponsored the Geophysical Analysis Group (GAG) in the Department of Geology and Geophysics. The GAG was made up of graduate students doing research in digital signal processing. In 1953 a consortium of oil and geophysical companies took over the sponsorship. At first the GAG used the MIT Whirlwind digital computer. In order to do the larger amount of computing required by the consortium, the Computer Service Section of the Raytheon Manufacturing Company was enlisted in 1953. The Raytheon people who played the key role were Dr. Richard Clippinger, Dr. Bernard Dimsdale, and Dr. Joseph H. Levin, all of whom were previously with the ENIAC, the world's first electronic digital computer. As originally built the ENIAC did not use programs stored in memory as a modern computer does. Instead the programming was done by rewiring the physical components for each new problem. In 1948 Clippinger was responsible for converting the ENIAC into the world's first stored-program computer. Prof. John von Neumann of the Institute of Advance Study acted as the consultant for this conversion. For the GAG work in 1953 Raytheon used the British Ferranti Mark 1 computer (which was the commercial version of the Manchester Mark 1 computer for which Alan Turing played a key role). This computer was installed at the University of Toronto to help in the design of the St. Lawrence Seaway. Raytheon was plagued by the frequent breakdowns of the computer, but still produced several hundred seismic deconvolutions for the summer GAG meeting in 1953. The consortium was pleased with the geophysical results but was disheartened by the unreliability of the current state of digital technology. As a result the GAG was directed to find analog ways to do deconvolution. Instead the GAG found that all of the analog methods, and in particular electric frequency filtering, could be done by digital signal processing. In fact, the digital way provided greater accuracy than the analog way. At the spring meeting in 1954 the GAG proposed that all analog processing be thrown out and replaced by digital signal processing. Raytheon was at the meeting and offered to obtain or build all the elements required for digital signal processing from input to output. The conversion to digital was not taken at the time. However that step did happen in the early 1960s, and exploration geophysics has the distinction of being the first science to experience a total digital revolution. Digital processing today provides seismic images of the interior of the Earth so startling that they compare to images of the stars made by the Hubble telescope. The digital method of deconvolution first developed in geophysics made possible the digital correction of the lens of the Hubble telescope.

Introduction

When a person goes to a new place, it seems to take longer to get there than to return. When the person takes the route for the first time, he is engaged in an act of problem solving. Subjective time passes more slowly. On the way back, he knows the route. Subjective time then passes more quickly. With the passage of time, people change. Interests change. Lives change. Priorities change. This story goes back in time a distance of over fifty years, and this return passage may seem quick and easy. However the original forward passage was slow and not so easy. One should not be lured into thinking that things were more or less the same in 1950 as they are today. A computer then was closer to the engines of Pascal, Leibniz, de Colmar, and Babbage than it would be to a computer of today. The changes wrought by computers since 1950 have no counterpart in all the centuries prior to 1950. When I was a boy, our home had a vacuum-tube radio, a heavy bulky device about three feet tall, two feet wide and a foot deep. But I was more fascinated by the crystal set, which was a small and light radio receiver. Its crystal detector was perfected by G. W. Pickard of Amesbury, Massachusetts (the town across the Merrimack River from Newburyport) who on November 20, 1906 patented the use of silicon in detectors. Today silicon has replaced vacuum tubes in electronics. A silicon computer chip weighing less than an ounce replaces by a million-fold, no, by a billion-fold, maybe a trillion-fold, the tons and tons of material that made up a computer of a half-century ago. In fact, a lot of things were different in boyhood. It is difficult to appreciate the greatness of the difference. At the grocery store there were no scanners. Instead the attendant wrote down the prices of the items on a brown paper bag and added the numbers up. Some added the numbers without even writing them down. Grammar schools in the 1930s were closer to the schools one hundred years before than to the elementary schools of today. A pupil had no computer, just a pencil and a pen. Of course, quill pens were not then in use, but wooden pens with metal penpoints were. The pupil had to dip the tip into an inkwell after every few words, and woe to the child that made an ink blot on the paper.

I entered MIT in 1946. A professor asked the class, "This is the Massachusetts Institute of Technology. What is technology?" No student answered. The professor responded, "You will develop technology." All the students had to decide upon a major subject. I chose mathematics. The mathematics majors were required to take a large number of mathematics courses, so we got to know the mathematics professors well and they got to know us. Prof. D. J. Struik was a geometer and also a historian of mathematics. He had many stories. He told us about Blaise Pascal (1623-1662) and his invention of a mechanical calculator. Pascal started on the project in 1642 when he was 19, and three years later he had a working machine. It was quite limited; it could add with some difficulty and subtract with more difficulty. Multiplication and division were beyond its capabilities. Gottfried Wilhelm Leibniz (1646-1716) is best known for calculus, but he also constructed the **Step Reckoner**, a device which, as well as performing additions and subtractions, could multiply, divide, and evaluate square roots by series of stepped additions. Charles Xavier Thomas de Colmar (1785-1870) made the first practically successful calculator. His machine worked on the stepped gear principle of Leibniz. The first patent for this device was granted in November 1820. Derivative devices were still being manufactured after 1900 and some were still in use in the 1940s. See Fig 1.

Fig. 1. The Stepped Reckoner of Leibnitz in 1674

In 1822 Charles Babbage (1791-1871) conceived the Difference Engine. Its purpose was to calculate mathematical tables automatically. The Difference Engine was only partially completed when Babbage conceived the idea of a more sophisticated machine called the Analytical Engine. This machine was a universal calculating engine, a machine that would perform any series of calculations that could be formulated for it. On several occasions Babbage was asked, "If you put into the machine wrong figures, will the right answers come out?" The Analytical Engine was not a logical extension of the Difference Engine concept, but radically different. In it he foresaw all the major components and functions of a modern electronic computer. The operation of the Analytical Engine was controlled by punched cards. The cards were not necessarily fed one after the other in constant succession, but sequences of cards could be reused if necessary (equivalent to a program loop), or depending on the result of a calculation, a conditional jump could be made. The Analytical Engine was never completed. Countess Ada Byron Lovelace, the daughter of one of Britain's greatest poets Lord Byron, was talented in music, languages and mathematics. She described the operation of the Analytical Engine with the words: "We may say most aptly that the Analytical Engine weaves algebraic patterns just as the Jacquard-loom weaves flowers and leaves."

Differential analyzer

The first-year students had to attend lectures in physics in the large auditorium under the great dome. Close by was a room that held the differential analyzer. Often I would walk by, but the heavy wooden door was always closed. Once I tried the door; it was locked. Simply walking in the presence of that machine was mesmerizing. It was the most advanced and best known analog computer at the time. Vannevar Bush started building the differential analyzer in 1930 at MIT. As time went on, he built improved versions. The differential analyzer was a Numerical Integrator (NI). In simple terms, the differential analyzer found the area under a given curve. A ***complex*** device, the differential analyzer was cumbersome, clumsy, and ***massive***. The final version at MIT weighed 100 tons. In addition to all of the mechanical elements (the integrators, torque amplifiers, drive belts, shafts, and gears), it contained 2000 vacuum tubes, thousands of relays, 150 motors, and approximately 200 miles of wire. It used shaft movement to represent variables, gears to multiply and divide, and differential gears to add and subtract. Integration was done by a sharply-edged wheel spinning at variable radius on a round rotating table. To provide amplification, the differential analyzer employed torque amplifiers which were based on the same principle as a ship's capstan. Because the differential analyzer was based upon the measurement of mechanical movements and distances, it was similar in concept to an automatic slide rule.

But for what problem was the differential analyzer used? To explain, we must look back to the First World War. When the Germans fired their new railway gun, the shell went almost twice as far as they had expected. The reason is that they had not taken into account that the drag on the shell was much reduced at the high altitudes reached by the trajectory. From that time on, the computation of accurate ballistic tables became essential. In Maryland, at the Ballistic Research Laboratories (BRL) of the Aberdeen Proving Ground, the U.S. Army Ordnance Department computed ballistic trajectories. Even Prof Norbert Wiener was involved in the computation of ballistic tables at Aberdeen during the First World War. These calculations were an attempt to mathematically model every possible field condition while taking into account the weight and shape of the shell and its propellant charge. The data were compiled into the firing tables that field gunners consulted in order to aim their weapons. In the early 1930s the Moore School of Electrical Engineering at the University of Pennsylvania formed a connection with the BRL. In 1934 a differential analyzer was constructed at the Moore School and another at the BRL, each with the full cooperation of MIT and Vannevar Bush. During the Second World War these two differential analyzers, as well as the ones at MIT, were used to compute firing tables. These machines were all kept busy on ballistic computations throughout the war. In addition several hundred young women were employed to do the same thing by using electrically driven desk calculators. Ballistics became the focus of computing, and MIT had computing securely within its grasp through the Bush differential analyzer. MIT's position of preeminence in computing could not be challenged.

ENIAC, the first large-scale electronic digital computer

Or could MIT's position be challenged? Engineers at the Moore School were thinking. During the war, they decided to design a computer that could do numerical integration (NI) more rapidly than the differential analyzer. The proposed machine would be electronic; that is, it would be an Electronic Numerical Integrator (ENI). And then someone added that it would be even more general still, and so the words "And Computer" were added. The machine was named the Electronic Numerical Integrator And Computer. Its acronym was ENIAC. When completed in 1946, the ENIAC was moved from the Moore School to the BRL at the Aberdeen Proving Ground. Dr. Joseph H. Levin was the Chief of the Machines Branch at Aberdeen. In this capacity he was in charge of its differential analyzer. Would the ENIAC displace the differential analyzer? Levin fought the good fight. He wrote the classic paper (Levin, 1948) which carried the differential analyzer to its greatest attainment.

The ENIAC was digital, but it was not a stored-program computer. The ENIAC was essentially a huge pile of parts. Signals were sent among the components by cables (wires), which were plugged in by hand. To solve a mathematical problem, components of the ENIAC would have to be assembled, mainly through wiring, into a special purpose calculator. After serving in the Army during World War II, Dr. Bernard Dimsdale took a position at Aberdeen early in 1947. On his first day he was handed a nonlinear partial differential equation and a stack of wiring diagrams about a foot thick. Dimsdale was told to compute. Dimsdale fought the good fight. He spent weeks on the ENIAC making wiring connections, and he set hundreds of switches. He connected input and output terminals so as to form digital trunks for the communication of numerical data. The units had to be set up to recognize when they were to operate and which particular operations were to be performed. There were no guidelines available, so everything was a major undertaking. When he threw the power switch on, the vacuum tubes blew out in large batches. The ENIAC had no power control device. Tubes were replaced time and again. He spent some more weeks in rewiring. No luck. The ENIAC was temperamental; it was a nervous machine. Dimsdale told everyone to be careful around it, and never to lean on anything. In time he found whole rows of unsoldered connections within the components. The output was the card punch, and from its chatter he could tell how things were going. He found that the machine was effective only late at night when most of the electric lights in the neighborhood were turned off. Only a perfectionist like Dimsdale had any chance at all. After some more attempts, he finally got the machine to work. It seemed like a miracle. In a few minutes the machine ground out the required answers for this particular mathematical problem. The next mathematical problem would requite a complete new assembly from scratch. It was clear that the ENIAC as designed was a white elephant.

Levin used the analog differential analyzer. Dimsdale used the digital ENIAC. They were the heavyweights. Would it be analog or digital? Dr. Richard F. Clippinger, the head of the Mathematics Division at Aberdeen, stepped in. In 1947 he set out to modify the ENIAC into a stored program computer. He had electronic engineers from Aberdeen permanently assemble the machine into a fixed configuration, a process that took some months. In essence, Clippinger took the assortment of parts that made up the original machine and from these parts built a stored-program computer. For four days a year, John von Neumann was a consultant to Aberdeen Proving Ground. Clippinger and Dimsdale would meet with him on these occasions and they would fill him in on the modifications they were making on the ENIAC. By the summer of 1948 Clippinger had succeeded in converting the ENIAC into the world's first stored-program computer with a programming language (Clippinger, 1948). The programs were fed into the machine on the function tables (the banks of switch-controlled resistor matrices originally designed to hold input data). The new method worked beautifully, but others wanted to go back to the original way. They said the ENIAC was at least six times faster with the old way. But Dimsdale came to the rescue. He said although that is true, it is not important. The old way requires some months to configure the ENIAC, and then a few minutes to do the calculations. The new way requires a few days to write the code, and a few hours to do the calculations. The old way of rewiring the machine for each problem was never used again. Instead a code would be written in the new programming language for each problem. For years it was said that John von Neumann had made this spectacular advance. However von Neumann's role in this achievement was that of an interested consultant; the genesis of the idea came from Clippinger. The IEEE Computer Society presents its Computer Pioneer Award to a person who made significant contributions to concepts and developments in the electronic computer field which have clearly advanced the state of the art in computing. The contributions must have taken place fifteen or more years earlier. In 1996 Richard Clippinger received the Computer Pioneer Award for his conversion of the ENIAC to a stored program computer. The record was finally set straight.

Undergraduates at MIT were required to be in the Reserve Officers Training Corps (ROTC) for the first two years of study unless they were war veterans. The second two years of ROTC were optional, but I stayed in ROTC in Ordnance. The Ordnance supplies and maintains all guns, ammunition and vehicles for the Army. In the summer of 1949, I was sent to the ROTC summer camp at Aberdeen Proving Ground in Maryland. On one Saturday morning those who were interested were given a tour of the ENIAC. It was then that I first met Jim Steward, who worked on the ENIAC. The ENIAC was made up of thirty units, each one eight feet tall, three feet deep, and from two to six feet wide. Lined up side by side, they stretched for eighty feet in a U along three sides of the room. The machine had 18,000 vacuum tubes, 70,000 resistors, and 6,000 switches, and consumed 140 kilowatts of power. The ENIAC included a cycling unit, twenty accumulators, an initiating unit, a high-speed multiplier, a combined division and square root unit, function tables, and input and output units. The function tables were made up of three panels. Data as well as instructions were entered on the function tables by dial switches which were set by hand. These switches selected the digits and signs for each of the 104 values of an independent variable that were stored in each table. In addition to the function tables, there were other ways of supplying the machine with information (data or instructions). The requisite numbers could be put into the machine by means of punch cards fed into the card reader, or by means of switches on the constant transmitter. I did not see Jim Steward again until 1962, when he was head of the Computing Laboratory at Amoco in Tulsa.

Fig.2. Aberdeen Proving Ground, August 1949: The German V1 rocket (and Robinson), the invention that led to communication by satellite.

I graduated first in mathematics with a bachelors degree on June 8, 1950. I also received a reserve commission as second lieutenant. I volunteered for active duty in the Army and was sent to the Ordnance School at Aberdeen Proving Ground. The course would take the summer and then we would be sent to Korea. Again at Aberdeen, I wanted to learn more about the ENIAC. Of course, everything about the ENIAC was secret but I made friends with a programmer. She was one of the bright young women with degrees in mathematics the Army sought to be programmers for the ENIAC. All she had available were unclassified documents, and they were out-of-date government manuals mostly on circuitry. These documents were enough to discourage anyone. I would make valiant attempts to read them but each time she soon persuaded me to put them aside. My first experience with programming came to no avail.

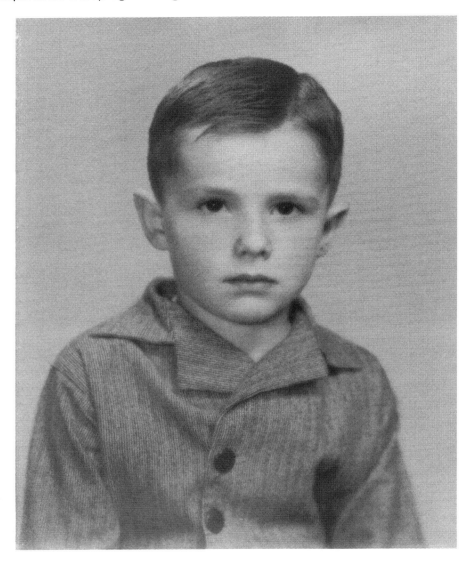

Fig. 3. Enders Robinson, May 31, 1935: the old way to do arithmetic.

Modern computer history begins with the ENIAC. Until 1952 the ENIAC was the main computer in the world for the solution of the scientific problems. The ENIAC logged in a total of 80,223 hours of operation in its lifetime from 1946 to 1955. In addition to ballistics, the ENIAC was used for other scientific endeavors including atomic energy calculations, weather prediction, wind tunnel design, cosmic ray studies, thermal ignition, and pseudo-random number generation. The ENIAC is reputed to have done more arithmetic than the entire human race had done prior to its construction. Included in this previous arithmetic were the additions and multiplications performed by every school child in history. I was one of those children.

MIT from the fall of 1950 to spring of 1951

When I graduated from the Ordnance School in September 1950, instead of being sent to Korea, I was assigned to the early-ready reserve unit at the Watertown Arsenal in Massachusetts. An early-ready unit was a reserve unit that the Army could activate and send anywhere on a 24-hours notice. Back in Massachusetts, I visited the MIT Mathematics Department. Prof. W. T. Martin, head of the Department, was happy to see me, and he gave me a quarter-time teaching assistantship and a quarter-time research assistantship. In this way I was able to start graduate school at MIT. For the teaching assistantship, I taught a class in calculus. I shared a beautiful office in the Mathematics Department with Chester H. Gordon who was working on his PhD dissertation *Tunnel Wall Effects for Non-Uniform Two Dimensional Motion of Thin Airfoils in Incompressible Flow*. When someone asked him about his progress, his answer would be: "Things take time."

For the research assistantship, I worked under Professors George Wadsworth and Norbert Wiener to apply time series methods to seismic exploration. Professor Wadsworth's field was weather prediction, his interest dating back to his successful efforts in World War II. Prof. Wadsworth had completed his PhD dissertation in 1933 on systems of partial differential equations and the geometry of algebraic pfaffians, but later his interest turned toward the field of mathematical statistics. (Johann Friedrich Pfaff obtained his doctorate at Göttingen in 1786. He was the dissertation advisor for both Carl Friedrich Gauss and August Möbius.) The story of how Wadsworth's acquired an interest in geophysics has almost become legend. In the late 1940s, Wadsworth shared a car pool with Patrick M. Hurley, who was a professor of geology, and others. They all lived in Lexington and traveled to MIT each day. On a number of occasions Robert R. Shrock, also a professor of geology, rode with them and learned firsthand how widely the conversation spread throughout the general area of instruction and research. One day Wadsworth and Hurley fell into a discussion about the use of mathematics in geology. As the story goes, Wadsworth was needling Hurley a little bit, chiding him because he thought not enough mathematics was being used in geology. Wadsworth was used to analyzing weather time-series data, which he described as data that "go up and down." Hurley said that seismic traces also "go up and down," and that geophysicists have to "eyeball" them in order to pick reflections. One day, on the way to the car pool, Wadsworth passed by the office of Hurley, who pulled down an issue of GEOPHYSICS with some pictures of wiggly-trace seismic records. "Let me take this along," said Wadsworth, "I'll get Joe Bryan to have a look at it." Joseph G. Bryan was a recent doctorate in statistical measurement theory from the Harvard School of Education, and was working with Wadsworth on weather prediction for the U.S. Air

Force. An inquiry was sent to the Magnolia Petroleum Company which provided eight seismic records. When I showed up, Dr. Bryan with a sigh of relief gladly handed me the eight records. Professor Wadsworth told me to find the reflections mathematically, and suggested using partial differential equations. My entire knowledge of geophysical exploration came from the movie **Gold Is Where You Find It which I saw as a boy. Except for** some scenes of mining operations I did not remember much about the film except that it starred the beautiful actress Olivia de Havilland. And then for years I pondered over the metaphor "Gold is where you find it." Gold is the elusive goal for which a person strives. And now for the first time I went to the Geology Library. The library had every book and journal on all aspects of geology, and many maps and drawings. I found GEOPHYSICS. I pored over the past issues. In *Exploration Geophysics* (Jakosky, 1950), I read: "The problem of primary importance in the study of the reflection seismogram is to recognize reflections on the records."

Professor Norbert Wiener was also overseeing the seismic research. He had a great interest in the applications of theory to practice. Nobody in the Mathematics Department wanted to go to lunch with him because "all he did was talk and talk." I did not mind. I listened. In the spring semesters Prof. Wiener would go to Mexico, and I was moved into his office to save space. There I was alone with Wiener's books and mementos. Although I was in the Mathematics Department, I wanted first to get a Master's Degree in the Economics Department under Professors Paul A. Samuelson and Robert Solow. Later each of them would win the Nobel Prize. While taking Samuelson's advanced graduate course on economic analysis in the spring semester, I worked out a mathematical model for the Schumpeter theory of economic innovations. I converted Schumpeter's verbal analysis into equations. I used Wiener's work together with classical time series analysis.

The problem was to find the innovations underlying economic time series. The crucial link was the recognition that the onset of an innovation, such as a new technological advance, cannot be predicted. Thus the onset of each innovation produces a definite and measurable prediction error. On this basis, the timing of the economic innovations can be found from the economic time series as follows. First compute the prediction operator for the given time series. Next apply the prediction operator to obtain the predicted values. However, the predicted values are not the object of the analysis. Instead, the prediction errors are desired. The prediction errors can be obtained by subtracting the actual values of the time series from the predicted values. These prediction errors represent the desired economic innovations. Could the same time series method work in exploration geophysics? My plan was to take the digitized seismic traces and treat them as economic time series. Then I would carry out the prediction error filtering. In modern terminology the process is called deconvolution. The prediction error series is the deconvolved time series.

MIT in the summer and fall of 1951

In the past Wadsworth had a full staff of people who were adept at using desk calculators. However, only Virginia Woodward was left of the original group. In the summer of 1951, Professor Wadsworth relented and let me have the use of her calculating expertise for a few weeks. I was on active duty in the Army at that time working on the gun books of the antiaircraft artillery used in World War II. Each large-caliber gun used in the war had a gun book in which was recorded each time the gun was fired together with pertinent notes. With the help of three enlisted men, all veterans of World War II, I spent the daylight hours in the subterranean vaults at the Watertown Arsenal where the records were stored. The fire control of these guns represented the area for which Professor Wiener had directed his work on prediction theory. I was now applying **the antithesis, namely prediction-error theory,** to seismic analysis. After finishing at Watertown in the evening, still in uniform I would take the old 1910 vintage streetcar (trolley) to MIT where I would start work. So, in both places, you might say, I worked in the dark. I laid out the required calculations at night and left them for Ginny to pick up in the morning. She faithfully did her work while I was at the Arsenal, and left the results for me to pick up that night. Ginny worked for some days on the Marchant desk calculator to set up and solve normal equations. Next I had her compute the prediction errors. Then one night I plotted the prediction errors (the deconvolved traces). The reflections stood out like a sore thumb. Deconvolution worked. It was August 1951.

I made an appointment to see Professor Wadsworth, and in a few weeks I was able to meet with him. He transferred me from seismic analysis to weather prediction, the deconvolution results notwithstanding. However, when Professor Hurley was shown the results he was ecstatic. In the fall semester 1951, I had to leave seismic research and work instead on the meteorological problem of measuring the characteristics of the coal-induced smog in London, which in peak outbursts was responsible for ill health and even death. Today London has clean air because of the use of North Sea natural gas instead of coal. The great discoveries of oil and natural gas in the North Sea were made possible in part by deconvolution.

In October 1951 Professor Hurley introduced me to Howard Briscoe, who was a geophysics undergraduate student. Briscoe was an outdoors person, a camper and a skiing enthusiast. He also knew how to code on the Whirlwind. He told me about Whirlwind. At the end of the war, MIT made plans to retain its preeminent position as the world's center of computing. A whole new stable of analog machines was planned around the differential analyzer. But surprisingly quickly the effort collapsed. In 1950 the MIT provost confessed to the MIT president that MIT has missed its chance to retain leadership in computing. And what was the reason? It was the ENIAC, and the host of digital computers that it spawned: the EDVAC, the ORDVAC, the UNIVAC, the Institute of

Advanced Study computer, the JOHNIAC, the MANIAC, the ILLIAC, the SILLIAC, the EDSAC, the Manchester Mark 1, and looming up, right at MIT, the Whirlwind. Let us explain. With the differential analyzer in mind, the government in 1943 gave MIT a contract to build a flight training simulator. Jay W. Forrester was the director of the Project, and the assistant director, Robert Everett, later became a founding father of the MITRE Corporation. For a real-time simulator, speed was essential. The proposed analog simulator was appropriately called Whirlwind. However an analog device turned out to be too slow to calculate the responses to a pilot's actions. In desperation Forrester went to see the ENIAC in November 1945. The result was that Forrester changed Whirlwind into a digital computer.

My recitation teacher in physics in 1946-1947 was Professor George E. Valley. The lectures had a large number of students; the recitation classes had a small number. I clearly remember Prof. Valley trying to teach us how to solve the difficult physics problems assigned as homework. In fact MIT, for the most part, just taught us how to solve problems. There were few conversations on the beauty of the universe. For that you would have to go to Harvard. At the MIT Radiation Laboratory in Building 20, Prof. Valley had developed the directed radar that played a strategic role in World War II. After the war he worked on the air defense of the United States using the radar technology. On a visit to Whirlwind in 1950 Prof. Valley realized that the answer would lie in the marriage of computers and communication. This idea was the germ that grew into the Internet. The U.S. Air Force took over the funding of Whirlwind, which became fully operational in 1951.Whirlwind was the prototype and test bed for a new system called SAGE that would provide computerized electronic defense against an air attack.

Fig. 4. The MIT Barta Building: "And they shall reap the whirlwind."

The Barta Building behind the MIT campus was the home for Project Whirlwind. The building was linked by telephone lines to radar sites. The computer occupied 2500 square feet on the second floor. The MIT Digital Computer Laboratory with its programming and maintenance personnel had offices on the first floor. Whirlwind was a single-address binary computer. It had 4,500 vacuum tubes and 14,800 diodes. Because short words helped real-time operations, Whirlwind had a 16-bit word structure instead of the longer formats geared for scientific computations. Initially the high-speed memory (RAM) was electrostatic storage with a size of 1,024 words. Within a few years the electrostatic storage was replaced by magnetic core memory, and the size was increased. Initially the add time was 20,000 additions per second (0.05 ms per addition), but it was increased to 50,000 additions per second. Power supplies were located in the building's basement and the roof was covered with air conditioning equipment to cool down the system. Power generation for the building was approximately 150 kilowatts. A system implemented by J. H. Laning and N. Zierler on Whirlwind in 1953 was the first algebraic compiler system. It used subscripted variables, function calls and expression translation. It was the first recognizable compiler with all modern features, but it was never ported to any other machine. IBM took note of the Whirlwind compiler in its subsequent development of FORTRAN. Whirlwind was a real-time computer that was at the heart of a communications network. Whirlwind had leapfrogged all of the other computers that had been spawned by the ENIAC. The stored-program ENIAC was the invention that brought forth computing as the confluence of the two streams of calculation and programming. Whirlwind was the invention that brought forth cybernetics as the confluence of the two streams of communication and computing.

MIT had regained leadership, but now it was in communication and computing. Project Whirlwind was to evolve into a continental air defense system that exceeded the Manhattan project in cost and scale. The system was called Semi-Automatic Ground Environment (SAGE). IBM built the computers, Burroughs developed communications, Western Electric constructed the concrete "Direction Center" buildings, and MIT (and, after 1958, a MIT-formed not-for-profit corporation called MITRE) provided system integration. By the time the system was fully deployed in 1963, the 23 Direction Centers and three Combat Centers were linked by long-distance telephone lines and radio contact to more than 100 interoperating air defense elements. At the heart of SAGE was the giant Whirlwind II (AN/FSQ-7) computer. Each of the Direction Centers was equipped with two Whirlwind II computers: one operating live and one operating in standby mode for additional reliability. SAGE required system integration on a scale previously unimagined. Whirlwind II ran the largest computer program written up to that time, with 500,000 lines of code. SAGE employed digitized radar data, long distance data communications via landlines and ground-to-air radio links, and featured a large collection of interactive display terminals. The program automated information flow, processed and presented data, and provided control information to the weapons systems. The communications devices from Burroughs allowed each center to communicate with other centers, creating the first large-scale computer network. SAGE was responsible for training more than 10,000 programmers in the 1950s, and many later worked for the Advanced Research Projects Agency (ARPA). SAGE pioneered the important technology which is used to facilitate Internet processing today; for example, the modem, the mouse in the form of a light gun, multi-tasking, array processing, computer learning, fault detection, and interactive computer graphics. When this technology was transported to ARPA, the result was ARPANET. The Internet sprang from ARPANET. The last of the Whirlwind II computers shut down in 1983, giving Whirlwind the record for practical operational longevity among all digital computers. But in a larger sense, Whirlwind never shut down; its technology drives the Internet. As Hosea 8:7 says, "For they have sown the wind, and they shall reap the whirlwind."

Whirlwind was the first step toward the still unfulfilled vision that Professor Wiener had put forth in his book: *Cybernetics, or control and communication in the animal and the machine* (Wiener, 1948). Chapter 3, entitled *Time series, information, and communication*, contains the mathematics which Howard Briscoe and I started to program on Whirlwind in the fall semester of 1951. Briscoe and I wrote various programs for digital filtering and deconvolution. I was 21 years old then; Briscoe was about the same age. Around the Digital Computer Laboratory there were few people who were much older. I never saw a professor enter there. In the meantime Professor Hurley was anxious to exploit the deconvolution results. I prepared a document, an extract of which reads:

> "The purpose of the study carried on at MIT during the summer of 1951 was to answer a few specific questions regarding the behavior of seismic records considered as time series. The data used were eight records each resulting from a single shot and consisting of four traces produced by the output of four geophones placed along a line with the center at the shot-point. These data were supplied by Magnolia Petroleum Co. The question to be answered is: Is it possible to determine the points where a deep reflection occurs in the record through purely statistical means by observing a change in the dynamics of the system at that point? The tentative answer to this question based entirely upon the analysis of the before mentioned records is as follows: Linear operators were constructed for the data. The operators were then utilized to predict the period during which the reflection occurred. In every case the errors of prediction increased very markedly during this period, and, after the interval of time during which the reflection occurred, the errors dropped back to approximately their previous values. On several of the records the deep reflection failed to occur as it had in most of the seismograms, but nevertheless, in these instances the errors of prediction jumped up in the same manner. This introduces a new approach into the problem of determining when additional energy is introduced into the system through reflection from a deep layer. Enclosed is a graph indicating the errors of prediction previous to the reflection, during the reflection, immediately after the reflection, and the beginning of a new reflection."

On November 1, 1951 Professor Hurley sent my document to the Magnolia Petroleum Company in Dallas. Magnolia was the production arm of the Socony Vacuum Oil Company, later renamed Mobil Oil. On November 29, 1951 D. H. Clewell, the Assistant Director of the Field Research Laboratories, sent Professor Hurley the response: "Your letter of November 1 has been circulated here at the Laboratories, and the results you presented are distinctly of interest. The curve you sent shows excellent signal-to-noise for a single trace, and a multiplicity of curves derived from geophone signals in a conventional reflection spread would appear to show great promise. We have no very good appreciation of the mechanical operations required for predicting the geophone signals and displaying the difference between predicted and measured signals. Unless instrumentation can be developed to do this rapidly, the method would probably be difficult to apply to commercial prospecting. Is it correct to assume that the operations stand a chance of being instrumented for rapid use?" I knew the answer to Clewell's question. The operations could be instrumented for rapid use on a digital computer. I set objectives. My first objective was to make deconvolution operable on a production basis by the use of Whirlwind. If this could be done, my second objective would be to demonstrate that deconvolution worked on an assortment of seismic records. If this succeeded, then my third objective would be to provide a geophysical model that justifies deconvolution.

GAG in the winter and spring of 1952

In the fall of 1951 Professor Hurley succeeded in raising $13,000 from the MIT President's Office to cover the costs of the first stage of an expanded program of the seismic project. I received the master's degree in economics in January 1952 and then transferred to the Department of Geology and Geophysics, accepting the appointment as Research Associate. The Geophysical Analysis Group (GAG) officially came into existence in February 1952. Stephen Simpson as well as Briscoe joined the GAG. Simpson was a graduate student in geophysics who had received his undergraduate degree in physics at Yale. Briscoe and I continued working on the Whirlwind codes. Unfortunately Briscoe had to leave for ROTC summer camp before the deconvolution code was finished. I completed it but the code would not work. Frantically I checked everything. In those early days, everything was written in the octal number system in machine language. The hand-written program was given to two typists, each of whom typed the program on paper tape in binary form. Then the two tapes were compared. If the tapes matched, it was assumed the typing was correct. The tape was left with the computer operator who would run it whenever time became available in a lull in the military needs or in maintenance. Maintenance of a vacuum tube computer would take about eight hours a day on good days. As a result one run a day at the machine was considered good. Upon request, the computer operator would print out the contents of memory (in octal) at the time the program failed. Because these memory dumps were so difficult to interpret, I found it better to have the program itself print out numerical flags along the way which would indicate approximately at what point the program failed. Finally after a couple of weeks I discovered the reason why the deconvolution program did not work. The reason was that there was a little spot on the coding sheet itself. Each typist mistook this spot for a comma, so this extraneous comma was punched into the paper tape. Once corrected the deconvolution code worked. On July 4, 1952 I told my brother about these troubles, and he remarked, "Computers will never work." Despite my brother's forebodings, the program worked to deconvolve some more seismic traces in time for a planned August meeting.

Meeting in the summer of 1952

The MIT Industrial Liaison held the meeting on August 6, 1952. The meeting was entitled a Conference on the Generalized Harmonic Analysis of Seismograms. The results of everything done to date were presented. Two reports were discussed: *Results of an Autocorrelation and Cross-Correlation Analysis of Seismic Records* and *A Prospectus on* the Application of Linear Operators to Seismology. Those attending were: L. Y. Faust (Amerada), H. F. Dunlap (Atlantic), R. B. Bowman and Dr. W. W. Garvin (California Research), R. R. Thompson (Carter), R. M. Bradley (Cities Service), W. E. N. Doty and J. M. Crawford (Continental), T. J. O'Donnell and W. C. Dean (Gulf), D. H. Gardner (Humble), Dr. W. J. Yost (Magnolia), R. G. Piety (Phillips), R. Vajk (Standard Oil Company, New Jersey), Dr. D. Silverman (Stanolind), W. Evans (Sun), H. J. Jones and D. B. Dubbert (Texas Instruments Company), Dr. E. Eisner (The Texas Company), C. A. Swartz and F. B. Coker (United Geophysical), and R. R. Shrock, P. M. Hurley, G. P. Wadsworth, Norman A. Haskell and E. A. Robinson (MIT). The invited guests were leading geophysicists from major geophysical companies and from all the major oil companies except Shell. Shell had a standing policy to go it alone. This pleasant meeting with outstanding and renowned geophysicists full of ideas and enthusiasm was a success. These geophysicists were an exceptional breed of scientists, and they lent an aura of excitement to the undertaking that was unequaled anywhere at MIT.

The first part of the meeting covered autocorrelation and crosscorrelation analysis. I remember asking if it were possible to use a controlled signal in seismic work, as is done in radar. The response was negative, but apparently Conoco thought otherwise. In Conoco Geophysics: The First Fifty Years, published by Conoco (November 25, 1975), the invention of VIBROSEIS is described in the section entitled "John Crawford and Bill Doty, Co-inventors of VIBROSEIS." It reads:

> "On August 6, 1952, W. E. N. (Bill) Doty attended the symposium, "Harmonic Analysis of Seismograms," presented at the Massachusetts Institute of Technology in Boston. Bill came away from this meeting with a firm feeling that the Information Theory Technique which had been described could be beneficially applied to Seismic Exploration. Returning to Ponca City, he immediately expressed this opinion to John Crawford. John concurred with Bill and the two of them set out to determine a practical means whereby crosscorrelation could be applied to seismic signals. The first breakthrough came with the suggestion by John on August 18 that a "sweep signal," that is, one which continually changes frequency in one direction during transmission, would provide the desired non-repetitive, long-duration signal. Thus, cross correlation of the transmitted and received signals could provide the basic requirement of the seismic system; i.e., travel time between transmission and reception of a signal."

The second part of the meeting covered the application of linear operators to seismology, which was the old terminology for deconvolution. There was a lot of interest, and the unanimous feeling was the companies should sponsor this research at MIT. Future plans for the GAG were made in the fall of 1952 under the leadership of Professor Hurley for MIT and Dr. Daniel Silverman of Stanolind for the oil and geophysical companies. The two reports discussed at the August 6, 1952 meeting were mimeographed and sent to the companies as MIT GAG Reports No. 1 and No. 2. Professor Hurley went out to gather support. I met with Professor Hurley in his office on October 9, 1952. He brought up points concerning a recent trip he had made to Dallas, Texas where he conferred with the Magnolia Petroleum Company and with Geophysical Service, Inc. He said that that the feelings expressed in Dallas were that the GAG should analyze in considerable detail one record. The interrelation of parameters should be studied with the view of determining optimum values of parameters. In addition, the effect of the shot hole variable (i.e., amount of powder, local characteristics of hole and explosion) should be studied. The records from Florida were also discussed. In particular, the question was asked: Are the ghosts and multiple reflections on these records "real" physical phenomena or are they due to the very narrow filter systems used? Another consideration was whether it would be worthwhile to compare error curves from Florida records with error curves from the Persian Gulf records. The Magnolia Petroleum Company's velocity logger was discussed. This machine determines the velocity of strata all the way down a drill hole. Professor Hurley said that Magnolia is correlating reflections with change in velocity and density.

Raytheon in the fall of 1952

In the fall of 1952, it was clear that the GAG would need quite a bit of machine time on Whirlwind to do the seismic processing. I applied for five hours per week; only one hour a week was granted. In practice the GAG did not even get that much time. The reason was that hardware improvements were still being made in Whirlwind so the machine had a lot of down days. At that time, the maintenance time on Whirlwind's memory alone was four hours per day, and the mean time between memory failures was two hours. We looked for an alterative, and found Raytheon. The Raytheon Manufacturing Company in Waltham, Massachusetts had recently established its Computer Services Section. Richard F. Clippinger was the Head of the Section. With him were his friends Bernard Dimsdale and Joseph H. Levin. Before entering Raytheon, Clippinger was responsible for the ENIAC, EDVAC, and ORDVAC computers at Aberdeen; Dimsdale was responsible for numerical analysis at Aberdeen; and Levin was responsible for the SEAC computer at the National Bureau of Standards. Looking back now after a time span of over fifty years, I might say that Clippinger was the relentless driver, Dimsdale was the absolute perfectionist, and Levin was a kind and loving person. All were powerful mathematicians; it was a pleasure and an honor to work with them.

The GAG had its first meeting with Raytheon on October 17, 1952. The GAG was doing mostly multichannel deconvolution. Matrix inversion had to be used for the solution of the normal equation in the multichannel case, because at that time the Levinson recursion was known only for the single channel case. The short register length (16 bits) on Whirlwind made accurate matrix inversion difficult even with double precision arithmetic. Unless the data were "well-behaved," the computations would cause overflow and the inversion would fail. The GAG was primarily interested in having Raytheon do the formation and the inversion of matrices, which was termed the "Half-Case." Raytheon would use a computer of longer word length, which would ease the overflow problem. The GAG felt that Whirlwind could effectively handle the remainder of the computations (the computation of prediction errors) effectively. Raytheon seemed anxious to do a greater percentage of the work and the GAG agreed to have Raytheon submit an estimate on two cases, one the "Half-Case Computation" and the other the "Full-Case Computation." Raytheon's motivation seemed to be connected with the nature of our research. This research was to prove or disprove the deconvolution method of seismogram analysis. If the method proved valid, Raytheon would be in a position to offer deconvolution services, backed by pertinent experience, directly to the oil industry. In addition Raytheon would be sufficiently familiar with the problem to design especially suitable computing equipment.

On October 28, 1952 Raytheon submitted an estimate. The computation of 1,000 full cases (with two traces each) would cost $12,400, or $12.40 per case. These figures were so low that a month later (November 25, 1952) MIT appropriated $1,000 for Raytheon to begin the necessary coding study. The purchase order reads:

> "Computing services covering coding study and preliminary code for seismogram analysis program. Deliver flow diagram and preliminary code on or before Jan. 1, 1953. Amount not to exceed $1,000.00. Purchased from Raytheon Manufacturing Company. T. R. Porter, Manager, Technical Sales."

On December 23, 1952 Raytheon delivered the flow diagram and preliminary code. I still have these papers; they are in the handwriting of Clippinger and are dated Dec. 17, 18 and 19, 1952, and initialed R.F.C.

In fact, Raytheon went beyond the $1,000 mark on assurances that a contract would be negotiated shortly after a project conference with the sponsoring oil companies was held. Raytheon, in turn, assured us that the code would be working properly as soon as we were ready to hand in data, about the first week in February 1953. The understanding of the mechanics of the arrangement was that the "cases" were to be passed in to Raytheon in small batches and that processing by Raytheon would take about two weeks for each batch. This is an important point. In research work, experiments designed to test a method should be designed from knowledge of the behavior of the previous experiments. If one has to design a series of experiments all at once, guessing the outcome of each, there is bound to be inefficiency and useless expense.

By February 1953 all of the oil and geophysical companies had joined in the venture and the GAG came under their sponsorship. One or two representatives from each sponsoring company made up the Advisory Committee. Some of the representatives were in geophysical research while the others were in geophysical operations. Two meetings of the GAG with the Advisory Committee were to take place each year; the winter meeting would be in the Southwest and the summer meeting at MIT. In all there were four such meetings in which I was involved: the Dallas meeting on January 30, 1953; the MIT meeting on August 12-13, 1953; the Tulsa meeting on March 29-30, 1954; and the MIT meeting on September 14, 1954. Once each meeting was over, I more or less had to run the GAG on my own until the next meeting. As a result all the students on the GAG would learn how to use computers. One of my first tasks was to teach Stephen Simpson how to program. He was a little reluctant at first, but all of a sudden the computer bug grasped him and he became one of the foremost programmers of all MIT, and the strongest advocate of computers.

Additive model and analog processing

Refection seismology operates on the echo principle. A shot of dynamite emits a source pulse which travels down into the earth where it is reflected from the subterranean strata. Seismometers on the surface pick up the reflected pulses. In those days the means of observing the lengths of time required for the pulses to travel the round trip from the source to the reflecting strata and back to the seismometers was provided by recording the seismometer outputs on a strip of moving photographic paper. Each trace on the paper represented the response of one seismometer to the shot. In addition to the energy derived from the source, the seismometers also pick up energy not derived from the source. This non-source energy would include such things as wind noise and highway traffic noise. However, such extraneous energy is generally held to a low level. It is usually so minor that it is not significant on seismic traces. As a result, virtually all the energy on an exploration record is due to the shot.

In the ideal case a trace would consist solely of the sequence of reflection pulses, which was called the signal. However, in addition to the desired reflections, the seismometers also pick up a lot of other energy. This other energy is unwanted. Its includes such disturbances as instrument response, direct waves, surface waves, refracted waves, diffracted waves, transverse waves, sustained strata vibration, ghosts, multiple reflections and reverberations. In those days this complexity of unwanted energy was called either interference or noise. The model used for a seismic trace was the *additive model*. In this model the trace is the sum of signal plus noise; that is,

$$\text{trace} = \text{signal} + \text{noise}$$

where the signal is the set of reflection pulses and noise is the interference. The signal was desired; the noise was the trouble-maker. Good records resulted when the noise level (the interference) was low. In such cases the interpreters could see the signal (the set of reflections) on the traces. Poor records resulted when the level of noise was high. In such cases the interpreters had trouble seeing the signal (the set of reflections) on the traces. The problem became one of recognizing the true reflections hidden in the confusion of the interference. In other words, the problem was one of separating signal (the reflections) from noise (the interference). Unfortunately, some geologically promising areas of exploration yielded seismic records on which few if any reflections could be picked visually. Seismograms that could be interpreted only with much uncertainty as well as records that could not be interpreted at all were called no-good (or interference) records.

The problem was the separation of signal and noise. In those days this problem was attacked by frequency filtering. Any waveform has a frequency spectrum. The spectrum has two components: the amplitude spectrum and the phase spectrum. For most studies the phase spectrum was not used. As an example, consider the case in which the amplitude spectrum of the noise peaks at 18 Hz and the amplitude spectrum of the signal peaks at 26 Hz. A bandpass filter centered at 26 Hz would pass the dominant frequencies of the signal and would reject the dominant frequencies of the noise. Thus the output of the bandpass filter would tend to preserve the signal and destroy the noise. Electric analog filters were used to do such frequency filtering. There were other ways used to enhance the signal. One of the most important was mixing. Mixing was the term used for the addition of two or more adjacent traces so as to form one output trace. A trace by itself was referred to as zero mixing, the sum of two traces was referred to as two channel mixing, and mixing weighted by a tapering function was referred to as graded mixing.

Originally the filtering and mixing were done in the field at the time of the recording of the seismic waves. By the early 1950's some oil companies had multichannel recording and reproducing equipment for the benefit of seismic crews operating in poor record areas. This service involved broadband recording of the seismic energy in reproducible form. Analysis could then be conducted back in the laboratory which was more conducive to detailed experimentation than the field. In order to suppress noise and accentuate signal, the broadband records would be run through various electric analog filters, such as high-pass, band-pass and low-pass. This approach represented the introduction of analog processing to seismic exploration.

Meeting in the winter of 1953

The winter meeting of the GAG with the Advisory Committee was held in Dallas on January 30, 1953. On the night before the meeting I had dinner with Professor Hurley. He said that oil companies are chiefly interested in finding oil. Existing techniques work about 95 percent of the time. Florida is an exception. In looking to the future, progressive companies realize that more powerful methods may be needed. This explains their interest in the GAG. Use of oil, exhaustion of reserves, and discovery are all going up exponentially. Oil company operations are limited by funds, but chiefly by trained personnel. One trained paleontologist may be of more marginal value to increasing production than one trained theoretical physicist. Also the lack of funds requires trained personnel to do lower caliber jobs, e.g. a geologist must cut his own thin sections. Many promising methods are never tried, e.g. the determination of minor elements by a spectroscope. Also much paleontology is never worked out because of the lack of personnel, micro-paleontology in particular, which must be worked out and classified from the very beginning in each area. Most geophysicists and geologists in the Texas area are from local schools and have obtained only B.S. degrees. Doctorate degrees are rare; Magnolia with three PhD's on their research staff probably has the most. Hence the geologists and geophysicists have a limited amount of theoretical knowledge. New PhD's are highly respected, although they still have to go through some practical training. And so his discourse went. He then brought up the blueberry analogy. He said the adage about blueberry picking probably holds in oil, namely, the slowest person who stayed at one bush picked more berries than fast people who kept running from bush to bush. For example, companies like Gulf and Magnolia who have expended much effort on research have not discovered oil at as good a rate as others who stick to conventional methods. He concluded by saying that picking where to drill a new well is a relative choice as there are many acceptable regions. Many wells must be drilled on geology alone because of the lack of seismic crews. In sedimentary basins oil is expected and is not an exceptional thing. In such a region a pure wildcat well has one chance in 18; and with the aid of geology and geophysics the chance is better.

The meeting started early the next morning. We told the cab driver: The Magnolia Building at Akard and Commerce Streets. The cab driver said he had a guy from New York yesterday who kept bragging about how quickly New York keeps putting up beautiful new buildings. Being a good Texan the cab driver drove the New Yorker past the Magnolia Building. The New Yorker asked: What is that magnificent building? Better than anything we have in New York. And the cab drive answered: I don't know. It wasn't there last week. I think I remember this story because Dallas made such a great impression on me. Texas was magic.

At the Dallas Advisory Committee Meeting on January 30, 1953, Dr. Daniel Silverman was the Committee Chairman, a position he held throughout the lifetime of the GAG. Those present at the meeting were L. Y. Faust (Amerada Petroleum Co.), H. F. Dunlap (Atlantic Refining Co.), N. A. Riley (California Research Corporation), R. R. Thomson (Carter Oil Co.), Richard Bradley (Cities Service Oil Co.), J. M. Crawford (Continental Oil Co.), L. F. Peters (Gulf Research and Development Co.), P. E. Haggerty (Texas

Instruments Co.), W. Jacque Yost (Magnolia Petroleum Co.), R. G. Piety (Phillips Petroleum Co.), D. Silverman (Stanolind Oil and Gas Co.), A. C. Winterhalter (Sun Oil Co.), B. D. Lee (The Texas Company) and P. M. Hurley and E. A. Robinson (MIT). Not at the meeting were O. H. Gardner (Humble Oil and Refining Co.), C. A. Swartz (United Geophysical Co.), and Henry Salvatori (Western Geophysical Co.). The agenda for the day's meeting was agreed upon. It was divided into two main divisions; the technical aspects of the prediction theory research, and the administration problems connected with the immediate program at MIT. Professor Hurley described the general characteristics of the results obtained in the past with the aim of indicating the various directions the research work might take in the immediate future. The results to date indicated that deconvolution (prediction-error filtering) did detect reflections that could be seen visually, and in addition it did detect at least some reflections that could not be seen visually. But this work was performed on relatively good records. The problem was to test deconvolution on more difficult records.

Two points of view were presented regarding the type of study to be assigned the highest priority. From one viewpoint, the prediction error curves (deconvolved traces) should be compared with various other methods for interpreting seismograms. The other viewpoint was that considerable geological, geophysical, and logging data from the area under study should be used in evaluating the prediction error curves. While the majority seemed to favor the former approach initially, it was agreed that the data should be in such a form that the latter approach could be followed whenever it seemed desirable to any of the interested groups. As a result, it was agreed to supply the MIT project with all the significant data pertinent to the area in which the seismograms under study were obtained. It was further agreed that the initial studies would be based upon seismograms from a reasonably simple geological section. The second point of agreement was that the first few seismograms to be submitted should come from reproducible records in order that at least three sets having different filtering and/or mixing could be supplied from the same original data. These would include: (i) an original recording of 12 traces through a 20-120 cps channel having faithful reproduction within this band; (ii) this same record after it had passed through a narrow band filter in the low frequency range; (iii) similarly for a higher frequency filter; and (iv) the best filter and/or mixing which the group supplying the data had been able to obtain.

It was agreed that these initial test areas should include at least five shot holes in a profile where the record quality did not change appreciably from shot to shot. Then, several seismograms would be obtained from a single shot hole with variable depth and size of the shots. All of these requirements were summarized. The Texas Company, Continental, and Magnolia each agreed to try to get a set of such seismograms together with the available geological data for the section released by their company's management and sent to Professor Hurley at MIT. At least one of these three sets would be studied so that a fairly detailed report can be made by MIT in June 1953. In addition to these sets, other types of sets were considered by the group. It was decided that sets of more complexity would then be supplied by other sponsors. Stanolind, Atlantic, and Cities Service each agreed to try to get suitable records released for this later study. Other companies would study their files and contact Professor Hurley if they have suitable records. I presented the computing scheme that MIT planned to use, including "operator" solutions to be done by Raytheon and the **prediction-error** process on Whirlwind. Initially, the GAG would plan to take about ten cases per seismogram. Since the capacity is estimated at 60 cases per month, this would mean six seismograms to be analyzed each month.

The task to be done was quite clear. The GAG would first develop a digital processing system with Raytheon that could handle a large number of cases, and then use the system to detect the reflections on the records supplied. There was general agreement on this objective and all the members of the advisory committee spoke with one voice. The purpose of the GAG was to verify the validity of deconvolution as a seismic processing scheme. The results were to appear in the next GAG reports, together with theoretical work on digital signal processing as applied to seismology. The Committee went along with the Raytheon proposal for the computing and left the details of the experimental procedure to the GAG. No budgetary changes for the GAG project were felt necessary. The Advisory Committee gave the GAG four months to carry out this task. Early in June 1953, the GAG would prepare a report covering this work. This report would be distributed to each participating company for study. The Advisory Committee would meet at MIT, at least ten days later, to discuss and examine the report. The Texas Company was the first to submit seismograms to the GAG for this purpose. On February 3, 1953, B. D. Lee of The Texas Company wrote to Prof. Hurley: "We are busy today running off the records which you have requested and we will forward them to you as soon as they have been washed and dried." On the next day he sent 18 seismograms (which we named Records 12.1 through 12.18) made up of six traces each. Another seismic record (which we named Record 12.0) was also sent.

GAG in the winter of 1953

In February 1953 Mark Smith and William Walsh joined the GAG as research assistants. Barbara Halpern became secretary and Irene Calnan became technical assistant. Simpson was finishing up his PhD dissertation so his available time was limited. I started teaching Smith and Walsh about computer programming. Raytheon and I were left do the seismic processing. The GAG moved into new quarters in Building 20, a wooden structure in which the MIT Radiation Laboratory had developed radar during the war. The view from our windows was of a grassless courtyard with some old dismantled radar equipment. One of the office doors did not work. There was not even a screwdriver handy. Yet Mark Smith (later vice president of Texas Instruments) fixed the door. He said, "In the GAG we do things with our bare hands."

At the onset of World War II, British scientists had developed microwave radar to detect enemy aircraft. However, they were unable to perfect or mass produce the magnetron tube which was the heart of the radar's function. At the suggestion of MIT's Radiation Laboratory, a meeting was arranged between Britain's leading scientists and Raytheon. Raytheon not only came up with radical changes that would simplify the manufacturing process, but also ways to improve the functioning of the radar. Impressed, Britain awarded, through the MIT Radiation Laboratory, "little" Raytheon a small contract to supply the magnetrons. At the same time it awarded "giant" Western Electric a large contract. By the end of the war, Raytheon was producing 80 percent of all magnetrons, leaving Western Electric, RCA, GE and other giants far behind. During the war Raytheon also developed the microwave SG radar, a shipboard radar that was far superior at sea to the radars carried in planes. Raytheon discovered microwave cooking in 1945, and in 1947 Raytheon demonstrated the world's first microwave oven. For the Office of Naval Research, Raytheon built the Hurricane computer. In 1948, Raytheon became the first company to develop a missile guidance system that could hit a flying target. In 1948, Raytheon also released the first commercially produced transistor, the CK703 point contact transistor. Raytheon followed this by the CK722 germanium junction transistor, the first transistor sold to the public. In 1954, Texas Instruments released the first commercially produced transistor radio. Raytheon responded the next year with its own version of the transistor radio, the 8TP-4. Transistors were to completely revolutionize computers and electronic technology.

On February 2, 1953 the GAG held a meeting with Raytheon representatives. A few days later Raytheon sent prices for the work involved in the programming, the reading, the computation, the supplying of operator coefficients, and the final charting of the error curves (deconvolved traces) for the seismograph records to be supplied by the GAG. The price of programming and analysis was $2,800 and the price per Half-Case Computation (assuming 50 half-case computations per month) was $7.50 each, and price per Full-Case Computation (assuming 200 full-case computations per month) was $15.00 each. Each would be for two values of prediction distance. Since a total of 250 cases per month would not be possible, an agreement was reached with Raytheon on February 9, 1953 whereby the GAG would pay $2800 for programming and analysis and order a total of 320 full-case computations at $16.50 each, with the understanding that half-case computations could be prorated. Thus the contract came to a total of $8,080 made up of $2,800 and $5,280. There was an understanding that there would be flexibility so changes could be made underway. Raytheon was willing to do this on the grounds that they were feeling their way in this type of computation. The total of 320 cases represented about five months computational work at the rate of about 60 cases per month. Thus 320 cases would cover the months of February through June 1953.

Raytheon decided to use a machine at the University of Toronto for the GAG computations. The Toronto machine was called FERUT (for Ferranti at UT). Raytheon selected this machine for this project after a careful survey of the few large scale electronic digital computers available for commercial computations. The FERUT operated in the binary number system. Its overall dimensions were two bays, each of which was 16 feet long, 8 feet high, and 4 feet wide, and a control desk. The power consumed was 27 kilowatts. The computer had about 4,000 vacuum tubes and 15,000 resistors. Its multiplication time was 2.2 ms (i.e., about 450 multiplications per second). Its addition time was 1.2 ms (i.e., about 833 additions per second). The input was punched teleprinter tape which was read photoelectrically and fed in at rate up to 200 characters per second. The output was punched teleprinter tape at 10 characters per second or direct printing by teleprinter at 6 characters per second. It had internal high speed electrostatic storage (RAM) of 256 words (a word being 40 binary digits, i.e., about 12.1 decimal digits). Its magnetic drum had storage for about 16,000 words.

Some of the advantageous aspects of the Ferranti Computer for seismogram analysis work were: a fairly satisfactory input speed, very satisfactory computational speed, and large drum storage. A disadvantage of the machine for this type of computation was its small electrostatic storage (RAM). For an extensive computation, such as the one under discussion, many instructions were required (some 1,000 instructions), as well as large amounts of data. When read in initially all this information was stored on the magnetic drum, and must later be transferred to the electrostatic storage for use in many successive relatively small blocks. The most important consequence of this fact was the difficulty of preparing the code and consequent possibilities of coding errors which must be located and corrected before the problem was run. Another limitation of the machine which was expected to be relieved sometime in the not too distant future was its slow output speed. While it was possible to reduce loss of time due to this cause by taking advantage of the fact that the machine could compute during printing, in any specific case other coding considerations sometimes limited the extent to which this could be done.

Spring of 1953 and the trip to Toronto
On February 17, 1953 the GAG submitted Job No. 1 to Raytheon. This job consisted of 60 half-case computations with two values of the prediction distance each. The breakdown was 35 half-case computations on Record 10.9 (Magnolia), 10 half-case computations on Record 7.5 (Atlantic), and 15 half-case computations on Record 12.0 (The Texas Company). The predictions and the error curves were to be done on Whirlwind. In a telephone conversation on March 3, 1953, Clippinger told me that

Raytheon will complete some cases in 3 weeks and the rest of the cases of Job No. 1 in 5 weeks. On March 9, 1953 the GAG submitted Job No. 2 to Raytheon. This job was on 18 records (Records 12.1 through 12.18) of The Texas Company. As of then no results had been forthcoming. On March 16, 1953 I telephoned Raytheon and spoke to Levin. He said that the Toronto machine was broken down all last week. Raytheon was still checking the code for the matrix solution. Meanwhile Levin was writing the error curve code. In a telephone conversation on March 20, 1953, Clippinger said he underestimated the amount of time it would take to get cases back to us. He said that the codes are not working because of machine errors and coding errors. However, he said that by May 15 the 320 cases would definitely be done. They have computed one 9 by 9 matrix solution by hand; this took 40 hours. They would not compute any more by hand at the present time. They were now ready to read our records. Ours was the only major computational problem that Raytheon had undertaken and top management was interested in the success of this problem. There was no need for concern on our part at this time.

I talked with Prof. Wadsworth on March 25, 1953. He suggested that the Advisory Committee Meeting should be postponed from June to September, and for me to write a theoretical paper by June that could be sent to the oil companies. This paper would include research on the theory of difference equations with numerical examples as well as other work along these lines. Professor Wadsworth also suggested that there should be a meeting to discuss the question of subjects for Ph.D. theses. An overall policy should be considered for the research work the half-time research assistants would be doing.

At a meeting on April 1, 1953, Raytheon said it still would take two more weeks to process the data. A realistic estimate of the delivery time of computational Jobs No. 1 and No. 2 would be May 1. On April 13, 1953 I saw Levin. He said that he saw Clippinger in Toronto two days earlier. Clippinger reported that he was getting along fine. A good part of the code was corrected and he wanted to come back in another week. Levin would go up the end of this week. The difficulty had not been fundamental. There were errors in coding. The machine was operating 24 hours per day, and now was enjoying about 50 hours of good time per week rather than the 4 to 6 hours of good time per week previously. The main project in Toronto was the St. Lawrence River waterway. This project received 3 full days of machine time per week. The rest of the time **was** distributed among all other problems, including ours.

On April 27, 1953 I talked by telephone with Clippinger who was back in Massachusetts. He said things were not going as well as Raytheon would like. He just had a call from Levin in Toronto. There were 20 subroutines in the problem. Of these there were 8 working, another 6 were pretty close to working, and there were about 4 Levin was working on. I asked if the cross-products code was working. He said yes, and that Levin was working on getting the operator coefficients from the inverse matrix. I said that if he could get that part working, we could do the rest on Whirlwind. I added that if things really looked hopeless we could postpone the Advisory Committee Meeting until September. The meeting was planned for the middle of June. Clippinger answered that by May 15, Raytheon should have an excellent idea of where things stood. We should not make plans to postpone the meeting. The chances on getting the material on June 1 were excellent. He was working day and night, and was going back to Toronto for 10 days, leaving the next day.

In a telephone conversation on May 8, 1953, Mr. Porter of Raytheon told me that he had received a telephone call from Canada in which he had been told that Raytheon had good time on the machine last night. Mr. Porter said that solutions may be expected within the next two weeks. In the spring of 1953, Raytheon was plagued with the unavailability of sufficient machine time, largely because of frequent breakdowns of the FERUT. It must be remembered that both the Whirlwind and Ferranti computers were newly designed and were still being tested. This was the first digital signal processing ever to be performed, the whole experience new even for seasoned computer veterans. These computers had no floating point arithmetic at that time, so there was always the problem of overflow unless the data were carefully scaled beforehand. Professor Wadsworth was visited with nightmares. He wrote to Professor Hurley, "Dear Pat, I woke up in the middle of the night worrying about the large expense that we are going to incur by having all the computations done at Raytheon this year and next. In order that I may sleep better during the night, would you please check over and be sure that we have sufficient money to carry this burden and that we have not used too much of it on staff." The result was that I was told to go to Toronto.

And so I went by night train to Toronto accompanied by Clippinger and Levin. The old railroad coach, vintage about 1890, was lit by only two overhead lamps hanging from the ceiling. The swinging back and forth created a dance of shadows as the steam engine chugged along into the dark and unknown. Clippinger started talking. I was captivated. He talked about Alan Turing. A brilliant original thinker, Turing published *On Computable Numbers* in 1934. This paper laid a theoretical foundation for computer principles. Formally a mathematician, Turing covered a whole spectrum of subjects, from philosophy and psychology to physics, chemistry and biology. He combined high-level thinking with hands-on experience with machinery and experiments.

Clippinger said that in 1948 the British government developed the Small-Scale Experimental Machine (SSEM) which, while simplistic, showed the potential for a stored-program electronic computer. At the University of Manchester the British quickly developed the Mark 1, a more powerful and usable machine designed primarily for scientific research. Turing came to the University of Manchester in September 1948. In the summer of 1949 he was instrumental in acquiring paper tape equipment for the Mark 1. The British government commissioned Ferranti Ltd. to produce the Mark 1, which turned out to be the first commercially available computer. The first Ferranti Mark 1 debuted in 1951 and the following year, the University of Toronto purchased the second Ferranti Mark 1 (the FERUT) which they were using to design the St. Lawrence Seaway.

This was a working trip. I wanted to help. Clippinger gave me a lesson in coding for the FERUT. He said that Turing was mainly responsible for the decision to use the base-32 numerical system. To do any serious programming, I would have to learn the following table of correspondence between the 32 digits of the number base, their numerical equivalent, and their equivalent in binary notation. Both the binary form and the base-32 form of numbers were written with the least significant digit to the left. This convention was for the convenience of the engineers.

0	00000	/		8	00010	½		16	00001	T		24	00011	O
1	10000	E		9	10010	D		17	10001	Z		25	10011	B
2	01000	@		10	01010	R		18	01001	L		26	01011	G
3	11000	A		11	11010	J		19	11001	W		27	11011	"
4	00100	:		12	00110	N		20	00101	H		28	00111	M
5	10100	S		13	10110	F		21	10101	Y		29	10111	X
6	01100	I		14	01110	C		22	01101	P		30	01111	V
7	11100	U		15	11110	K		23	11101	Q		31	11111	£

Clippinger said that the 40 digit binary number

01010 00011 10011 01100 00110 10100 00011 00011

would be written more concisely as the 8 digit base-32 number: ROBINSON. He said that a 20-bit instruction was written as four characters and a storage address as two. He told me that the 5-hole tape could be read directly. He said that you can read the information on the display tube easily, particularly in relation to instructions, as a 20-bit line on a display tube was laid out in four groups of 5 bits, each of which corresponded directly with a base-32 character. To Clippinger, all this was duck soup.

Now came the work. The fun was over. I was to check out a subroutine that was not quite working. I held the sheets in my cold hands. I would get so far, and then lose track. Programming in the base-32 system seemed archaic. I was used to the simple and powerful Whirlwind language. The railway carriage rocked from side to side, and lunged back and forth. Like Robinson in Daniel Defoe's novel, the feeling came over me that: "We knew nothing where we were, or upon what land it was we were driven - whether an island or the main, whether inhabited or not inhabited." Clippinger and Levin sat there in the dim light diligently working on the programs. Finally at Levin's encouragement I was able to leave them to their labors, and I slipped off to the sleeping car. I barely got to sleep when I was being shaken by two Canadian policemen. The train was at the Canadian border and they needed to see my passport.

Once in Toronto, we gulped down breakfast and then went directly to the computer. The computer was in an old run-down university building. The furnishings were sparse, but I did find a small table at which I could work. I was determined to get that subroutine working. We worked all the day and the following night as well. In the middle of the night, they ran the computer codes that had been previously written by Dimsdale back in Massachusetts. Dimsdale's codes worked on the first try, most likely the only time such a miracle ever happened on this arcane computer. We ran the subroutine with my corrections. It did not work. For the next few hours I made more corrections. We ran it again. It still did not work. Clippinger said that eating every four hours eliminates the need for sleep. I did not believe it. A small nearby all-night diner supplied this requirement, and the food did taste good. Another try and still my code did not work. But, as Ralph Waldo Emerson said, "Bad times have a scientific value. These are occasions a good learner would not miss."

When the sun rose on that second day, a blessing (at least for me) happened. The university said the computer would be unavailable for part of the day. My joy was unbridled. I could not wait to get in bed. We went to the shabby room that we shared upstairs in an old small two-story wooden house. The floors creaked. It might be described as some sort of primitive bed-and-breakfast without the breakfast. Fortunately I had the cot bed that was to one side of the room. It was hard and lumpy. The shades were drawn but, instead of sleeping, Clippinger sat in bed going over the computer results obtained so far. I slept in fits and starts. Too soon it was time to go back to that dread computer and the diabolical code devised by Alan Turing. I sat at my table and worked on the subroutine. Those few precious hours of sleep had revived me. Clippinger relished each moment unaware of the passage of time. Levin set a straight course. Things were beginning to work. I made a couple more unsuccessful tries. About 2 AM the next morning, I had another chance on the machine. This time the subroutine worked. I felt the exhaustion. Levin came to my rescue and directed me to a cold wooden bench hidden somewhere in the dark recesses of the old building where I could lie down. Soon I fell into a deep sleep, only interrupted by dreams of computers, computers floating on a sea of seismic waves. And the waves were made up of wavelets, wavelets everywhere all in a random sea. Then all at once I was awakened by Clippinger running in. It was first light, the crack of dawn. He exclaimed all the programs were working. Still half asleep, I went out and looked at the lights flashing on the console. Clippinger and Levin could read them easily. I could not read them. To me the output in the base-32 devised by Turing was still unintelligible. I would have to wait until the numbers were plotted. Now Clippinger and Levin ran a large batch of the GAG data. The cases were ground out one by one. I looked forward to the train ride back to Boston.

meeting in the summer of 1953

On July 1, 1953 the GAG held a meeting with Raytheon at MIT. Raytheon said that as of the present time they have completed 56 half-case computations and 17 full-case computations. Clippinger presented the costs incurred by Raytheon to date. They were:

Costs of analysis, coding and checking in machine	$26,130
Machine Rental (at $100 per hour of good time)	
a. Checking	$2,640
b. Production of 56 half cases and 17 full cases	$2,970
Administrative Costs	$9,750
Reading of Records	$3,900
Graphing	$1,170
Travel	$3,000
Equipment	$1,000
Total	**$50,560**

Out of the total time used on the machine, 70 percent was no good, for which they were not charged. When the machine went down for a week, the work of Dimsdale, Clippinger and Levin plus the work of two or three woman assistants was wasted for that period. Also because of the deadline, the coding had to be divided up among the three. As a result there was inefficiency in that they would not know what the other person was doing when one was in Canada and the other in Massachusetts.

The professors thought that the funds would be better used for accepted academic research. Prof. Shrock later remarked, "It was not surprising that there was a question about the future of high-speed computers; even experienced scientists and engineers did not foresee what was to come. I had to clear up the whole financial mess before the meeting with the Advisory Committee now scheduled to take place on August 12-13, 1953. I met with T. R. Porter who was the manager of technical sales at Raytheon. The GAG had asked Raytheon to do extra things that were not covered in the original contract. In a letter to me on August 5, 1953 Porter wrote:

> "With reference to our conversation and discussion regarding the contract under which we are now operating covering the costs of computing services for the seismograph analysis program, we wish to offer the following solution to the situation as it now stands." The solution was a new contract price of $9180.

The old contract price was $8080. The total addition was $1100, and that amount covered the extra work that we had asked Raytheon to do. Porter concluded the letter with: "In the meantime, we are continuing this work on the supposition that the above will be agreeable with you."

Raytheon had developed a fully operational deconvolution system. According to the IEEE History Center, Raytheon offered to the industry at large what must have been the first commercial digital signal processing service. Never before had computers been used to process large amounts of digital data. Before this time, computers had been used to solve mathematical equations which involved little actual data. The Ferranti computer itself was a severely limiting factor. Its layout was not suited for digital processing, and yet Raytheon had completed the task. The Ferranti with its long word length, slow speed, and slow output was good for computing the deconvolution operator (the half-case) but not good for performing the deconvolution (the remaining portion of the full case). On the other hand, Whirlwind with its short word length, fast speed, and fast output was not good for computing the deconvolution operator but good for performing the deconvolution. Both computers had a small RAM (the Ferranti with 256 words, and Whirlwind with 1024 words). According to Raytheon, twenty-four man months of effort were required to program seismic deconvolution and to check the codes on the Ferranti computer. A year earlier, Howard Briscoe and I had completed an admittedly much less-powerful programming task on Whirlwind. When Briscoe and I started in 1951, there was just primitive machine language, and we had to write our own double precision code. In its way, our work influenced the thinking of the Digital Computer Laboratory in its development of Whirlwind as a computer to handle large amounts of air defense data.

On July 8, 1953 we submitted MIT GAG Report No. 3, *Case Study of Henderson County Seismic Record, Part I* to the Advisory Committee. This report contained computational results on Magnolia Petroleum Co. Record 10.9. This record was acquired and digitized by the GAG before the Advisory Committee Meeting on January 30, 1953. In Job No.1, 35 half-cases for this record were submitted to Raytheon. Because there were two values of prediction distance for each half-case, there would be a total of 70 deconvolution operators in all. The first twenty-eight sets of operator coefficients were returned to the GAG by Raytheon on May 26, and additional sets were returned to the GAG on June 16. For these sets of operator coefficients the GAG computed on Whirlwind the prediction error curves included in this report. Error curves for operator coefficients supplied to us by Raytheon after June 16 could not be included in this report because of lack of sufficient operating time on Whirlwind. The record was shot in Henderson County, Texas, where about sixty feet of loose Carrizo sand is underlain by Wilcox sandy clay with lignite stringers. Magnolia considered this a problem area because of the loose sand. Record 10.9 was an interference record that exhibited no clear reflections. However, Magnolia had marked five reflection times on the top trace. A different shooting procedure, which showed the reflections, provided the basis for indicating these refection times. Deconvolution easily picked up all the reflections on Record 10.9.

On July 21, 1953 we submitted MIT GAG Report No. 4, *Linear Operator Study of a Texas Company Seismic Profile, Part I* to the Advisory Committee. This report contained computational results on the records that The Texas Company sent to the GAG in February 1953 (Records 12.0 -12.18). The ancillary information was a velocity survey from a well located approximately 9,000 feet on strike from shot point C11X and an electric well log at a well approximately 300 feet northeast of shot point C11X. These interference records had a highly ringing character. As a result, the autocorrelations were also highly ringing. The attendant large values of the autocorrelation coefficients made the matrix inversions difficult. This complication is the reason Raytheon had to scramble and reprogram a much more accurate and more costly matrix inversion. This imperative cost valuable time in the spring that we had not counted upon. However we were still able to run 30 deconvolutions on each of 10 seismic records. In other words we had run 300 deconvolutions in all. Each digitized trace and each deconvolved trace had about 600 points, which represents 1.5 seconds of seismic time at a spacing of 2.5 ms. In the 300 deconvolved traces there were 300 times 600, or 180,000 points to plot by hand. Corners were cut to get the job done in time. A seismic attribute of the deconvolved trace was plotted, not the trace itself. Each value of the attribute was based upon ten consecutive values. Only every tenth point of the attribute was computed and plotted, because the complete plot would require ten times the work. The deconvolution results looked good. The deconvolution removed the ringing and gave a consistent set of reflections.

On August 4, 1953 we submitted MIT GAG Report No. 5, *On the Theory and Practice of Linear Operators in Seismic Analysis* to the Advisory Committee. This report contained research work done by the Geophysical Analysis Group since February 1953. Section 7 was *Discussion of machine solution of seismogram analysis program* by R. F. Clippinger and J. H. Levin of the Computer Services Section, Raytheon Manufacturing Co. Section 7 first discussed the short range prospects of price reductions: "It is anticipated that future production costs will undergo substantial reductions. Clerical costs for tape preparation (a rather intricate procedure requiring extreme care to eliminate any possibility of error) have been reduced as personnel became more experienced, and are expected to undergo still further reductions. Supervisory costs have similarly undergone reductions, and may also be expected to decrease further. In addition to reduction of labor costs, there exist numerous possibilities for reduction of machine time per case. At present 5 minutes of machine time are required for a half case and 15 minutes for a full case. Only a relatively small part of this time is used in actual computing. For full cases, for example, computing takes about 5 minutes, and printing about 10 minutes. This situation is expected to improve with the introduction of a parallel high speed printer in the not too distant future. This will decrease printing time to 25 per cent of its present figure, or better. At present the cost of output printing for a full case is approximately $18. At the current rental rate this could be expected to be reduced to $4.50, or less, a reduction of at least $13.50. If one assumes that the improved facility results in increasing the rental by as much as $20 per hour, the printing cost would still be reduced to $5.40, or less. A number of possibilities exist for reducing the cost of solution on FERUT by amending the program. For example, the program may be modified so that the computer will take in the master tapes corresponding to the traces, and for each case will call for parameters and other identification information from a short supervisory tape. The proper portions of the traces will then be selected, and the computations carried out. When all required computations are completed, a new set of traces would be called in. This type of revision would eliminate the necessity of preparing specific data input tapes for each case. This is only one of several kinds of coding improvements that would result in cost reductions."

Section 7 then discussed the prospects of long range improvements: "From a long range point of view it might be worthwhile to seriously consider the possibility of doing this problem on a machine having magnetic tape input and having digital to analog facilities for output. It is understood that seismogram recordings are already made in some cases on magnetic tape. With the type of equipment under consideration it should be possible to feed the recordings directly into the machine and to program the machine for analyzing these recordings. The output would be converted from digital to analog form and recording pens would draw the error curves (deconvolved traces) directly. There is good reason to believe that a long range program of development along these lines might result in prices below $20 per full case."

In Section 8, the deconvolutions done by hand in the summer of 1951 on the original eight Magnolia records (now named Records 10.1 through 10.8) were redone on Whirlwind and the complete plots of the deconvolved traces were given. Everything worked fine.

The summer meeting of GAG with the Advisory Committee took place on August 12-13, 1953 at MIT. Those attending were L. Y. Faust (Amerada), H. F. Dunlap (Atlantic), R. B. Bowman and W. W. Garvin (California Research), R. R. Thompson (Carter), R. M. Bradley (Cities Service), J. M. Crawford and W. E. N. Doty (Continental), T. J. O'Donnell and W. C. Dean (Gulf), D. H. Gardner (Humble), W. J. Yost (Magnolia), R. G. Piety (Phillips), R. Vajk (Standard Oil Company, New Jersey), D. Silverman (Stanolind), W. T. Evans (Sun), H. J. Jones and D. B. Dubbert (Texas Instruments), E. Eisner (The Texas Company), C. A. Swartz and F. B. Coker (United Geophysical), R. R. Shrock, P. M. Hurley, G. P.

Wadsworth, N. A. Haskell, E. A. Robinson, S. M. Simpson and M. K. Smith (MIT) and R. F. Clippinger, B. Dimsdale and J. H. Levin (Raytheon).

The GAG presented the computer results and new theoretical material. The focus of attention turned to deconvolution of the interference (ringing) records given in GAG Report No. 4. At the winter meeting on January 30, 1953 I had given the impression that the computations would go smoothly based upon our experience with Whirlwind. On Whirlwind the Air Force always used parts, such as vacuum tubes, of the highest quality **even** though they were much more expensive. Project Whirlwind had a large operating budget. FERUT operated on a shoestring. The maintenance personnel at Whirlwind were always bustling about. In comparison FERUT seemed deserted. At this summer meeting on August 12-13, 1953 we kept mentioning all of the machine downtime on the FERUT. The representatives were rightly discouraged. However, the computing feat in itself was remarkable. No reflections at all had been marked on any of these records. The study showed that the deconvolution removed the reverberations and yielded a consistent set of reflections. This achievement was a turning point. For the first time the Committee entered into a lively and heated discussion. All at once everyone became involved in one way or another in this venture. No one liked the way in which the deconvolved traces were graphed. This poor presentation was a drawback. The numerical values of the traces and of the deconvolved traces were given as backup material, but just the sight of this mass of numbers was daunting. Attention turned to how the results should be displayed. There was considerable discussion. The committee suggested to the GAG that the deconvolved trace should always be plotted and never the attribute. A uniform plotting scale should be used and the traces should be grouped on a single large sheet for easier study. A suggestion was made that automatic plotting equipment be investigated. The GAG said it planned to use the oscilloscope screen on Whirlwind that was capable of displaying real-time text and graphics.

And the Lord said,

> "Behold, the people is one, and they have all one language; and this they begin to do, and now nothing will be restrained from them, which they have imagined to do. Go to, let us go down, and there confound their language, that they may not understand one another's speech."

So the Lord scattered them abroad from thence upon the face of the earth, and they left off to build the city (*Genesis 11*). Geophysicists were not a homogeneous group, at least not the members of this committee. There were field geophysics and there were research geophysicists. Their education was in geophysics, or in geology, or in physics, or in electrical engineering, or in business. At the Dallas Meeting on January 30, 1953, the Advisory Committee decided that the GAG would test deconvolution on a large number of cases. In other words, the purpose of the GAG was to verify the validity of deconvolution as a seismic processing scheme. There was general agreement on this objective and they spoke with one voice. But now, six months later, there was no such single-minded objective. Each person had to reconcile the new digital way of thinking with his own experience. As a result, a whole potpourri of research projects was thrust forward, from theoretical physics to computation of tables. Before, the committee was one, and they had all one language; and deconvolution they began to do, and nothing would be restrained from them. But now their language was confounded, they did not understand one another's speech. They were scattered abroad, and they left off building deconvolution.

I thought that this scattering abroad into uncharted territory was useful and exciting. To understand geophysics one has to understand the different languages of science. The theoretical discussions were wide ranging. There were questions asked about the properties of the linear operators and the relationship of these properties to conventional filter theory. The representatives wanted the GAG to study the statistical character of the noise itself as it appears on the seismic record. They talked about the energy loss of a seismic wave, and whether it is the result of visco-elastic damping or the result of scattering from a distribution of inhomogeneities in the earth. They discussed the relationship of the behavior of seismic energy in a complex earth which contained many scatterers to the concept of entropy in thermodynamics. It was mentioned that research being done elsewhere on pulses of light diffusing through fog might have some bearing on these ideas. It was suggested that the GAG set up a physical model in which the waves would be reflected from various reflectors and scatterers. And so went the theoretical discussions.

The relationship between the deconvolution operator and the correlation function was discussed in terms of the theory. It was suggested that a study of the correlation functions for a given record should precede the calculation of the deconvolution operators. The present computer programs did not provide the entire correlation function, but only those coefficients used in the calculation of the deconvolution operator. More study of the relation between these coefficients and the complete correlation function should be made. The committee wanted the GAG to start computing the filter characteristics of deconvolution operators on Whirlwind. The Fourier analyzer of the Carter Oil Company was mentioned. It was suggested that the GAG should specify electric analog filters that were equivalent to the deconvolution operators. A way to do deconvolution by electric filters was desired. Then the existing equipment for the analog filtering of seismic records could be used. Two related points were discussed. One point was the computation of an average operator for an entire record. It was suggested that a particular record or set of records be used for this purpose. In such a study, various methods for obtaining an average operator would be compared. The other point was the use of an average operator on various traces. The objective would be to find sets of deconvolution time-domain operators that could be realized by electric frequency filters. The position of many of the members of the Committee was clear. They liked deconvolution; they did not like digital. They would be happy if the GAG were to find an equivalent analog process for deconvolution.

Attention turned to the results recently published in the July issue of GEOPHYSICS by Frank and Doty (1953) of Continental. The article discussed an interference record from a poor record area. In accordance with the additive model, a sequence of artificial pulses is superimposed at intervals along the interference record. In other words each new trace is made up of the interference trace plus the added superimposed pulses. The added pulses represent the signal, and the original interference record represents the noise. To suppress the noise, Frank and Doty developed new methods of frequency filtering based upon the signal-to-noise ratio. They reported that "the difference in results is so striking, in many cases, that the interpreting personnel are hesitant to accept the improved results as data." The article made a strong case for analog seismic processing with electric frequency filters. The general feeling was that frequency filtering held the answer. There was discussion on the use the additive model. This model was well accepted as the one to be used. The representatives wanted to take interference records and then artificially introduce fictitious reflection signals. The upshot was that Bill Doty agreed either to supply a set of his Continental records or ask Magnolia to supply similar records. Since the Atlantic interference records were ready for computations, it was suggested that work should be started on them with artificial refection pulses added. Then, it was suggested, a second set from Continental or Magnolia should be studied. To me the true reflections were hidden in the interference record, so why deal with superimposed artificial reflections at all?

The Raytheon representatives discussed their computational work. They emphasized that the big computer load was that of data handling and correlation work rather than the solution of simultaneous equations. Raytheon also described the service they could provide to interested companies now that the deconvolution programs were developed. They proposed that the data be recorded on magnetic tape so it could be directly read into the computer. They also could rent a better computer or build a computer for the computations. A plotting device could be directly connected to the computer. Several people emphasized the importance of such computer experience as a by-product from all this work. Raytheon was trying to sell seismic processing to the oil companies. However, at that point in time the companies either individually or as a whole were not ready to launch into such a venture.

Prof. Wadsworth discussed some of the difficulties to be expected when the operator coefficients became too large. He also emphasized the strong correlation existing among the various terms chosen and how this produced a certain indefiniteness in the operators. Finally, he outlined a much broader problem concerned with the relationship between the prediction work and the solution of the complete boundary value problem for seismic wave propagation. During the various sessions of the meeting, many good ideas had been put forth. At the last session of the meeting, I summarized the suggestions that had been made for future work. I was to mail this list, together with appropriate explanatory notes to all participating companies. Each company would then return a copy of this list to MIT along with their suggestions as to the relative emphasis they want placed on these items. In summary, the oil and geophysical companies were pleased with the deconvolution results but **were** disheartened by the unreliability of the current state of digital technology. The consensus was that the GAG should find analog ways to do deconvolution.

Treitel and the return to reason

There was no way to carry out all the individual research projects discussed in the August 12-13, 1953 meeting that the various members of the committee wanted. After the meeting, I drew up a review of all the items and the questions that were raised in the discussions. Certain additional problems as well as recommendations were included in this review. The review was mailed to the Advisory Committee for evaluation and comment. It was stated that any suggestions as to the priority to be given to the items would be welcome. For this elaborate review we only have a record of two of the responses, both poised in general terms. One was from Atlantic; the other was from Magnolia. My return letter to Magnolia read as follows: "Thank you for your letter of October 7, 1953. We find that your comments are very helpful in helping us plan our course of action. We agree with you that our outline of priorities is too ambitious for the time remaining before December, and we shall attempt to confine our work sufficiently to give meaningful results. We have already undertaken work relating to items in Section I-A and Item 10 of I-B. At this time we have had comments only from one other company. This company indicated that work should be pursued on Item 1 of Section II-B. We feel that you have a good understanding of the problems we are working on, and as a result your comments are very valuable to us."

Item 1 of Section II B was: "Picking of Weak Reflections in a Controlled Experiment. In this problem a controlled wavelet is superimposed on all traces of a "no- record" seismogram and linear operators are chosen to detect this artificial reflection. Signal-to-noise ratios and signal-to-noise frequency differences may be carefully controlled so that a comparison of results with other techniques may be made. Since this approach has been used with filtering techniques by Doty and Frank of Continental, it is convenient to use the same records and signals employed in that study. This relieves the MIT group from making the frequency and amplitude analysis necessary for setting up the problem. Also the experiment may be carried out with existing automatic computational facilities. The MIT group can carry out this experiment on the "no-record" seismograms supplied by the Atlantic Refining Company. In this case reflections would have to be introduced numerically and a study of frequency characteristics would be necessitated. As yet the group does not have automatic facilities for computing spectra but it does plan to have digital computer programs for doing this in the near future." Within weeks the GAG finished coding these programs on Whirlwind.

Thomas Edison said, "Our greatest weakness lies in giving up. The most certain way to succeed is always to try just one more time." Our deconvolution programs were working. One more time we would try to convince the companies of the practical value of deconvolution. If we succeeded, deconvolution would cease to be a research curiosity and instead would become a commercial product used in oil exploration. As a result, I decided not to add artificial reflections on the Atlantic ringing records as the Advisory Committee wanted, but instead to deconvolve them as they were recorded. Raytheon was anxious to finish up the contract. I had Mark Smith choose some deconvolution cases for these records. One of his handwritten notes says:

> "Motivation for choosing operators and operator intervals on Records 7.7, 7.8, 7.9. Two operator intervals selected as characteristic of record noise on 7.7, i.e., no evident reflections. One each on 7.8 and 7.9. The average period of the oscillations seems to indicate that 8 lags would be a good choice on the predicted trace, and the neighboring traces were chosen for maximum cross-correlation. Also selected to shut Raytheon up."

In September 1953 the GAG took on four new research assistants. They were David Bowker, Robert Bowman, Freeman Gilbert, and May Turyn. In February 1954 Sven Treitel joined the GAG. During the fall of 1953 the GAG undertook a training program for the new research assistants. This program consisted of regular conferences and discussion periods with the new members and the presentation of a course in the statistics of time series with geophysical applications. Sven Treitel also participated in this course. His wisdom and foresight were to open up an entire new era for the GAG. A sympathetic person he had the understanding and the good judgment that were much needed. Digital projects were assigned to the new GAG members. In particular, to Freeman Gilbert I assigned the task of doing the digital frequency filtering on the Continental records with their artificially added signals. I assigned to Robert Bowman the task of deconvolving the Atlantic no-good ringing records.

Meeting in the spring of 1954

On March 10, 1954 the GAG submitted MIT GAG Report No. 6, *Further Research on Linear Operators in Seismic Analysis*. This report represented work done since August 1953. The meeting of the GAG with the Advisory Committee took place at the Stanolind Research Center in Tulsa on March 29-30, 1954. Those attending were W. T. Born, A. Wolf, and K. S. Cressman (Amerada), H. F. Dunlap (Atlantic), W. W. Garvin (California Research), R. R. Thompson and G. M. Webster (Carter), E. W. Johnson and R. M. Bradley

(Cities Service), J. M. Crawford, C. J. Clark, and W. E. N. Doty (Continental), T. J. O'Donnell and W. C. Dean (Gulf), W. J. Yost (Magnolia), R. G. Piety, R. B. Rice and S. E. Elliott (Phillips), H. F. Sagoci (Standard Oil Company of Texas), D. Silverman, J. D. Eisler, and L. P. Goetz (Stanolind), A. J. Siegert (Consultant to Stanolind from Institute of Advanced Study), A. C. Winterhalter, W. T. Evans, and W. F. Brown, Jr. (Sun), H. J. Jones, R. J. Graebner and E. J. Stulken (Texas Instruments), B. D. Lee and E. Eisner (The Texas Company), C. A. Swartz (United Geophysical), P. M. Hurley, E. A. Robinson, S. M. Simpson and M. K. Smith (MIT), and R. F. Clippinger and J. H. Levin (Raytheon).

A plethora of new questions from the company representatives were addressed. The GAG presented the advances in digital signal processing given in GAG Report No. 6, not the least was the demonstration that a digital filter could do the same job as an analog electric filter, and in fact with greater accuracy. Howard Briscoe was not there, but his report was presented. It gave a survey of current available computing machinery and data handling devices. In one more attempt to convince the representatives that deconvolution could be commercially implemented, Clippinger and Levin came to Tulsa and made a strong case. They passed out the report *Utilization of Electronic Digital Computers in Analysis of Seismograms* by R. F. Clippinger, B. Dimsdale, and J. H. Levin. The report described the role of Raytheon in programming, coding, and computational tasks relating to the GAG work. It said that the Raytheon computer service was ready to perform deconvolution for the industry and gave prices for the service. Raytheon was also ready either to obtain or to build the digital computers that were most suitable for seismic work. In particular, Raytheon proposed using the new IBM 701 computer. Raytheon proposed to input the seismic data to the computer by magnetic tape. Again Raytheon tried to sell seismic processing to the oil companies. However, the companies were still not ready.

At the meeting, the GAG also presented the results in digital seismic processing given in GAG Report No. 6. Mark Smith spoke on his work on filter characteristics of linear operators, methods of determining the optimum linear operator or filter, and directional filtering properties of multiple seismometer groups. Freeman Gilbert was not there but his work was presented. He had completed the requested Continental study and had obtained positive results. His report dealt with digital filtering when the amplitude spectra of noise and signal are known separately, and it showed that the digital results were better than those of analog electric filtering. Doty later commented that digital filtering was not very useful because it did not seem to be able to do much better than analog electric filtering would do in the separation of seismic signal from noise. However, the GAG's establishment that digital filters on a computer could do what electric analog filters could do was an important breakthrough in itself. Many people in electrical engineering as well as in geophysics did not accept this proposition until years later. When the GAG computed tables of time-domain operators for highpass, low-pass and band-pass filtering, few people believed that time-domain operators could do frequency filtering at all. Professor Wadsworth later pointed out that a considerable achievement of the GAG was in relating linear operators to filter theory in more detail and more specifically than had been previously done by any other group.

Robert Bowman was not there but his work was presented. Using the Raytheon services and Whirlwind, Bowman did an excellent job of deconvolving the ringing interference seismograms of the Atlantic Refining Company. He wrote, "It is clear that all the visual reflections on the seismograms are retained after the applications of the linear operators; that is, peaks in the error curves indicate intervals of time where reflected energy is present. These results indicate that, on seismograms of this type, linear operators can be designed to separate reflected energy from non-reflected energy. The results are consistent with the reflections shown on the seismograms, and in addition the results show a marked degree of statistical regularity. The fact the operators in this study did perform so well under the handicap of computational techniques that at best were unrefined is encouraging. If, for example, more lags were used in each operator and information from more than two traces was used, greater discrreasonably expected." Deconvolution had removed the reverberations. These were the "no-record" seismograms that Dunlap had supplied to the GAG. Dunlap spoke up and said that the success of deconvolution on these ringing seismic records is an example of where deconvolution was a benefit. Cecil Green (1980) wrote: "As director of GSI (Geophysical Service Inc.) research, Ken Burg very soon recognized the future potential of the emerging computer revolution. Also during the 1950s, we see him very wisely adapting the newly recognized statistical communication theory to reflection seismology with the direct help of such then current Ph.D. graduates in geophysics from MIT as Mark Smith, Milo Backus, Lawrence Strickland, Freeman Gilbert, and Robert Bowman. This special group was truly instrumental in converting exploration seismology to digital technology in the early 1960s."

For analog seismic processing, the seismic traces were recorded in a reproducible form in the field and then they were brought to the laboratory. In the laboratory there were assortments of electric filters and other devices. In addition some companies had Fourier analyzers, either mechanical or electronic. We recall that in its original form, the ENIAC was an assortment of parts. Dimsdale was given a differential equation and a stack of wiring diagrams, and then he was told to compute. In the geophysical laboratory the geophysicist was given a seismic profile and a stack of filter diagrams, and then he was told to enhance. It took time for the geophysicist to set up the analog equipment so as to get the best results in the enhancement. Once that was done the actual running took just a mater of minutes. But the setup would only work for this particular profile. The next seismic profile would require an entirely new setup. The oil companies, at least some of them, wanted the GAG to find the analog equivalent of deconvolution in terms of frequency filtering. Then deconvolution could be added as another feature of their seismic analog processing scheme. Even if this were done, all the trials and tribulations of the setup of analog equipment would still be there.

I always looked forward to the Advisory Committee Meetings. This meeting, like all the others, was pleasant and exciting. The attendees were enthusiastic. They were full of ideas, both practical and visionary. I was impressed by Tulsa and the Stanolind Research Center, as I was impressed by Dallas and Magnolia the year before. I was captivated by the scope and beauty of exploration geophysics. At the summer meeting on August 12-13, 1953 at MIT, the GAG was directed to find analog ways to do deconvolution. If the GAG had come to this meeting and announced that we have found an assortment of analog frequency filters that could do deconvolution, the oil companies would have been delighted. Instead we said that we have found that digital time-domain filters can do everything that analog frequency filters can do. We even went one step further. We said that all of the analog methods could be done by digital signal processing. In fact, the digital way provided greater accuracy than the analog way. In effect, we proposed that the oil companies abandon their analog processing all together, and replace it with digital processing. Clippinger said that Raytheon was ready to obtain or build all the elements required for digital signal processing from input to output. Like Frankenstein in Mary Shelley's book, Clippinger had built a monster for the Army from an assortment of parts. It was the rebuilt ENIAC, the first operational stored-program digital computer. Mary Shelley opens with the sentence. "You will rejoice to hear that no disaster has accompanied the commencement of an enterprise which you have regarded with such evil forebodings." Now in 1954 Clippinger was in Tulsa ready to build a monster for geophysical exploration. It would be the first operational digital seismic processing system. The oil and geophysical company representatives were not ready to undertake digital seismic processing at this time. They were discouraged because an excursion into digital seismic processing would require new effort and cost real money, and still it might fail because of the unreliability of the existing computers. On the other hand, I believed in digital processing. All of the analog equipment in an oil company laboratory could be replaced by one high-speed, stored-program electronic digital computer. Then deconvolution and everything else (the corrections, gain control, adjustments, mixing, filtering, correlation and spectral analysis, etc.) could be done under program control by this one computer. But the acceptance of digital seismic processing was not to be, at least not in 1954.

Leo Tolstoy wrote, "The two most powerful warriors are patience and time." Computers were in their infancy. I knew that the available digital computers were not entirely suitable for geophysical processing. However, each year from 1946 to the present year 1954, there was a constant stream of improvements in computers and this development was accelerating each year. Oil exploration is a serous business. With patience and with time, the oil and geophysics companies would carry out the conversion to digital processing. It would happen when the need for hard-to-find oil was great enough to justify the investment necessary to turn no-record seismograms into meaningful data. Meanwhile the door to exploration geophysics was open in front of me. When I finished my degree I wanted to work for an oil company.

Meeting in the summer of 1954

This failure to convince the oil companies about the value of digital seismic processing reinforced the qualms at MIT. Established professors as well as administration looked somewhat askance at anything digital. I owe much to Sven Treitel who came to the rescue. He gave encouragement to continue the course and not to go off into a labyrinth of sidetracks. The mathematics of digital processing had to be expressed in geophysical language. I turned my efforts to my third objective: the provision of a geophysical model that justifies deconvolution. I knew that time was of the essence in finishing up my PhD dissertation on which I had already done considerable work. New initiatives were started for the other members of the GAG, while I worked diligently on my dissertation (Robinson, 1954). It was reproduced as MIT GAG Report No. 7, *Predictive decomposition of time series with applications to seismic exploration*, dated July 12, 1954. In mathematics I integrated the works of Wold (1938) and Kolmogorov (1941) on time series analysis with that of Wiener (1949). Wold was a statistician and an economist. I learned of his work while I was studying in the Economics Department. His predictive decomposition theorem is an existence theorem that represents any stationary time series as being made up of a regular component and a singular component. An example of a singular component is a pure sine wave. The singular component is completely predictable. The regular component, which is only partially predictable, is in the form of a moving average. I started out with the empirical knowledge of deconvolution. I showed that the regular component may be considered to be additively composed of many overlapping wavelets. These wavelets all have the same stable minimum-phase form. The arrival times and strengths of these wavelets are random and uncorrelated with one another. The result is the seismic convolutional model

$$\text{trace} = \text{noise} * \text{signal}$$

where the asterisk is the symbol for convolution, where the random noise is the reflectivity (the sequence of refection coefficients), and the deterministic signal is the wavelet. The wavelet represents the dynamic modifications made to the reflection pulse by instrumentation and by mechanisms within the earth. An example would be a reverberation wavelet. Admittedly this model is a simplification. I looked at the convolutional model and then figured out how the deconvolution operator worked. It turned out that the deconvolution operator would have to be the inverse of the wavelet. For example, the deconvolution operator would be the inverse of the reverberation wavelet. The deconvolution operator is given as the solution of the normal equations. I then had to show that the deconvolution operator so computed is indeed the inverse wavelet. The deconvolved trace would be the noise (the reflectivity). Finally I had to integrate all of this with the temporal and spectral analyses of Kolmogorov and Wiener. The minimum-phase concept had only been worked out for continuous time. I did the whole thing for discrete time: the use of the z-transform, the unit circle, the polynomial factorization. It all fitted together. The important thing is that the wavelet and the reflectivity left the realm of seismic theory. They could now be numerically computed from the seismic trace. This could not be done by analog means; digital was a necessity.

The oil and geophysical companies were well along in their development of analog seismic processing with frequency filtering. Analog seismic processing was based on the additive model. The deconvolution work in the spring and summer of 1953 on the reverberating seismic records taught an important lesson. For a seismic trace, there was something wrong with the additive model. Instead, the seismic trace needs the convolutional model. Reflectivity is different at each place in the world, and so can be treated as random noise. A reverberation has the same mathematical structure everywhere, and so can be treated as deterministic signal. Let us give an example. There is a fleet of ships hidden in a cover of fog or smoke. First, suppose that the cover is fog. The fog and the ships have no physical connection. We call the fleet of ships the signal. We call the fog the noise. What one sees is the sum of signal and noise. This is the additive model. We need a device that reduces the fog (the noise) and brings out the signal (the ships). This is the approach of frequency filtering. Second, suppose the cover is smoke. Each ship is sending off a smoke screen which plummets out in a tail from the stern of the ship. The smoke and the ships have a physical connection. We have no information about the location of the ships, so we consider them the noise. However we know exactly how a smoke screen works, so we call the smoke screen the signal. What one sees is the convolution of noise and signal. This is the convolutional model. We need a device that turns off the smoke screen emitted by each ship. Such a device is the deconvolution operator.

In the *additive model*, the trace is the *sum* of signal and noise; that is, trace = signal + noise, where the signal is the reflectivity and noise is the interference. The noise and signal have no connection. In the convolutional model, the seismic trace is the additive sum of wavelets arriving with random strengths and arrival times. The trace is the *convolution* of noise and signal; that is, trace = noise * signal, where the asterisk is the symbol for convolution, where the noise is the reflectivity, and the signal is the wavelet. The noise and signal have a connection; each wavelet is attached to a reflection coefficient. The convolutional model turns the seismic world upside down. Addition becomes convolution, signal becomes noise, noise becomes signal, and analog processing becomes digital processing.

Before I could obtain my PhD, I had to satisfy the academic requirement of attending the MIT undergraduate geology summer camp in Nova Scotia. That took a good part of the summer. After that I had to spend time on active duty in the Army. The Advisory Committee Meeting was held at MIT on September 14, 1954; it was the last meeting in which I participated. The people attending were H. F. Dunlap (Atlantic Refining Co.), L. Y. Faust and W. T. Born (Amerada Petroleum Co.), J. J. Roark (Carter Oil Company), R.M. Bradley (Cities Service Oil Co.), C. J. Clark, J. M. Crawford and W. E. N. Doty(Continental Oil Co.), M.K. Smith (Geophysical Service Inc.), W.C. Dean and T. J. O'Donnell (Gulf Research & Development Co.), M.R. MacPhail and W. M. Rush, Jr. (Humble Oil & Refining Co.), J. E. White (Magnolia Petroleum Co.), S. E. Elliott and R. G. Piety (Phillips Petroleum Co.), R. Runge and D. Silverman (Stanolind Oil & Gas Co.), W. F. Brown, Jr. (Sun Oil Company), H. J. Jones (Texas Instruments Corp.), R. A. Peterson (United Geophysical Co.), R. L. Wentworth (MIT Industrial Liaison Office), R. R. Shrock, P. M. Hurley, G. P. Wadsworth, J. G. Bryan, E. A. Robinson, S. M. Simpson, Robert Bowman, D. R. Grine, D. E. Bowker, K. Vozoff, T. S. Neves, and M. Lopez-Linares (MIT). At the meeting I presented my dissertation results (the seismic convolutional model as the basis for deconvolution). H. F. Dunlap acting for the Advisory Committee wrote, "It was generally agreed between the sponsors present that the work showed considerable promise, and the sponsors were well pleased with what had been accomplished." The GAG had met the three objectives set after Clewell's letter of November 29, 1951. The GAG had (1) instrumented deconvolution by digital computer, (2) demonstrated the efficacy of deconvolution on an assortment of seismograms, and (3) provided the convolutional model to justify deconvolution. The GAG was shipshape. I went to work for Gulf Oil Company on a seismic crew stationed in Lamesa, Texas where I started learning that oil is where you find it.

On October 7, 1954 I sent a copy of my dissertation to Professor Herman Wold in Uppsala, Sweden. He was one of the early pioneers of time series analysis. His reply sent on October 18, 1954 was forwarded to me in Lamesa. He wrote to me as follows:

> "First of all I wish to congratulate you on your thesis and excellent work with several interesting results and equally distinguished by the thorough treatment and clarity of exposition. You may imagine that I am happy to see my theorem of predictive decomposition subjected to such a brilliant review in the light of the subsequent development. And I am touched in seeing with what scrupulous care you have given reference to priority to results in my thesis that were novel at the time. You kindly invite me to give criticism and comments, and offer to submit my remarks to those who are receiving your thesis. Actually I have little or nothing to criticize. My predictive decomposition was primarily intended as an existence theorem, the emphasis being upon the distinction between the regular and the singular component, and the interpretation of earlier

approaches as special cases of the stationary process. I was aware that there was a close relationship between the decomposition and the properties of the spectral function, but I did not enter upon this problem, for the simple reason that I did not master the general methods of spectral theory. The applications (seismic deconvolution) in **your** Chapter 6 are very impressive. I hope the contact now established will continue, and in particular I should like to hear your reaction on the above comments. Further I hope to make your personal acquaintance some day. Is there a chance that you might come over to Europe during the near future? In such a case, please do not forget you have a friend in Uppsala."

This letter was the start of a life-long friendship with Professor Wold. "If you can look into the seeds of time, and say which grain will grow and which will not, speak then to me" (Shakespeare). Great strides were continually being made in digital computers. With the introduction of transistorized computers, like the IBM 7090 and the Control Data 1604, both computer technology and computer applications were again in the ascendancy. In 1959 Jack Kilby of Texas Instruments patented the first integrated circuit (IC). Robert Noyce at Fairchild sold the first commercial IC chips in quantity in 1961. The conversion to digital seismic processing did start to happen in the early 1960s and exploration geophysics became the first of any science to experience the digital revolution. The oil and geophysical companies began using deconvolution and other digital signal processing methods on all exploration seismic records. Provinces for oil exploration that yielded only no-record seismograms were now unlocked. Included were great offshore prospects whose seismograms were typically clouded by the reverberations of the water layer. Raytheon, through Seismograph Service Company and the work of Dale Stone, Bob Geyer and others, took its rightful pace as a leader in seismic processing. The enthusiasm for digital seismic processing has continued uninterrupted to this day. The changes wrought in geophysical exploration are comparable to the changes wrought in astronomy with the invention of the telescope. The exciting story of exploration geophysics from its early beginnings is well told in the excellent and comprehensive book of Lawyer, Bates, and Rice (2001).

In 1954 the directorship of the GAG was turned over to the competent hands of Professor Stephen Simpson. Simpson was a top person in digital computers and was continually coming up with valuable new ideas in geophysics. He always put the concerns of the students first. He stayed up many nights helping students in their studies and research. Like Ted Madden, Steve Simpson became an institution in MIT geophysics. Sven Treitel was a member of the GAG right up to when the project came to an official end in 1957. In the next article Sven Treitel tells the story of the GAG from 1954 on. He is the one who gave life to the GAG while a member and then even after its demise. He resurrected the objectives of the GAG, and the two of us, as well as many others, have carried on the tradition of the GAG over the years.

Conclusion

The success of reflection seismology in discovering petroleum depends upon the generation of accurate pictures of the interior of the earth. Digital processing makes these images possible. Throughout the article we have given the names of the people directly involved in the early development of digital seismic processing. In the background there were others who provided significant help and encouragement. Notable are Milton B. Dobrin and Norman Ricker of the oil industry; John Tukey, Claude E. Shannon, and H. W. Bode of the Bell Telephone Laboratories; and Prof. David Durand and Prof. John Nash of MIT. Most important of all was the support provided by the Society of Exploration Geophysicists in those past days.

Acknowledgements

My appreciation goes to Sven Treitel for his help in this undertaking. I want to thank Jerry Schuster, the editor of GEOPHYSICS, for his enthusiastic support and valuable insight. He represents the many hard-working geophysicists whose ability and vision are propelling geophysics to ever new and exciting heights. I want to give special thanks to Jerry's talented and accomplished wife, Susan, who painstakingly went through the manuscript and made significant improvements. As always, I am indebted to Dean Clark, Editor of *The Leading Edge*, for his guidance. Also I express my thanks to Dolores Proubasta and Sylvie Dale of *The Leading E*dge. I want to thank Judy Wall of the SEG for her kindness and proficiency, and for helping me get through the intricacies of modern publication.

References

Clippinger, R.F., 1948, A logical coding system applied to the ENIAC: Aberdeen BRL Report No. 673.

Frank, H. R. and W. E. N. Doty, 1953, Signal-to-noise ratio improvements by filtering and mixing: Geophysics, **18**, 587-604.

Green, C., 1980, Biography of Kenneth E. Burg: SEG Virtual Museum, seg.org.

Jakosky, J. J., 1950, Exploration geophysics: Trija Publishing Co.

Kolmogorov, A., 1941, Interpolation und Extrapolation von stationaren zufalligen Folgen: Bull. Acad. Sci. URSS, Ser. Math., 5, 3-14.

Lawyer, L. C., C. C. Bates, and R. B. Rice, 2001, Geophysics in the affairs of mankind: Society of Exploration Geophysicists.

Levin, J. H., 1948, On the Approximate Solution of a Partial Differential Equation on the Differential Analyzer: Mathematical Tables and Other Aids to Computation, Volume 3, Number 23

Robinson, E. A., 1954, Predictive decomposition of time series with applications to seismic exploration: MIT Ph.D. Thesis

Wiener, N., 1948, Cybernetics, or control and communication in the animal and the machine: John Wiley.

Wiener, N., 1949, The extrapolation, interpolation and smoothing of stationary time series with engineering applications. John Wiley.

Wold, H., 1938, A study in the analysis of stationary time series: Almqvist and Wiksells.

Extended Resolution by 3-D Holographic Seismic Imaging

by Enders A. Robinson

Offshore Technology Conference, Houston, Texas, May 4-7, 1998

Introduction

Photography is the art of making photographs of an object. A photograph is a picture made by a camera. Light reflected from a given point on the object is directed by the camera's lens to the corresponding point on light-sensitive film. Thus there is a one-to-one relationship between points on the object and points on the photograph film. Holography is the art of making holograms of an object. A hologram is produced by making a recording on a two-dimensional light-sensitive plate or film. When developed the plate becomes the hologram. The hologram itself is not an image; it is the recording of a wavefield. It is essentially unintelligible when seen in regular light. The surface of the developed hologram consists of a very fine, seemingly random pattern, which appears to bear no relationship to the object.

A hologram can be illuminated in order to display a fully three-dimensional image of the object. When illuminated, with the object gone, the hologram produces the wavefield produced by the object, so a virtual image of the object is formed. The image can be seen without the aid of special glasses. The image is a representation of the "whole" object, showing it in three dimensions. Inexpensive holographic images are found on credit cards and ID cards where they help prevent copying. More impressive are large holograms that produce a 3-D image that you can walk around to see from all angles. If a viewer walks around this image, he sees its image from different perspectives even as he would see the real object. The reason is that the whole object has been recorded at every point on the hologram. A hologram is a two-dimensional photographic plate that allows us to see a faithful image of an object in three dimensions.

All the information about an object is encoded on the hologram by using a combination of magnitude, frequency, and phase modulation. When a laser beam is later directed through the developed hologram (with the object removed), a virtual three dimensional image of the object unfolds from the hologram. Each point on the object diffracts light to every point on the hologram. Any object can be regarded as made up of a multitude of point objects. Each point object produces its own pattern on the hologram plate. The responses of all such point objects are added by the principle of superposition. In this way, the wavefield of a three-dimensional object is recorded on the hologram.

Let us give an essential fact about a hologram. Cutting a piece from the hologram and sending the laser beam through the fragment also produces an image of the whole object, although this image may not be quite as sharp. Let us now discuss why every piece of a hologram contains the entire picture. Each diffraction point of the object sends out waves that reach every point on the hologram. As a result each point on the hologram contains a contribution from every point on the object. It follows that every point on the hologram contains the entire picture. Thus when either the entire hologram is illuminated, or just a section of it, we see the image of the entire object. The characteristic that each part of a hologram contains the entire picture has widespread implications in seismology.

Of course the more points used on the hologram, the better the quality of the picture. Let us explain. Each point in a photograph represents light scattered from a single point of the object. When a photograph is cut in half, each piece shows half of the object. Each point on a holographic recording includes information about light scattered from every point of the object. When a hologram is cut in half, the whole object can still be seen in each piece. It can be thought of as viewing an object outside a house first through a large window, and then through a small window. The viewer can see entire object through the large window. The viewer still can see the object through the small window, but now he must move the head from side to side to see that entire object

In summary, a hologram is a recording of microscopic interference fringes, and appears as a hodgepodge of whirly lines. When the hologram is placed in a beam of laser light (with the object gone) the light rays are bent by the hologram to produce rays identical to the original rays diffracted by the object. When viewed by the eye the bent rays produce the same effect as the original diffracted rays. When we look through the hologram we see a full realistic three-dimensional virtual image.

Seismology is the art of making seismograms of an object, namely a volume of the subterranean earth. The dictionary defines an earthquake seismogram as the record made by a seismograph or seismometer. In the early days, an exploration seismogram would consist of a few traces recorded on photographic paper. Even today the word "seismogram" brings up memories of old paper records, long since gone. Now we would like to use the word "seismogram" to mean all of the seismic data acquired in a survey. Such a seismogram would consist of many millions of traces from thousands of shots, all of which are recorded in digital memory. Seismic acquisition is the step of recording the seismogram. Seismic processing is the step of filtering out unwanted information and then forming an image of the object (the subterranean earth).

A seismogram is a hologram
Optical holography is intrinsically a method of acquisition, not processing. The hologram acquires information about a three-dimensional object on a two-dimensional plate. When the hologram is illuminated, an optical image of the three-dimensional object is formed. The seismogram acquires information about a three-dimensional object on a

two-dimensional datum. When the seismogram is processed and imaged, a computer image of the three-dimensional object is formed.

The following statements illustrate the duality:

Holography is the art of making holograms of an object.

Seismology is the art of making seismograms of an object.

In this duality, "hologram" corresponds to "seismogram." The result is that *a seismogram is a hologram*. Of course, a seismogram is not an optical hologram (which uses light waves). A seismogram is a seismic hologram (which uses seismic waves). Optical holography uses light waves which travel in straight lines through the air. Seismology uses seismic waves which travel in all sorts of ways through the earth.

Optical holography is a method of recording on a plane (the hologram) a pattern due to the interference of a reference beam with light diffracted from an object. When the hologram is illuminated, the entire picture of the object in three-dimensional space is obtained as a virtual image. In the way of analogy, the recorded seismic data on the horizontal datum plane at the surface of the earth is a pattern due to the seismic waves reflected and diffracted from of the subsurface geologic structure. In other words, the entirety of the recorded seismic data is a hologram. It follow that when this hologram is correctly processed and imaged, the entire picture of subsurface is obtained as a three-dimensional image.

The understanding of this correspondence opens up new vistas in seismic exploration, and in particular justifies important cost saving measures in acquisition (Robinson, 1998). Holistic methods allow wavefield images to achieve resolution beyond that predicted by conventional digital processing techniques. When a hologram is illuminated or a seismic section is imaged, each depicts the entire image of the unattainable object. Moreover, any part of the hologram also depicts the entire image of the object. The same is true in the seismic case. Holistic imaging is a process in which any part of the seismic section produces the entire image of the subsurface. The image might not be quite as clear, but the same fine structure will be present. For example if we record a seismogram with 2 million seismic traces, we obtain a certain image. If we wish to save money we could instead record a "decimated seismogram" with 1 million seismic traces by skipping every other trace. We obtain essentially the same image in either case.

Let us now discuss why every piece of a hologram contains the entire picture. Each diffraction point of the object sends out waves that reach every point on the hologram. As a result each point on the hologram contains a contribution from every point on the object. It follows that every piece of the hologram contains the entire picture. Thus when either the entire hologram is illuminated, or just a section of it, we see the image of the entire object. Of course the more points used on the hologram, the better the quality of the picture. The characteristic that each part of a hologram contains the entire picture has wide-spread implications in seismology. In seismic holography we can eliminate not just a section of made of adjacent points but by a section made up of every other point, or every third point, etc. Such a uniform procedure is called *systematic decimation*. All decimation must be applied under the general rule as given by Neidell; namely, "Adequate sampling spatially and in depth or time are necessary for interpretive visibility; they must be considered together."

The implication is that in a seismic survey the number of shot points and detectors in many cases can be reduced without adversely affecting the results. Using this holistic approach, fewer traces are needed to obtain a desired resolution in images of the subsurface. The cost savings makes the holistic approach advantageous in acquisition. Rudy Prince and Norman Neidell were the first to use this holistic idea in the field (Neidell and Prince, 1998). They tested decimation in several different ways in the processing of a 3D survey. In the late 1990s, they successfully used the holistic method in the field. On one survey they saved $11m. Many discoveries have since been made from that data set. As Neidell generously wrote to me, "You were the one pushing for data decimation. I was in love with resolution. The concept of modifying the field practice is entirely your contribution. I was more interested in higher frequencies." Without Neidell's pioneering work, none of this would have been done.

In shifting our seismic guidelines and paradigms to the point of view of holography, many of the unnecessary restrictions and limitations that have been accepted as essentially insurmountable barriers can be removed. Holographic seismic imaging can achieve resolution beyond that given by the ordinary Nyquist criteria as applied to the individual variables. The fine details in geologic structure that fall through the cracks in conventional processing can be captured in holistic processing. The compressive sensing (CS) method in use today is a form of holistic imaging in which random decimation is used instead of systematic decimation.

Optical holography

Holography represents a method of recording on a plane (the hologram) a pattern due to the interference of a reference beam with light diffracted from an object. When the hologram is illuminated, the entire picture of the object in three dimensional space is obtained as a virtual image. An essential principle is that a seismogram is a hologram. The understanding of this principle opens up new vistas in seismic exploration, and in particular justifies important cost saving measures in acquisition and processing methods. When a hologram is illuminated or a seismic section is migrated, each depicts the entire image of the unattainable object. Moreover, any part of the hologram also depicts the entire image of the object. The same is true in the seismic case if conventional migration is replaced by holographic seismic imaging, also known as holistic migration. Holistic migration is a process in which any part of the seismic section produces the entire image of the subsurface. Holistic methods allow wavefield images to achieve resolution beyond that predicted by conventional digital processing techniques. The image might not be quite as clear, but the same fine structure will be present. The implication is that in a seismic survey the number of shot points and detectors can be greatly reduced without adversely affecting the results. Holographic seismic imaging provides the extended resolution needed to attain a better image of the subsurface.

The reflection seismic method is an instrument to find the structure of an inaccessible body, the subsurface geology. Because the rock layers are transparent to seismic waves, the recorded seismic time sections contain not only the primary reflections from the geologic interfaces, but the multiple reflections as well. The purpose of deconvolution, stacking, and related seismic processing methods is to produce multiple-free time sections and also to obtain a velocity function of the subsurface. The purpose of migration is to find a three-dimensional (3-D) picture or image of the subsurface from the multiple-free time sections according to the velocity function. Cost is a major factor in the design of 3-D surveys. Neidell (Ref. 1) has challenged traditionally views, and has introduced methods that allow extended resolution in seismic imaging as compared to conventional methods.

The purpose of this paper is to give a theoretical basis for the new methods of imaging known as holographic seismic imaging, or simply as holistic migration. They are addressed from the viewpoint of imaging technology, and in particular the theory of holography. Holography is the doorway that leads to better methods of seismic imaging. This doorway gives access to the fulfillment of the imaginative methods required to obtain the best possible images of the subsurface. Holography involves the recording and the illumination of a hologram in order to produce a 3-D image of a body. In shifting our seismic guidelines and paradigms to the point of view of holography, many of the unnecessary restrictions and limitations that have been accepted as essentially insurmountable barriers can be removed. Holographic seismic imaging can achieve resolution beyond that given by conventional methods of migration.

Holistic migration offers lower overall cost. Suppose that a given number of shot points and detectors yields a certain resolution of the subsurface structure under conventional migration. Then only one-half or one-fourth as many shot points and detectors can give the same resolution under holistic migration. Because the cost of a seismic survey depends directly upon the number of shot points and detectors used, the holistic method can reduce the cost of a 3-D seismic survey greatly, often to one-fourth the previous cost, or less. The fine details in geologic structure that fall through the cracks in conventional processing are captured in holistic processing.

Holography

The basic theory of geometrical optics describes how optical elements such as lenses, mirrors, and prisms modify the direction of light rays. Physical optics extends the theoretical treatment of optical systems by incorporating the wave nature of light. A basic assumption is that light waves propagate in an isotropic media with simple harmonic motion and satisfy the scalar wave equation. In the solution of the wave equation, the temporal part of the electromagnetic wave is generally suppressed, because no detector has sufficient bandwidth to respond directly to the amplitude fluctuations at light frequencies. Also the relative phase is generally ignored. With these conventions, the complex transmittance of an optical element can be represented by a complex function of the space variables. The complex transmittances of several optical elements in series multiply, as would be expected.

The Fresnel zone pattern is fundamental to holography. As originally conceived by Gabor (Ref. 2), holography was a way to correct the aberrations of an electron beam microscope. Gabor realized that a two-dimensional interference pattern represented by the Fresnel zone contains information about the position of an object in three-dimensional space. The information is recorded on film so that the image can be reconstructed at visible wavelengths after the aberrations are corrected. The Gabor hologram uses a reference beam collinear with the signal beam. The basic problem is that this arrangement does not allow the signal beam to be cleanly reconstructed because the desired information spatially overlaps other terms, such as the bias.

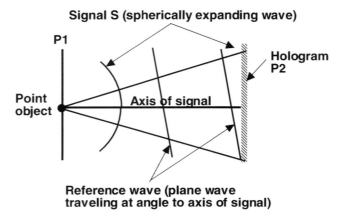

Fig. 1. Recording of an off-axis hologram for a point source.

This situation can be corrected by using an off-axis reference wavefront (**Fig. 1**). This arrangement is similar to the Gabor arrangement, except that the reference beam is no longer collinear with the axis of the signal beam. The hologram is made by illuminating a photosensitive medium such as photographic film for a certain exposure time. It contains all the information needed to reproduce the wave field of the object. Let the R (which is a complex function of the space variables) represent the reference beam, and similarly let the S (which also is a complex function of the space variables) represent the signal beam. In the case represented in the figure, S is a spherically expanding wave emanating from a point object. Let a superscript asterisk represent the complex conjugate. The intensity I recorded on the photographic film (the hologram) is

$$I = (R + S)(R + S)^*$$

which is

$$I = (R\,R^{**} + S\,S^*) + R^*S + R\,S^*$$

The term is parentheses is a real function, which we denote by A. Thus mathematically the recorded hologram is

$$I = A + R^*S + R\,S^*$$

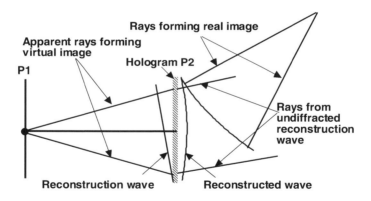

Fig. 2. Reconstruction of the off-axis hologram for a point source.

The hologram is reconstructed by illuminating it with a replica of the reference beam R. This beam is now called the reconstruction beam (**Fig. 2**). The illuminated hologram produces the signal

$$RI = RA + RR^*S + RR\,S^*$$

which propagates outward to the right of the hologram. Denote the real quantity RR^* by the symbol B. Then the above signal becomes

$$RI = RA + BS + RR\,S^*$$

This equation shows that three wavefronts are released from the hologram. Because A is real, the first term RA (the undiffracted reconstruction wave) has the same form as the reconstruction wave R, but with some attenuation as introduced by the term A. The undiffracted reconstruction wave does not suffer from diffraction, but continues to propagate in the same direction as R. Because B is real, the second term BS (the reconstructed wave) has the same form as the original spherical signal beam S, but with some attenuation as introduced by the term B. The reconstructed wave propagates to the right of the hologram as though the spherically expanding wave had never been intercepted. This reconstructed wave produces a virtual image, as seen from the right of the hologram, of the original point object. In the figure, the apparent rays associated with the virtual image are shown to the left of the hologram. The last term $RR\,S^*$ represents a wave propagating toward the right at twice the angle of the reconstruction beam R. The spherical phase factor of $RR\,S^*$ has the opposite sign produced by the conjugation operation. This conjugate wavefront represents a convergent wave that forms a real image of the original signal. At some distance to the right of the hologram, the three beams no longer overlap, thus producing a clean reconstruction of the signal.

All the information about a point object is encoded in the hologram by using a combination of magnitude, frequency, and phase modulation. Any object can be regarded as made up of a multitude of point objects. Each of such point objects produces its own pattern at the hologram plane. The responses of all such point sources are added at the plane of the hologram by the principle of superposition. The hologram reconstruction distinguishes each point object because its associated spatial frequency shifts upward or downward, within the passband, according to whether the particular point object produces a larger or smaller angle with respect to the reference beam. Thus, in this way, three-dimensional objects are recorded on a hologram.

The hologram

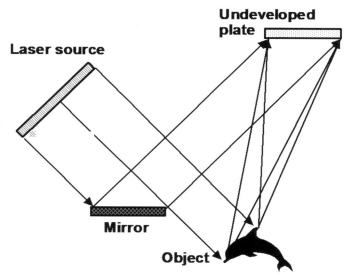

Fig. 3. In holography no lens is used, so no image is formed. Each point on the object diffracts light to every point on the hologram.

Holograms can be recorded under a wide range of geometrical and physical conditions. Here, one of the basic types of holograms is described (**Fig. 3**). The hologram is made by shining laser light at an object. Half of the laser beam never hits the object because it is reflected from a mirror placed in its path. This reflected light, which constitutes the reference beam, is directed to a photographic plate. The other half of the laser beam finds the object. Each point on the object acts as a diffraction point and spreads light in all directions. The diffracted light from a point on the object reaches every point on the undeveloped plate. When the two halves of the laser light meet at the plate, they interfere with each other. The resulting interference pattern is recorded on the plate.

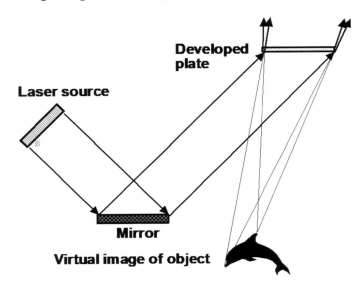

Fig. 4. When illuminated, with the object gone, the hologram produces the wavefield produced by the object, so a virtual image of the object is formed.

When developed the plate becomes the hologram (**Fig. 4**). When a laser beam is later directed through the hologram (with the object removed), a virtual image of the object unfolds from the wave pattern and projects three dimensionally in space. If a viewer walks around this chimerical object, he sees its image from different perspectives even as he would see the real object. The reason is that the whole object has been recorded at every point of the interference pattern on the hologram. A hologram is a two-dimensional photographic plate that allows us to see a faithful reproduction of a scene in three dimensions.

Cutting a piece from the hologram and sending the laser beam through the fragment also produces an image of the whole object, although this image may not be quite as sharp. Let us now discuss why every piece of a hologram contains the entire picture. Each diffraction point of the object sends out waves that reach every point on the hologram. As a result each point on the hologram contains a contribution from every point on the object. It follows that every point on the hologram contains the entire picture. Thus when either the entire hologram is illuminated, or just a section of it, we see the image of the entire object. Of course the more points used on the hologram, the better the quality of the picture. The characteristic that each part of a hologram contains the entire picture has wide-spread implications in seismology.

In an ordinary camera, a lens is used to form an image of the object on the plane of the photograph film (**Fig. 5**). Light reflected from a given point on the object is directed by the lens to the corresponding point on the film. Thus there is a one-to-one relationship between points on the object and points on the photograph film. Moreover, all the light that reaches the film comes from the object. There is no secondary source as in the case of a hologram in which half of the laser light (the reference beam) is reflected from the mirror and does not reach the object. Let us now compare the ordinary camera with holography. In making a hologram, no image-forming lens is used. Thus each point on the object diffracts light to every point on the hologram plate. Thus there is a one-to-many relationship between a given point on the object and all the points on the hologram plate. Thus every part of the hologram plate is exposed to light diffracted from every part of the object. In addition the total light that reaches the hologram plate is made up of two parts, namely the part of the beam (the reference beam) that is reflected from the mirror and the part of the beam (the signal beam) that is used to illuminate the object. These two parts produce the interference pattern recorded on the hologram. That is, one set of wavefronts (the reference beam) is from the light reflected by the mirror, and the other set of wavefronts (the signal beam) is from the light diffracted by the object. The hologram is the recording of the interference pattern resulting from the combination of these two sets of wavefronts.

A hologram is a photograph of microscopic interference fringes, and appears as a hodgepodge of whirly lines. When the hologram is placed in a beam of laser light (with the object gone) the light rays are bent by the hologram to produce rays identical to the original rays diffracted by the object. When viewed by the eye the bent (or diffracted) rays produce the same effect as the original diffracted rays. When we look through the hologram we see a full realistic three-dimensional virtual image as if we were viewing the object through a window. When we move our eyes and look down the sides of the object, and when we lower our eyes and look underneath the object, parallax is evident as in real life. The entire wavefield on our side of the hologram has been reconstructed by the illumination of the hologram by the laser light. We see the object as a virtual image, even though the original object is no longer present.

Seismic surveys

Migration starts with the surface seismic time sections, that is, the wavefield made up of reflections incident upon the surface of the Earth. Migration involves two theoretical constructs: (1) wavefield reconstruction and (2) imaging. Wavefield reconstruction is the determination of the wavefield over a region of interest. Imaging involves the making of a picture of the geometrical distribution of the reflecting surfaces within the medium. In the process of migration, the wavefield within the earth is first reconstructed from the surface seismic time sections by use of various approximations to the wave equation and/or the associated eikonal equation. Then the reconstructed wavefield is imaged to produce the migrated depth sections that give the required 3-D image of the subsurface layering. This process of migration is well-suited to computer calculation.

A reflected event occurs on the seismic trace at its two-way traveltime. Each seismic trace is characterized by its source position and its receiver position. An equi-time surface for an event occurring at a two-way traveltime on a trace is defined as the locus of all possible diffraction points in the subsurface that yield the given two-way traveltime for the source/receiver pair of the trace. Each source point, receiver point, and traveltime together with the velocity function defines an equi-time surface. In the constant velocity case, the equi-time surface is a semi-ellipsoid.

Migration is the process of constructing the depth sections from the time sections. The migration of seismic data is performed routinely in seismic processing regimes. Various techniques for migration are commonly available. The basic theory of migration can be explained in terms of diffraction curves and equi-time curves. For purposes of exposition, it is easier to consider the 2-D case, where the seismic data are taken along a single surface line, and where the underlying earth structure is regarded as two dimensional. The two spatial dimensions are the horizontal coordinate x and the depth coordinate z. The variable x can take on any positive or negative value, but the variable z must be positive. Also, time t must be positive. Because z and t must be positive, there is a certain duality between them. There is nothing in our exposition that cannot be extended to three spatial dimensions; the extension is straightforward and involves no new principles.

In seismic work the sources and receivers are at the surface of the earth and reflectors are at depth. A certain type of idealization deserves special study, namely, the case of a point reflector, which is also called a point diffractor. When such a diffraction point is illuminated by a surface source, the diffraction point acts as a secondary source and hence sets off outgoing wave motion in all directions. Any reflecting surface may be considered as being made up of a dense set of point diffractors. The time coordinate of each event on a trace gives the two-way traveltime from the given source to an unknown diffraction point and back to the given receiver. Although the position of the diffraction point is unknown, it is known that it must lie somewhere on the curve defined by the given source, the given receiver, and the given two-way traveltime. As we have seen, the locus of the totality of diffraction points, all of which have the same traveltime for the given source/receiver pair, is called the equi-time surface, which in the present 2-D case reduces to a curve. An equi-time curve is defined by the source and receiver positions and the traveltime of an event on the seismic trace recorded for that source/receiver pair. In other words, an equi-time curve gives the spatial positions of all possible diffraction points associated with a given source, receiver and traveltime of an event. The equi-time curve for each event on a seismic trace can be computed. The actual diffraction point that produced that event must lie at some point on that curve.

The recorded seismic sections form the starting point for migration. A seismic section is made up of traces, each of which is defined by a source and receiver pair. The wave equation describes the motion of the waves generated by the source. However, the seismic section does not correspond to a wavefield resulting from any single experiment because the sources are excited sequentially, not simultaneously. A seismic trace records the two-way traveltimes that originate from a given surface source. The raypaths proceed from the given surface source to all possible diffractors. The raypaths then proceed back to a given surface receiver. The seismic sections contain the traces for all the source-receiver pairs used in the survey.

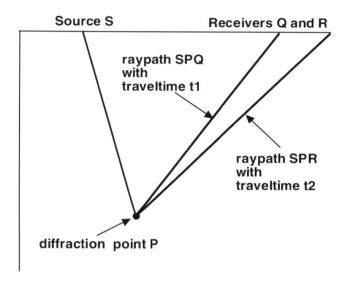

Fig. 6. Diffraction point. The seismic rays diffracted from the subsurface point P are directed to all points on the earth's surface, such as points Q and R.

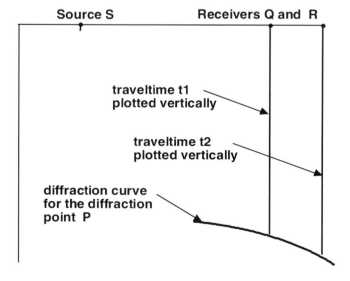

Fig. 7. Seismic traces. The returned signal from the diffraction point gives a hyperbolic-shaped diffraction curve. The geologic structure can be considered as composed of many diffraction points. The resulting seismic section is the superposition of all the corresponding diffraction curves.

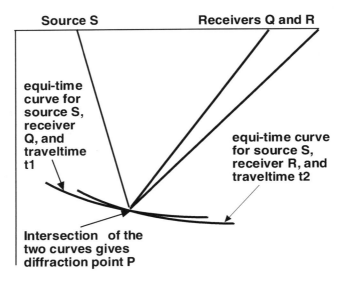

Fig. 8. A representation of the process of migration. For each of traces Q and R, the amplitude value for the given traveltime is mapped into the subsurface along the entire equi-time curve, that is, the curve formed by the loci of points for which the traveltime from source to diffraction point and back to receiver is constant.

Let us describe the type of Kirchhoff migration known as equi-time migration. For simplicity, consider the case of a single diffraction point in the 2-D case (**Fig. 6**). Rays from a diffraction point reach all points on the earth's surface. Each trace records the diffracted event for a given source point and a given receiver point. The seismic traveltime curve for the rays from a point diffractor is called the diffraction curve (**Fig. 7**). The diffraction curve is the seismic section for the point diffractor in question. Take the traveltime of each reflected event on the trace and compute the equi-time curve for the given source and receiver (**Fig. 8**). The intersection of all these equi-time curves gives the true spatial position of the diffraction point.

Now take the general case. Each reflected event has an equi-time surface. Place the given reflected event on every point of the equi-time surface. Repeat this process with equi-time surfaces for each and every data point of the seismic time sections. By the linear superposition principle, the result gives the migrated (or true-reflector) depth sections. That is, the migrated depth sections are found by the superposition of all the equi-time surfaces. In summary, Kirchhoff equi-time migration takes the value of a possible reflected event and places this value evenly along its equi-time surface. The equi-time migrated depth volume is the sum of all the possible equi-time surfaces.

The seismic section as a hologram

The migration methods described to this point represent the existing way that migration is done (conventional migration). The use of the holographic principle in migration defines a new method of migration, appropriately called holistic migration, or holographic seismic imaging. Seismic surveys are taken on the surface of the earth in order to determine the underlying three-dimensional structure. The sources and receivers are at grid points on the surface of the earth, and correspond to the holographic plate. The reflecting horizons are the interfaces between the sedimentary rock layers within the earth. These reflecting horizons represent the geologic object to be imaged. Waves reflected from the subsurface structure are returned to the receiving instruments on the surface and recorded as seismic traces. The collection of all the traces makes up the seismic time sections.

The seismic time sections are the counterpart of the developed holographic plate. In fact, the seismic time sections constitute a hologram in the true meaning of the word. The way of carrying out a seismic survey is, of course, different from the way a hologram is made. In holography, electromagnetic (light) waves are used. In the seismic case, acoustic (sound) waves are used. The laser waves are extremely narrow-band, and are, in fact, almost pure sine waves. In contrast, seismic waves are broadband pulse-type waves. An important feature of seismic exploration is that there is an absolute reference time (the time of the shot); this feature makes it unnecessary to use a reference beam as in holography. On the photographic plate making up the hologram, only the intensity pattern of the interference is recorded. As previously shown, the component of the intensity pattern that contains the virtual image is R^*S. When illuminated by the reconstruction wave, this component yields the reconstructed wave $R\,R^*S = BS$. When this reconstructed wave is viewed and imaged by eye, the virtual image is seen in the mind of the beholder. In seismic exploration the whole time-varying signal pattern at the earth's surface is recorded as seismic traces. In holography, the exterior of an opaque object is imaged. In seismology, the entire interior structure of the earth is imaged because solid rock is transparent to seismic waves. The wavefront reconstruction aspect of migration corresponds to the illumination of a hologram, and the imaging aspect of migration corresponds to the viewing of the hologram.

The term *imaging* refers to the formation of a computer image. For the geophysicist, the required image is one that faithfully depicts the subsurface structure of the Earth. Seismic imaging may be roughly divided into two parts, namely *signal enhancement* and *event movement*. Signal enhancement, discussed in the previous section, entails the separation of the primary reflections (the desired signals) from the signal-generated noise (the undesired signals). In this section we discuss event movement. The more common terminology for event movement is seismic *migration*. Each primary reflection on the enhanced trace must be moved (or migrated) to the spatial position of the reflecting point at depth. In other words, each amplitude value on the enhanced trace is moved to its proper spatial location (the depth point). Migration can be accomplished by the superposition of the processed traces. The superposition is similar to that used in Huygens's construction. See Fig. 4 and Fig 5. There is one added benefit of superposition, namely superposition is one of the most effective ways to accentuate signals and suppress noise. The superposition is designed to return the primary reflections to their spatial locations. The signal-generated noise still remaining on the traces is out of step with the primaries. Consequently the superposition of a huge number of processed traces results in the destruction of much of the remaining signal-generated noise. The superposition provides the desired digital image of the underground structure of the Earth.

If the reflecting interfaces are horizontal (or nearly so) the waves going straight down will be reflected nearly straight up. Thus the wave motion will be essentially vertical. If the time axes on the records are placed in the vertical position, time will appear in the same direction as the raypaths. By using the correct wave velocity, the time axis can be converted into the depth axis. The result is that the primary reflections show the locations of the reflecting interfaces. Thus in areas that have nearly level reflecting horizons the primary reflections as recorded essentially show the correct depth positions of the subsurface interfaces. However in areas that have a more complicated subsurface structure, the primary reflections as recorded in time do not show the correct depth positions of the subsurface interfaces. As a result the wave equation must be used in order to move (or migrate) the primary reflections to their proper spatial positions in depth. If one is satisfied with using ray theory instead of wave theory, then the eikonal equation can be used instead of the wave equation.

Historically the movement (migration) of reflected events to their proper locations in space was carried out manually, sometimes making use of elaborate drawing instruments. The computer implementation of migration involves massive data handling. All the traces must be amalgamation either by wave-equation methods or by the associated ray theory methods. Such methods involve a lot of data handing, which in the last century generally overloaded the limited capacities of the available computers. As a result, it was necessary to break the migration problem down into smaller parts. Thus migration was done by a sequence of approximate operations, such as stacking, followed by normal-moveout, followed by dip-moveout, and then followed by migration after stack. The process of time migration was often used, which improved the records in time but stopped short of putting the events in their proper spatial positions. All sorts of modifications and adjustment were made to improve these piecemeal operations. This approach made seismic migration a complicated discipline, an art as much as a science. The use of this art required much insight. Three-dimensional seismic imaging was rarely used because of the prohibitive costs involved. In the 1990s great improvements in instrumentation and computers resulted in light compact geophysical field equipment and affordable computers of great speed and massive capacity. Geophysicists rapidly took advantage of this new capacity. Instead of the modest number of sources and receivers used in two-dimensional seismic processing, the tremendous number required for three dimensional processing started to be used on a regular basis in field operations. Computers today are large enough to handle three-dimensional imaging. As a result, 3D methods are commonly used, and the resulting subsurface images are of extraordinary quality. Three-dimensional event movement (or migration) can be carried out by time-honored methods as those used in the Huygens construction. Such migration methods generally go under the name of prestack migration. Three-dimensional prestack migration significantly improves seismic interpretation because the locations of geological structures, especially faults, are given much more accurately. In addition, migration collapses diffractions from secondary sources such as reflector terminations against faults and corrects the so-called bow ties to show the synclinal structure.

Let us now give an outline of how three-dimensional imaging is done. The three-dimensional volume (x,y,z) represents the Earth, where (x,y) represents the surface coordinates and z represents the depth coordinate. On the surface plane (x,y) the sources and receivers are arranged in a two-dimensional grid. The (two-way) traveltime t is the duration of the passage of a primary reflection down from the source (x_s, y_s) to a depth point (x,y,z) and then up to the receiver (x_r, y_r). A digital trace is a discrete sequence of amplitudes as a function of discrete traveltime. Thus the amplitude $f(x_s, y_s, x_r, y_r, t)$ represents the sum of all primary reflections with traveltime t originating from source x_s, y_s and recorded at receiver x_r, y_r. There are many admissible depth points (x,y,z) that can contribute to this amplitude. See Fig. 6. All of these admissible depth points must be taken into account. The digital process called migration takes the given amplitude $f(x_s, y_s, x_r, y_r, t)$ and moves (i.e., migrates) this amplitude to each and every admissible depth point (x,y,z). This process is done for all the amplitudes on each primaries-only trace. The results are then summed, and, behold, an image of the geologic structure $g(x,y,z)$ emerges. The principle used in that of Huygens, in which the summation of all the individual responses yields the correct overall response.

In summary, migration is a digital operation in which the reflections on the seismic traces are moved to their correct locations in space. Migration requires the primary reflected events. What else is required? The answer is the seismic velocity function

$v(x,y,z)$. The velocity function is required to determine the raypaths of the admissible reflections. The velocity function gives the wave velocity at each point in the given volume of the Earth under exploration. The word *velocity* generally connotes a vector, with magnitude equal to the rate (a scalar) at which a wave travels through a medium and with direction equal to the direction of movement. When velocity is a scalar, the term "speed" is often used instead, but not in geophysics. Seismic velocity (or wave velocity) should more accurately be called speed. Wave velocity can be determined from laboratory measurements, acoustic logs, and vertical seismic profiles or from velocity analysis of seismic data. Wave velocity can vary vertically and laterally in isotropic media. In anisotropic media it can also vary azimuthally. Wave velocity tends to increase with depth in the Earth because of compaction. Here we consider only isotropic media so at a given point the wave velocity is the same in all directions. From now on we will merely say velocity when we mean wave velocity.

Seismic migration

The term imaging refers to the formation of a computer image. For the geophysicist, the required image is one that faithfully depicts the subsurface structure of the Earth. Seismic imaging may be roughly divided into two parts, namely signal enhancement and event movement. Signal enhancement, discussed in the previous section, entails the separation of the primary reflections (the desired signals) from the signal-generated noise (the undesired signals). In this section we discuss event movement.

The more common terminology for event movement is seismic migration. Each primary reflection on the enhanced trace must be moved (or migrated) to the spatial position of the reflecting point at depth. In other words, each amplitude value on the enhanced trace is moved to its proper spatial location (the depth point). Migration can be accomplished by the superposition of the processed traces. The superposition is similar to that used in Huygens's construction. There is one added benefit of superposition, namely superposition is one of the most effective ways to accentuate signals and suppress noise. The superposition is designed to return the primary reflections to their spatial locations. The signal-generated noise still remaining on the traces is out of step with the primaries. Consequently the superposition of a huge number of processed traces results in the destruction of much of the remaining signal-generated noise. The superposition provides the desired digital image of the underground structure of the Earth.

If the reflecting interfaces are horizontal (or nearly so) the waves going straight down will be reflected nearly straight up. Thus the wave motion will be essentially vertical. If the time axes on the records are placed in the vertical position, time will appear in the same direction as the raypaths. By using the correct wave velocity, the time axis can be converted into the depth axis. The result is that the primary reflections show the locations of the reflecting interfaces. Thus in areas that have nearly level reflecting horizons the primary reflections as recorded essentially show the correct depth positions of the subsurface interfaces. However in areas that have a more complicated subsurface structure, the primary reflections as recorded in time do not show the correct depth positions of the subsurface interfaces. As a result the wave equation must be used in order to move (or migrate) the primary reflections to their proper spatial positions in depth. If one is satisfied with using ray theory instead of wave theory, then the eikonal equation can be used instead of the wave equation.

Historically the movement (migration) of reflected events to their proper locations in space was carried out manually, sometimes making use of elaborate drawing instruments. The computer implementation of migration involves massive data handling. All the traces must be amalgamation either by wave-equation methods or by the associated ray theory methods. Such methods involve a lot of data handing, which in the last century generally overloaded the limited capacities of the available computers. As a result, it was necessary to break the migration problem down into smaller parts. Thus migration was done by a sequence of approximate operations, such as stacking, followed by normal-moveout, followed by dip-moveout, and then followed by migration after stack. The process of time migration was often used, which improved the records in time but stopped short of putting the events in their proper spatial positions. All sorts of modifications and adjustment were made to improve these piecemeal operations. This approach made seismic migration a complicated discipline, an art as much as a science. The use of this art required much insight. Three-dimensional seismic imaging was rarely used because of the prohibitive costs involved. In the 1990s great improvements in instrumentation and computers resulted in light compact geophysical field equipment and affordable computers of great speed and massive capacity. Geophysicists rapidly took advantage of this new capacity. Instead of the modest number of sources and receivers used in two-dimensional seismic processing, the tremendous number required for three dimensional processing started to be used on a regular basis in field operations. Computers today are large enough to handle three-dimensional imaging. As a result, 3D methods are commonly used, and the resulting subsurface images are of extraordinary quality. Three-dimensional event movement (or migration) can be carried out by time-honored methods as those used in the Huygens construction. Such migration methods generally go under the name of prestack migration. Three-dimensional prestack migration significantly improves seismic interpretation because the locations of geological structures, especially faults, are given much more accurately. In addition, migration collapses diffractions from secondary sources such as reflector terminations against faults and corrects the so-called bow ties to show the synclinal structure.

Miigration is a digital operation in which the reflections on the seismic traces are moved to their correct locations in space. Migration requires the primary reflected events. What else is required? The answer is the seismic velocity function. The velocity function is required to determine the raypaths of the admissible reflections. The velocity function gives the wave velocity at each point in the given volume of the Earth under exploration. The word velocity generally connotes a vector, with magnitude equal to the rate (a scalar) at which a wave travels through a medium and with direction equal to the direction of movement. When velocity is a scalar, the term "speed" is often used instead, but not in geophysics. Seismic velocity (or wave velocity) should more accurately be called speed. Wave velocity can be determined from laboratory measurements, acoustic logs, and vertical seismic profiles or from velocity analysis of seismic data. Wave velocity can vary vertically and laterally in isotropic media. In anisotropic media it can also vary azimuthally. Wave velocity tends to increase with depth in the Earth because of compaction. Here we consider only isotropic media so at a given point the wave velocity is the same in all directions. From now on we will merely say velocity when we mean wave velocity.

In summary, seismic migration is the process by which seismic events are geometrically re-located in either space or time to the location the event occurred in the subsurface rather than the location that it was recorded at the surface, thereby creating a true image of the subsurface. This process is necessary to overcome the limitations of geophysical methods imposed by areas of complex geology, such as: faults, salt bodies, folding, etc. Migration moves dipping reflectors to their true subsurface positions and collapses diffractions, resulting in a migrated image that typically has an increased spatial resolution and resolves areas of complex geology A form of migration is one of the standard data processing techniques for reflection-based geophysical methods (seismic reflection and ground-penetrating radar)

Seismic waves are elastic waves that propagate through the Earth with a finite velocity, governed by the elastic properties of the rock in which they are travelling. At an interface between two rock types, with different acoustic impedances, the seismic energy is either refracted, reflected back towards the surface or attenuated by the medium. The reflected energy arrives at the surface and is recorded by geophones that are placed at a known distance away from the source of the waves. When a geophysicist views the recorded energy from the geophone, they know both the travel time and the distance between the source and the receiver, but not the distance down to the reflector. Time migration is applied to seismic data in time coordinates. This type of migration makes the assumption of only mild lateral velocity variations and this breaks down in the presence of most interesting and complex subsurface structures, particularly salt. Depth Migration is applied to seismic data in depth (regular Cartesian) coordinates, which must be calculated from seismic data in time coordinates. This method does therefore require a velocity model, making it resource-intensive because building a seismic velocity model is a long and iterative process. The significant advantage to this migration method is that it can be successfully used in areas with lateral velocity variations, which tend to be the areas that are most interesting to petroleum geologists. The goal of migration is to ultimately increase spatial resolution and one of the basic assumptions made about the seismic data is that it only shows primary reflections and all noise has been removed. In order to ensure maximum resolution (and therefore maximum uplift in image quality) the data should be sufficiently pre-processed before migration. Noise that may be easy to distinguish pre-migration could be smeared across the entire aperture length during migration, reducing image sharpness and clarity.

A further basic consideration is whether to use 2D or 3D migration. If the seismic data has an element of cross-dip (a layer that dips perpendicular to the line of acquisition) then the primary reflection will originate from out-of-plane and 2D migration cannot put the energy back to its origin. In this case, 3D migration is needed to attain the best possible image.

Holistic migration

Conventional migration fails to recognize that a seismic section is a hologram. A portion of a hologram can produce the same picture as the entire hologram. Suppose, for cost reasons, a 2-D survey must be laid out with detector spacing equal to 2 spatial units. It is a common assumption that this spacing of two units governs the Nyquist frequency, so the processing is done at a spacing of two units. Accordingly, by use of conventional migration, the resolution at depth is forced to be two spatial units. If it is desired that the resolution at depth be one spatial unit, then the common belief is that detectors must be laid out at a one spatial unit spacing. The cost of a 2-D survey with one-unit spacing is about twice the cost of the survey with two-unit spacing. Thus, according to commonly accepted beliefs, to double precision, one must double cost, or thereabouts. This situation need not be so. One can double precision without any appreciable increase in cost. Alternatively, one can obtain the same precision at the half the cost. The way is to use holistic migration in seismic processing instead of conventional migration.

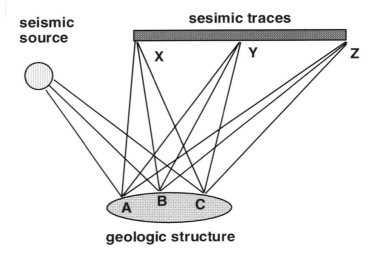

Fig. 9. Each seismic trace contains information about every geological diffraction point.

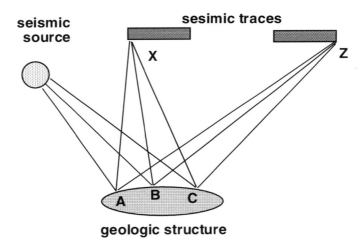

Fig. 10. Each seismic trace still contains information about every geological diffraction point even when every other trace is cut out.

Observe that the seismic section from a two-unit sampling is a subset of the seismic section with one-unit sampling (**Figs. 9 and 10**). That is, the two-unit section can be obtained from the one-unit section by taking every other trace. In other words, the two-unit section (piece of the hologram) is obtained by cutting a piece from the one-unit section (the hologram). Because the piece of a hologram gives the same image (in detail) as the hologram, the same detailed subsurface image is produced by the seismic section with two-unit sampling as by the more costly seismic section with one-unit sampling.

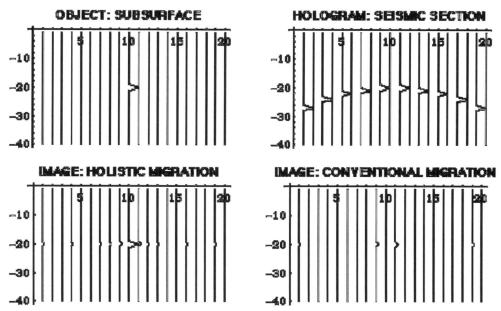

Fig. 11. The object is a point diffractor. Two methods of migration are applied to the seismic section. Only holistic migration is successful in detecting the point diffractor.

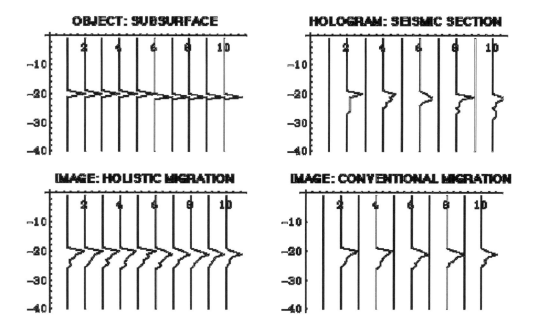

Fig. 12. The object is a sharp diffracting edge. Two methods of migration are applied to the seismic section. Only holistic migration is successful in detecting the location of the fault.

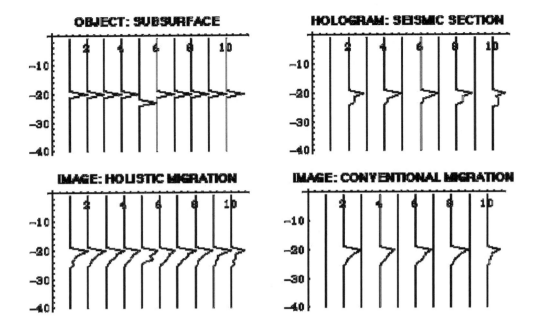

Fig. 13. The object is a small flaw on an interface. Two methods of migration are applied to the seismic section. Only holistic migration is successful in detecting the flaw.

Three examples comparing conventional migration with holistic migration follow. In each example the same seismic section is used for both conventional migration and holistic migration. The first example is the case of a point diffractor (**Fig. 11**). Diffractions differ from true reflections in that the energy from a shot returns from or near the point diffractor without appearing to obey the reflection law (incidence angle equals reflection angle). Any reflector may be considered as made up of a continuum of diffraction points lying on locus of the reflector. In the example shown in the figure, the given point diffractor falls through the cracks of conventional migration, but is easily found by holistic migration. The second example is that of a sharp diffracting edge at a fault. (**Fig. 12**). The final example is the case of a small flaw on an interface (**Fig. 13**).

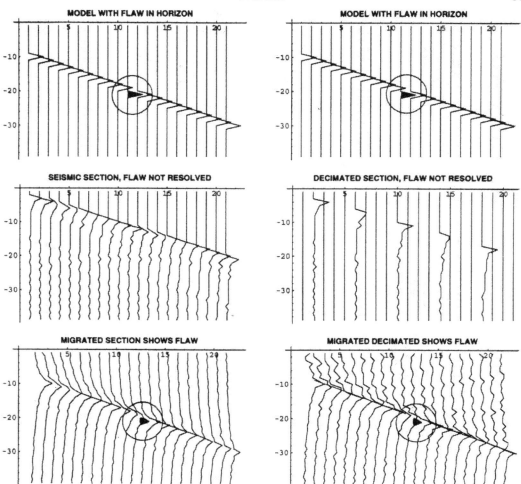

Fig. 14. The top two diagrams show the same geology. The middle two diagrams show a dense seismic section and a decimated section. The bottom two diagrams show the respective migration results. In both case the geologic flaw is detecte

In Fig. 14, he top two diagrams are identical. Each shows the same geology, namely a sloping horizon which is straight except for slight flaw. (b) The middle two diagrams show seismic sections for this geology. The one on the left shows the dense seismic section. The one on the right shows the decimated section with 75 percent of its traces gone. (c) The bottom two diagrams show the migration results. The one on the left is the conventional migration of the dense seismic section. The one on the right is the holographic migration of the decimated seismic section. In both case the geologic flaw is detected. In this case, the acquisition of only 25 percent of the traces gives a migration result almost as good as the acquisition of 100 percent of the traces.

Conclusion

In principle, a hologram and a seismic section are the same. When a hologram is illuminated or a seismic section is migrated, each depicts the entire image of the unattainable object. Moreover, any part of the hologram also depicts the entire image of the object. The same is true in the seismic case if conventional migration is replaced by holistic migration. As a result, holographic seismic imaging allows subsurface images to achieve resolution beyond that predicted by conventional digital processing techniques.

References

Dobrin, M. B., A. L. Ingalls, and J. A. Long, 1965, Velocity and frequency filtering of seismic data using laser light, *Geophysics* vol. 30, pp. 1144–1178..

Gabor, Dennis, A new microscopic principle, 1948, *Nature*, vol. 161, No. 4098, pp. 777-778

Neidell, Norman S., 1997, Perceptions in seismic imaging. Part 1: Kirchhoff migration operators in space and offset time, an appreciation, *The Leading Edge*, vol. 16, pp. 1005-1006.

Neidell, Norman S., 1997, Perceptions in seismic imaging. Part 2: Reflective and diffractive contributions to seismic imaging, *The Leading Edge*, vol. 16, pp. 1121-1123.

Neidell, Norman S., 1997, Perceptions in seismic imaging. Part 3: Kirchhoff seismic imaging, A transform view, *The Leading Edge*, vol. 16, pp. 1241-1243.

Neidell, Norman S., 1997, Perceptions in seismic imaging. Part 4: Resolution considerations in imaging propagation media as distinct from wavefields, *The Leading Edge*, vol. 16, pp. 1412-1415.

Neidell, N. S., and E. R. Prince Jr., 1998, West Cameron 3D Transition Zone seismic survey: A practical proof of concept for extended resolution imaging: OTC Paper 8678.

Robinson, E. A., 1998, Further to Norman Neidell's series–Holistic migration: *The Leading Edge*, 17, 313–314.

Preface
Mike Perz and Gary Margrave

Mike Perz (ARCIS Seismic Solutions) and Gary Margrave (University of Calgary) wrote "Assessing the Impact of Robinson's First Deconvolution Paper" (*CSEG Recorder*, February 2005). Some of its highlights are:

It is difficult to overestimate the importance and depth of Enders Robinson's contributions to geophysical signal processing. Early among these, and indispensable in modern data processing, is the theory of spiking deconvolution as set forth in a classic paper in 1957 titled *Predictive Decomposition of Seismic Traces*. Appearing in *Geophysics* and authored solely by Robinson, this paper triggered a revolution in data processing by demonstrating that

> (1) the seismic wavelet could be estimated directly from the seismic trace itself and
>
> (2) an effective inverse for this wavelet can be designed and applied.

This process has come to be called deconvolution and the resulting deconvolved trace usually shows a dramatic improvement in temporal resolution as well as an apparent reduction in strength of coherent noises like ground roll."

Today, the details of deconvolution theory are a standard component in the education of a geophysicist and it is not our intent to review them here. Rather, we intend to concentrate on Robinson's paper and, with the acute perspective of hindsight, comment upon the clarity of its vision and its relevance to our present understanding. In doing so, we hope to answer such questions as (1) Who were Robinson's major influences in developing his 1957 paper? (2) Did Robinson get it right from the beginning or were there significant missing ingredients? and (3) Do we understand the theory today in the same terms as were originally used?

In a section entitled *Wavelet Theory*, Robinson describes the 1940 theory of Ricker that the seismogram can be regarded as an elaborate wavelet complex. Though never stated explicitly, this theory is clearly a convolutional theory as it explicitly builds a seismogram as a superposition of many wavelets, with different strengths and arrival times. It is also recognizably a nonstationary convolutional theory since it recognizes the wavelet as a traveling wavelet, the shape of which is determined by the nature of the absorption spectrum of the earth for elastic waves. Robinson goes on to explicitly invoke the minimum-phase assumption, much as we would today, and characterizes such a wavelet as a one-sided transient which damps with a certain degree of rapidity. Later, the minimum-phase wavelet is defined as that which results from the Wold-Kolomogorov factorization of the power spectrum. Robinson's equation for the minimum phase $\theta(\omega)$ is an explicit prescription for constructing the minimum-phase spectrum and it is completely equivalent to our modern statement that the minimum-phase spectrum is the Hilbert transform of the logarithm of the amplitude spectrum. However, Robinson's equation for the minimum phase $\theta(\omega)$ is presented in a form that would be very efficient for numerical calculations in that it takes advantages of available symmetries such as the power spectrum being the same for positive and negative frequencies.

Interestingly, it appears that Robinson's primary motivation for invoking the minimum phase assumption was not physical reasonableness, but rather the fact that minimum phase sequences possessed certain desirable mathematical properties which we'll describe below. In 1966, over ten years after completing his thesis, he provided a physical justification for the minimum phase assumption by noting that certain physically plausible wave propagation effects—notably the source ghost and the water-bottom reverberation pulse-train, could be reasonably modeled via minimum phase sequences. In that same *Geophysics* paper he writes, "At the time of the writing of my thesis at MIT, some (physically-rooted) checks of the above (minimum phase) model were made but were necessarily of a limited nature because of the data and computing facilities ..."

And so we see that by connecting the seismic trace to Wold via Ricker, Robinson has made the two key assumptions which together form the cornerstone of today's deconvolution algorithms, namely that the wavelet is minimum phase, and that the reflectivity is white (i.e. unpredictable). Today, we're sufficiently familiar with the concept of white reflectivity that we often take the idea for granted, but one could imagine that the notion of ascribing a purely random behaviour to something as intrinsically deterministic as geology would be quite a stretch in 1957! At least it would have been without the mathematical bolstering of the Wold decomposition theorem.

After this analysis, we feel that the deconvolution algorithm of Robinson's 1957 paper has withstood the "test of time" far better that the vast majority of geophysical innovations. It is not just that the physical analysis was sound, but also the proposed algorithm has proven very robust in the presence of the many complications found in real data. While our modern understanding has matured somewhat and both surface-consistent and nonstationary extensions of Robinson's method have been developed, we are still fundamentally in agreement with the trace model (proposed by Ricker and championed by Robinson) and with the perspective of minimum-phase prediction error filtering for wavelet deconvolution. It is certainly true that these ideas are approximations to the complexity of real seismic data, and approximations, by their very nature, are not at all unique. However, in a field changing as rapidly as exploration geophysics, the longevity of an idea is often directly related to the intangible art and wisdom of the approximation. By thriving for 50 years, Robinson's deconvolution demonstrates a very high level of both wisdom and art.

John Nash, a beautiful mind

Instructors at MIT Mathematics Department from 1949
(I have included only those who are shown possessing a PhD in the MIT catalogue of the year.-- Haynes Miller)

1948
Julian Herman Blau
Felix Earl Browder   Rutgers Univ
Friedrich Ignaz Mountner
John David Newburgh

1949
Tom Mike Apostol   Caltech
Earl Alexander Coddington   UCLA
Bernard William Lindgren
George Springer   Indiana University

1950
Robert Duncan Luce   UC Irvine
Walter Rudin   University of Wisconsin
Isadore Manual Singer   MIT

1951
George Francis Denton Duff   University of Toronto
John Nash   Princeton University

1952
James B. Serrin   University of Minnesota
Gerald Washnitzer   Princeton University

1953
Joseph Harold Sampson   Johns Hopkins University
David L. Wallace

1954
Glen Earl Baxter
James Cassidy Fox
Sigurdur Helgason   MIT

1955
Arthur Paul Mattuck   MIT
William Francis Reynolds   Tufts University
Enders Anthony Robinson   MIT

The following is from Interview with Enders Robinson by Canadian Society of Exploration Geophysicists:

October 2005. Enders was the invited inaugural speaker for the 2005 CSEG (Canadian Society of Exploration Geophysicists) "DoodleTrain" held in Calgary, Alberta, Canada in the first week of November, and kicked off that educational week with his illuminating talk entitled 'Geophysical Exploration – Past and Future.'

Enders Robinson is a very familiar name in geophysics. All geophysicists have studied digital signal processing of seismic records, which was originally developed by Enders. Amongst the many different firsts that Enders may have to his credit, he is known most of all for his pioneering work on deconvolution. Fondly, he is called 'Father of Deconvolution.'

Enders has received several awards, most notably the SEG's Medal Award and EAGE's Conrad Schlumberger Award in 1969, SEG Honorary membership in 1983, Donald G. Fink Prize Award of IEEE in 1984, was elected to the National Academy of Engineering in 1988 and the SEG's highest honour, the Maurice Ewing Medal in 2001.

Enders holds an endowed Chair at Columbia University. He has written more than 25 books on digital signal analysis, seismic data processing and wavelet estimation, and published over 60 papers.

Larry Lines (University of Calgary) and Satinder Chopra sat down with Enders a day before he delivered his "DoodleTrain" inaugural talk and asked Enders to go down his memory lane and share some of his experiences and accomplishments.

The following is an excerpt from the CSEG interview concerning John Nash.

Larry: *You mentioned John Nash and you probably read the book – A Beautiful Mind – and saw the movie. How authentic is the movie or the book?*

Enders: Sylvia Nassar, the author, dedicated the book to Alicia Larde Nash, who is John's wife. Alicia has devoted her life to John and she well deserves the recognition that both the book and the movie give her. For the academic year 1955-1956 I was an instructor in the MIT mathematics department, and John Nash was an assistant professor. And that's when I got to know John well, although I had known him before that. We became good friends for we had a common interest in economic analysis. He would come to my office about 5 or 6 PM and say let's go and eat. Often Alicia would join us. In July 1956 I went to New York and worked for Standard Oil Company (New Jersey). John took a leave from

MIT to spend the academic year 1956-1957 at the Institute of Advanced Study in Princeton. He chose to live in Manhattan and commute to Princeton on the train. His first apartment, in a low rent area just outside of Greenwich Village, was what is known as a cold-water flat. A heavy iron bathtub was bolted down in the middle of the kitchen floor. He told me that water heated on the stove could be transferred more easily to a bathtub placed there than somewhere else. Soon Alicia moved to New York, and John and Alicia were married in February 1957. They rented a nice apartment near New York University from a professor on academic leave. The apartment was large and cheerful, and the walls were lined with bookcases filled with the books of the absent professor. I would have dinner there with John and Alicia. Everything was perfect. However John was being recast into the likeness of a "respectable" professor. John did not fit the mold. John and Alicia went back to MIT and I ended up in Mathematics at the University of Wisconsin. I still remember the last postcard that I received from John. It was 1958. Among other recommendations, he wrote in large letters, "Sell New Jersey Zinc." The mines of that ill-fated company were a mile deep and as black as pitch. The postcard seemed like an omen. I went back to Massachusetts for Christmas 1958 to be with family. John telephoned me to go to a Christmas party in Cambridge given by Andrew Gleason, a Harvard mathematics professor who is justly famous for his work on one of Hilbert's unsolved problems. Alicia and John picked me up in their car, and we went to the party and had a good time. To me, John was just the same as always. After the party they drove me back. A few months later, in April 1959, I learned that John had been sent to McLean Hospital, a psychiatric hospital. This was beginning of a downward journey that over the next several years subjected John to hospitalization and to drug and shock treatments. The movie shows one such treatment, grim. The movie is a script written from the book slanted with a Hollywood viewpoint. Entirely fictitious scenes were added to the movie for effect. John was neither as eccentric nor as glamorous as the movie portrays. Along with others, I believe that John's condition was not as bad as imagined. I feel that the treatments were worse than the ailment. Instead John should have been allowed to revert to his old ways with no set schedule either at work or at home. He was better off in the cold-water flat. The treatments took away his memory and he was finished as a mathematician. A comparable case is that of Ernest Hemmingway, the writer, who was hospitalized and given shock treatments. The result was that Hemmingway lost his memory, and his life as a writer was

> finished. The pity was that people looked upon John as a distinguished professor who should act as such. They thought that the treatments would render him "normal." They did not truly understand the sensitive and somewhat childlike person underneath and they would not accept John as he was. Today we, as a people, are much more forgiving, and the old destructive types of shock treatments are no longer used.

[Note added in 2019: In retrospect, it seems that John and Alicia wanting to see me at Christmas 1958 was almost like a cry for help. I had often been with them in the year before their marriage and the year after their marriage. They would seek my advice. One particular instance occurred in New York in 1957 after they were just married. The Courant Institute of Applied Mathematics at New York University had offered John Nash a very attractive professorship which he was tempted to accept. Unfortunately I took the position that he should return to MIT. That was a mistake. The harmless idiosyncrasies of John Nash would hardly have been noticed in the free-for-all of Manhattan. Even in Christmas 1958 I was completely unaware that such a tragedy could befall someone so kind and naïve as John Nash.]

Tadeusz J. Ulrych

In GEOPHYSICS, Vol. 64, No. 5, September-October 1999, Tadeusz J. Ulrych (University of British Columbia, Vancouver, British Columbia V6T 1Z5, Canada) writes:

> The earth's reflectivity is one of the principal targets of seismic exploration for oil and gas. It exhibits some fascinating properties. It is blue. It is fractal. In all probability, it reflects the output of a chaotic generator. I examine some of these characteristics here. Specifically, I look at the statistical properties of a canonical chaotic model, and I examine the effect of multiples on the statistical properties of seismograms generated from primary reflectivities.

> This article is a tribute to Enders Robinson. He is a pioneer who has inspired many. He inspires many to this day. I am one of them.

Bill Mueller

On Thursday, July 10, 2008, Bill Mueller (Antlers Exploration, "We See Things Others Don't") writes:

> Dear Enders: In the middle 1960's I was a geophysics major at the University of Tulsa. Most of my geophysics courses were taught at night by research geophysicists from Pan American Petroleum Company (Amoco) Research center in Tulsa. I understood that they all worked with you and they brought us the

cutting edgework that you were doing at the time on signal processing, especially deconvolution.

I was way, way ahead of most of the industry when I graduated and it was that background helped me immensely in starting a geophysics career that is now approaching 40 years

Again, Thanks. Bill

Medical imaging

by Enders A. Robinson

Feedback

The promise of medical imaging is the discovery of that which we yet know not of. In the late 1950s, the first transistorized digital computers were manufactured. As a result, the decade of the 1960s saw the conversion of the oil exploration industry from analog filtering to digital signal processing. The mathematical inverse process known as deconvolution made it possible to explore successfully in all areas of the earth including the areas under the seas.

Deconvolution requires massive parallel processing. The computer industry accommodated and developed special-purpose digital signal processing (DSP) computers, which at the time were called array processors (also known as vector processors). As time went on, these DSP computers were replaced by microchips, as were all digital computers. In 1986 the National Academy of Engineering (NAE) of the United States of America elected Enders Robinson as member with the citation:

> "For pioneering contributions that have led to the evolution of seismic processing from hand digitization of the 1950s to today's custom deconvolution chip"

The hand digitization of the 1950s was the forerunner of what was to come. Practically all communications today are done with digital data. The telephone is digital, the television is digital, the cinema is digital, the music is digital, the camera is digital. Now in the second decade of the twenty-first century, DSP chips are everywhere. The deconvolution chip is the prototype digital signal processing (DSP) chip. Usually the NAE credits new members for such things as "innovative research" or "revolutionary discoveries." Certainly such chips are vital, but why would the NAE mention a chip and not mention seemingly more important mathematical research?

The National Academy foresaw what many others did not foresee. In 1986 the National Academy realized that the era of mathematical numeral analysis was losing its position at the forefront of computing. Instead the era of communication was at the beginning of its meteoric rise to ascendency.

Communication and the attendant imaging require massive usage of digital signal processing. Today in 2015, digital signal processing is a powerful technology used everywhere. This technology is universally possible because of inexpensive and tiny DSP (Digital Signal Processing) chips. DSP chips are an integral part of audio and video systems, television, telephones, cameras, radar, sonar, transmission fiber cable, automobiles, airplanes, ships, space vehicles, programmable heart pacemakers, other medical devices, and all types of automation in manufacturing and logistics.

Digital Signal Processing (DSP) chips are used to satisfy the insatiable needs for communication among people and for the regulation and control of machines and devices. DSP chips take real-world signals like position, voice, audio, video, pressure, temperature, and medical readings to process them digitally in order to produce the desired results. Every time you use a mobile phone, you are using a DSP chip. Every time you drive an automobile, you are using several dozen DSP chips. The new medical devices that monitor you heath all use DSP chips.

However, in today's world we want more. We no longer want the old cell phone but we want a smart phone that plays not just off-the-shelf movies but movies of events taking place. All is fine with the mathematics. The same mathematics is just as useful. What is needed is plethora of sensors that can record the live action in place. The sensors have become tiny, inexpensive and light. Seventy years ago they might use 10 sensors for each source point; today they can use up to one million. The quality of the images goes up accordingly. There are plans to put up not just one big earth satellite but a whole array of small satellites that will image closely-spaced pointe on the earth to amazing accuracy.

Medical imaging is the most promising development in the offing. Medical imaging is the technique and process of creating visual representations of the interior of a body for clinical analysis and medical intervention. Medical imaging seeks to reveal internal structures hidden by the skin and bones, as well as to diagnose and treat disease. Medical imaging includes imaging technologies such as X-ray radiography, magnetic resonance imaging, medical ultrasonography or ultrasound, endoscopy, medical photography and positron emission tomography.

Medical imaging is a set of techniques that noninvasively produce images of the internal aspect of the body. In this restricted sense, medical imaging can be seen as the solution of mathematical inverse problems. Deconvolution is the main tool that is used to insure accurate images. This means that cause (the properties of living tissue) is inferred from effect (the observed signal). In the case of medical ultrasonography, the probe consists of ultrasonic pressure waves and echoes that go inside the tissue to show the internal structure. The term noninvasive is used to denote a procedure where no instrument is introduced into a patient's body which is the case for most imaging techniques used.

The key to the use of waves to detect the unknown interior structure is reflection. Medical ultrasonography uses high frequency broadband sound waves in the megahertz (10^6 Hz) range. The sound waves are introduced into the body. The waves are reflected by tissue. The reflected waves are processed by a computer to produce images. Today medical ultrasonography includes imaging the abdominal organs, heart, breast, muscles, tendons, arteries and veins. The high frequency sound waves are sent into the tissue in a multilayered bodily structure. The signal is attenuated and returned at separate intervals. The paths of reflected sound waves in the body are mathematically the same as in the paths of reflected seismic waves in the subsurface of the earth.

The concepts of ultrasound differ from other medical imaging modalities in the fact that it is operated by the transmission and receipt of sound waves. Ultrasound was first used to image unborn babies; the early medical pioneers worked closely with the geophysicists.

At present, ultrasound provides less detail than techniques such as CT or MRI. However, it has several advantages which make it ideal. For example, it depicts moving structures in real-time and it emits no harmful radiation. Ultrasound is safe to use and does not appear to cause any adverse effects. It is also inexpensive and quick to perform. Ultrasound scanners can be taken to critically ill patients in intensive care units, avoiding the danger caused while moving the patient to the radiology department. The real time moving image obtained can be used to guide drainage and biopsy procedures. Doppler capabilities on modern scanners allow the blood flow in arteries and veins to be assessed.

An oil field is like a great pulsating entity made up of stratigraphic layers interspersed with movements of naturally occurring water, oil and gas together with injected fluids. The weathered rock that makes up the surface layers presents a great natural barrier to the penetrating seismic signals. This barrier is overcome by permanently placing transmitters and receivers at depth at several hundreds of feet within the earth.

In a similar way, a human body is like a great pulsating entity made up of tissue layers and bone interspersed with movements of naturally occurring blood, water and other fluids. The human skin presents a great natural barrier to the penetrating ultrasonic signals. This barrier can be overcome by permanently placing transmitters and receivers within the body. Ideally, on your smart phone, you could see what is going on inside mind and body of everything in real time. How much do we want to know? What are the limits?

A servomechanism is a device which acts continually on the basis of information to attain a specified goal in the face of A servomechanism makes use of feedback. Feedback comes in two varieties: (1) negative feedback and (2) positive feedback. Feedback is called negative when it decreases any departure from a given bearing. Feedback is called positive when it increases any departure from a given bearing. A positive feedback mechanism is the exact opposite of a negative feedback mechanism.

With negative feedback, the output reduces the original stimulus. In a positive feedback system, the output enhances the original stimulus.

Negative feedback can be used to make the large output signal of an amplifier conform closely in shape to the small input. Negative feedback amplifiers were extremely important in communication systems long before the day of cybernetics. An example of negative feedback would be the bodily mechanism that controls of glucose (blood sugar) by insulin. When blood sugar rises, receptors in the body detect the change. As a result, the pancreas secretes insulin into the blood. The effect is the lowering of glucose. Once the glucose level reaches homeostasis, the pancreas stops releasing insulin.

The key is that a negative feedback mechanism inhibits the original stimulus and a positive feedback mechanism enhances it. An example of a positive feedback would be the mechanism of blood clotting. A vessel is damaged. Platelets begin clinging to the injured place. Chemicals are released that attract more platelets. The platelets keep accumulating and releasing chemicals until a clot is made. In his book Cybernetics, Wiener puts great emphasis on negative feedback as an element of nervous control and on its failure as an explanation of disabilities, such as tremors of the hand, which are ascribed to failures of a negative feedback system of the body.

We can easily think of other examples of feedback. The thermostat on the wall uses negative feedback. The autopilots of airplanes use negative feedback in manipulating the controls in order to keep the compass and altimeter readings at assigned values. The thermostat on the wall measures the temperature of the room and turns the furnace off or on so as to maintain the temperature at a constant value.

Physiological parameters must remain within a narrow range for a person to survive. Negative feedback loops within the body keep physiological parameters such as heart rate within the target range. For example, the average resting heart rate should remain in the target range from 60 to 100 beats per minute. A negative feedback loop works by adjusting an output, such as heart rate, in response to a change in input, such as blood pressure. A basic loop consists of a receptor, a control center and an effector. In this case, the receptor measures blood pressure, the control center is the brain, effector is the heart muscle.

If a person is at rest and blood pressure increases, pressure receptors in the carotid arteries detect this change in input and send nerve impulses to the medulla of the brain. This action tells the brain to reduce nerve impulses that stimulate the heart muscle to contract. The heart contracts more slowly and the heart rate decreases, causing blood pressure to decrease to within target levels.

When exercising there is an increase in heart rate and blood pressure. The body increases blood flow to muscle tissue in response to the increased demand for oxygen.

The homeostatic set points of heart rate and blood pressure are therefore "reset" higher. Vigorous exercise can make heart rate increase to as much as 180 beats per minute or more. Negative feedback loops act to maintain heart rate and blood pressure within these new higher target ranges. After exercise the muscle tissues no longer demand as much oxygen so homeostatic set points are reset back to the original target.

Human beings use negative feedback in controlling their motions to achieve certain ends. For example, a person uses negative feedback from eye to hand in guiding a pen across the paper, and negative feedback from ear to tongue and lips in learning to speak. The animal uses negative feedback to maintain bodily temperature despite the outside temperature. It uses negative feedback to maintain constant chemical properties of the blood and tissues. Homeostasis is the ability to keep body within a narrow range of limits despite environmental conditions outside of the body. There are many negative feedback pathways in biological systems, including: temperature regulation, blood pressure regulation, blood sugar regulation, and thyroid regulation.

The physiological system of a higher animal must maintain internal stability. Homeostasis refers to the ability of an organism or a cell to regulate its internal conditions so as to stabilize health and functioning, regardless of the outside conditions. Homeostasis is achieved by an arrangement of feedback loops. Homeostasis preserves the internal state at which the human body operates best. The human body has its own internal controllers for maintaining its temperature, pH, hormone levels, blood sugar and other internal variable levels. We sweat to cool off when hot, and we shiver to warm up when cold. In entomology, homeostasis is the ability of members of a colony of social insects to behave cooperatively to produce a desired result, such as when bees coordinate the fanning of their wings to cool the hive.

The wavelet

It was clear that in 1953 the oil company geophysicists were not particularly interested in learning about the complexities of digital signal processing. The idiom "as easy as pie" is used to describe a pleasurable and simple task. The idiom refers to eating a piece of apple pie. The first attempt of the GAG was to make, **not the theory** of deconvolution, but **instead the computation** of deconvolution as easy as pie. The digital computer achieved this goal. In 1953, Raytheon was ready to perform seismic deconvolution. The oil companies could outsource their seismic records to Raytheon. However, at that time, the oil company geophysicists, for the most part, showed signs of computer anxiety. The oil companies liked the way that they were already doing things. To abandon their familiar analog methods and venture forth into the unknown domain of digital techniques did not appeal to them. They did not take advantage of computer service that Raytheon offered.

In research the GAG was exploring the complexities of multichannel deconvolution. The GAG was obsessed with the problem of locating hidden reflections. That was achieved by the digital process of deconvolution. The GAG and Raytheon had computed hundreds of digitally-deconvolved seismic traces. The hidden reflections were revealed. The discussion in 1953 was: "The world is analog, so the GAG should devise an analog version of deconvolution? Find an analog way to do deconvolution and then the oil companies will consider it. " Nothing had changed in 1953; analog was still supreme.

Frederic Chopin (1810-1849) was a Polish composer and a virtuoso pianist of the Romantic era. His genius was "without equal in his generation." Chopin wrote:

> "Simplicity is the final achievement. After one has played a vast quantity of notes and more notes, it is simplicity that emerges as the crowning reward of art."

The GAG computations "played a vast quantity" of deconvolved seismic traces. But what was the "simplicity that emerges as the crowning reward of art?" And then the answer came! **The "simplicity" is the wavelet.** The wavelet is the final achievement. More specifically, the existence of a physical seismic minimum-delay wavelet was affirmed by computation. From the time of Pythagoras until then wavelets were either actually seen on the water or mentally seen as mathematical constructs. No wavelet had ever before been computed from observational data. The physical wavelet (shown in Figure 10.) computed from seismic data was the highpoint in my PhD thesis in 1954.

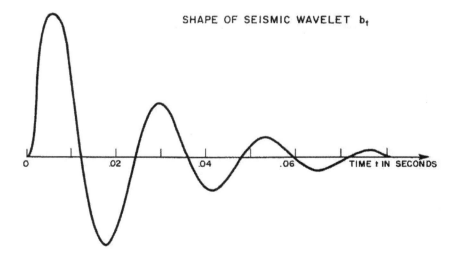

Figure 10. Depiction of the first physical wavelet ever computed from observational data. "Seeing is believing."

Geophysicists took up the digital wavelet in research and have produced remarkable results. More papers are written on wavelets today than those on deconvolution. In the early 1980s Jean P. Morlet, a French geophysicist, applied wavelet knowledge to devise the cycle-octave transform, known as the wavelet transform.

The word "wavelet" goes back to Christiaan Huygens in 1690. There is a traditional story that as a boy Huygens watched the water on the canals in Holland near his house. Wavefronts were running before his eyes. How were successive wavefronts related? In answer, Huygens reasoned that a wavefront is formed by all the wavelets emanating from the previous wavefront. Huygens Principle appears in every elementary physics book. It states that light propagates as waves and every point on a wavefront is a source of spherical wavelets. The wavefront at any instant is the envelope of spherical wavelets emanating from the wavefront at the prior instant.

For simplicity, consider the case of a homogeneous isotropic medium, so all the secondary spherical wavelets have the same radius. In such a case, the medium represents a linear space-invariant system. In engineering terms, the wavefront at the initial time is the input to the system, the wavelet is the impulse response of the system, and the wavefront at some later time is the output of the system. Thus Huygens principle, in fact, states that the wavefront at some later time (i.e. the output) is equal to the convolution of the wavefront at the initial time (i.e. the input) with the wavelet (i.e. the impulse response). In other words, Huygens principle is a spatial convolutional model in which the wavelet plays the key role. Despite the prominence of this principle, the Huygens wavelet always remained as a conceptual concept in the historical development of physics. Two centuries had to pass before Huygens concept of wavelet was given mathematical form. In mathematical terms, the Green's function is the solution of the wave equation with an impulsive source function. The Green's function is the wavelet.

For example, in seismic exploration at sea the water layer acts as an imperfect lens that masks the reflections from depth. In other words, reverberation in the water layer hides the signals coming from the geologic interfaces. The reverberation, which is a slowly damped oscillation, represents the wavelet. For such a case, the **convolutional model** states the recorded seismic trace is the convolution of the reverberation wavelet with the reflected signals coming from depth. Having the convolutional model of the trace, the next step is to deconvolve the trace. In other words, the next step is to unscramble the trace to get back the components. The deconvolution operator is the inverse of the seismic wavelet. Deconvolution removes the wavelet, thereby making the recorded trace reverberation-free.

The **convolutional model** would be the basis used for making Wiener's mathematics as easy as pie. The two physical quantities are (1) the impulses (e.g., the reflectivity of the underground interfaces) and (2) the wavelet (e.g., the seismic wavelet). The convolution model is: The seismic trace is the convolution of these two quantities.

Deconvolution

The Greek philosopher Plato presented the *Allegory of the Cave* in his work *The Republic*. It is a dialogue between Plato's brother Glaucon and Plato's mentor Socrates. The story is narrated by the Socrates. Socrates describes a gathering of people who have lived chained to the wall of a cave all of their lives. They are constricted so they can see only the face of a blank wall. They watch the shadows projected on the wall by objects passing in front of a fire behind them. They give names to these shadows. The shadows are as close as the people get to viewing reality. Socrates then explains how the philosopher is like a person who is freed from the chains. He can now see what is behind. The philosopher perceives the true form of the objects rather than the shadows as seen by the people. The philosopher comes to understand that the shadows on the wall do not make up reality at all. The reality consists of the objects themselves.

Let us describe this situation in mathematical terms. The shadow projected by a point source represents the wavelet. The shadows projected by an object passing in front of the fire represent the convolution of the object and the wavelet. The philosopher, in effect, deconvolves the shadows on the wall. In other words, he removes the wavelet from the shadows and thereby can see the objects in their reality.

The allegory is related to Plato's Theory of Forms. The material world is known to us through sensation. Plato's Forms possess the highest and most fundamental kind of reality. In mathematical terms, we perceive the material world by means of remote sensing. For example, physicists see images in the bubble chamber, but not the elementary particles themselves. Geophysicists see seismic images, but not the underground earth itself. The received images correspond to Plato's shadows. Deconvolution removes the interfering wavelets from the received images. The deconvolved images correspond to Plato's' reality.

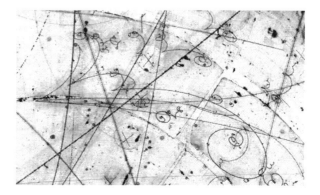

Fig. 1. Particle tracks in bubble chamber

Geophysicists used to live chained in a cave, so constricted so they could only see the face of a blank wall. The geophysicists could look at the seismic reflections projected on the wall by the underground structure of the earth. They ascribed forms of the underground earth but they would mistake appearance for reality. Digital Signal Processing (DSP) freed geophysicists from the cave. They began to understand that seismic reflection data is not constitutive of reality. Geophysicists deconvolved the reflection data and thereby obtained the true form of the underground structure of earth. They found Plato's reality. Deconvolution is now used in all fields of science.

Let us give another example. A person speaks into a mobile telephone. Inside the telephone is a DSP (Digital Signal Processing) chip. The chip deconvolves the speaker's voice. The deconvolved signal is transmitted and is received by the listener's mobile telephone. Its DSP chip re-convolves the signal thereby reproducing the speaker's voice.

Genome and proteome

A gene is the basic physical unit of heredity. A gene is a linear sequence of nucleotides along a segment of DNA that provides the coded instructions for synthesis of RNA, which, when translated into protein, leads to the expression of hereditary character.

A chromosome is any of several threadlike bodies, consisting of chromatin, that carry the genes in a linear order. The human species has 23 pairs, designated 1 to 22 in order of decreasing size and X and Y for the female and male sex chromosomes respectively. A *genome* is a full set of chromosomes; it encompasses all the inheritable traits of an organism. The genome embodies the genetic material of a living thing. A genome represents the entire set of hereditary instructions for building, running, and maintaining the organism, and passing life on to the next generation. In most living things, the genome is made of a chemical called DNA. In brief, the genome is divided into chromosomes, chromosomes contain genes, and genes are made of DNA.

Each species has its own distinctive genome. There are genomes for dogs, for wheat, for cows, for bacteria. Genomes belong to species, but they also belong to individuals. Every living thing has a unique genome. A person's genome is different from that of every other person. In fact, a person's genome is different from that of every other person who has ever lived. Though unique, a person's genome is still recognizably as a human genome. The difference is simply a matter of degree: The genome differences between two people are much smaller than the genome differences between people and apes. There are 20,300 genes of the known human genome,

Genomes are found in cells, which are the microscopic structures that make up all organisms. In a human there are cells in the muscles, cells in the brain, the cells in the blood, and so on. There are trillions of cells in a human body. With a few exceptions, each of these cells contains a copy of the person's genome. There are huge numbers of genomes in each person's body, in each apple tree, in each whale, in each mushroom, and in each bird: The world is full of genomes. A genome contains information that affects every aspect of behavior and physiology. A person's genome governs the way the person cooks food, digests food, talks, sings, and sleeps.

A genome alone does not make a person, because people are also influenced by human culture and hundreds of other aspects of environment. However, the fact remains that there is no living thing without a genome. Each human being contains a slightly different version of the human genome, but all human genomes are similar enough that we can learn about the human genome in general by studying the genomes of one or a few individual people. The human genome give insights into why some people die of one disease and others die of another disease, why some people like crowds and others do not, why some people are heavy while others are thin.

Let us now turn to proteins. The *proteome* is defined as the set of proteins expressed in a specific cell, given a particular set of conditions. Within a given human proteome, the number of proteins can be as large as 2 million.

Proteins are macromolecules made up of long chains of amino acids. The amino acid chain is constructed when the cellular machinery translates RNA transcripts from DNA in the cell's nucleus. The transfer of information within cells commonly follows this path

$$DNA \to RNA \to protein$$

A protein is any of numerous, highly varied organic molecules constituting a large portion of the mass of every life form and necessary in the diet of all animals and other non-photosynthesizing organisms. A protein is composed of 20 or more amino acids linked in a genetically controlled linear sequence into one or more long polypeptide chains. The final shape and other properties of each protein is determined by the side chains of the amino acids and their chemical attachments. Proteins include such specialized forms as collagen for supportive tissue, hemoglobin for transport, antibodies for immune defense, and enzymes for metabolism.

Proteins provide the control for cellular machinery. They serve a variety of functions within the cell, and there are thousands of distinct proteins and peptides in almost every organism. This great variety comes from a phenomenon known as alternative splicing, in which a particular gene in a cell's DNA can create multiple protein types, based on the demands of the cell at a given time.

The goal of proteomics is to analyze the varying proteomes of an organism at different times, in order to highlight differences between them. In other words, proteomics evaluates the structure and function of biological systems. The protein content of a cancerous cell is often different from that of a healthy cell. Certain proteins in the cancerous cell may not be present in the healthy cell, making these unique proteins good candidates for anti-cancer drugs.

In Platonic terms, the genome represents the reality. The proteome represents the shadows on the wall. The shadows are obtained by convolving the reality with the wavelet. The reality is obtained by deconvolving the shadows by the wavelet.

Microbes

The entire microbe ensemble in the biosphere may be considered as an analog device. A microorganism (or microbe) is a microscopic living organism, which may be single celled or multicellular. Microbiology is the study of microorganisms. Microbes are diverse and include all the bacteria and archaea and almost all the protozoa. They also include some fungi, algae, and certain animals, such as rotifers. Viruses are often classified as microorganisms, despite the fact they are considered as nonliving. Without microbes, life on Earth as we know it would not be possible.

Microbes are found in many places on earth. They live in every part of the biosphere, including soil, hot springs, "seven miles deep" in the ocean, 40 miles high in the atmosphere, and inside rocks down within the Earth's crust. Microbes, under certain test conditions, have been observed to live in the vacuum of outer space. Microbes are adaptable to all sorts of conditions, and survive wherever they are. They thrive in the Mariana Trench, which is the deepest part in the oceans. They thrive inside rocks deep below the sea floor. They thrive hundreds of feet within the Antarctic ice. Microbes play a crucial role in the Earth's ecology. They decompose substances. They are a vital part of the nitrogen cycle. Airborne microbes play a role in the weather. Microbes are increasingly used in biotechnology. Some microorganisms are pathogenic and cause disease and even death in plants and animals.

Microbes were the first forms of life to develop on Earth. They appeared on Earth approximately 3 to 4 billion years ago. True multicellular organisms that solve the problem of regenerating a whole organism from germ cells appeared much later. The vertebrates have only been around for the past half billon years. Microbes tend to have a relatively fast rate of evolution. Most of the microbes reproduce rapidly. Bacteria are also able to freely exchange genes through conjugation, transformation and transduction, even between widely divergent species. This horizontal gene transfer, coupled with a high mutation rate, allows microbes quickly to learn to survive in new environments. This ability has led to the development of strains of bacteria resistant to medical antibiotics.

Microbes can be found throughout the ocean, from rocks and sediments beneath the seafloor, across the vast stretches of open water, to intertidal and surf zones. The diversity and number of microbes in the ocean far exceed that of macroscopic life, and many employ unique life strategies not seen anywhere else on Earth. Some microbes are photosynthetic, deriving their energy from the sun. At deep-ocean sites and around hydrothermal vents and seeps, microbes derive energy from chemical reactions and not the sun. Some microbes prey on others; some obtain carbon from inorganic sources; some are scavengers that feed on dead organisms or other waste organic matter. Certain microbes in the seas can eat hydrocarbons, such as naturally seeping petroleum and petroleum from spills. In other words, fossil life (petroleum) feeds present life (bacteria and animals that eat bacteria).

Ocean microbes play an important role in Earth's biogeochemical cycles, particularly the carbon, nitrogen, phosphorus, iron, and sulfur cycles. They also form the very base of the marine food chain, recycle nutrients and organic matter, and produce things needed by higher organisms to grow and survive. Many have evolved over millions of years to form symbiotic relationships with animals that allow the host animals to live in harsh or otherwise toxic environments, such as the hot, sulfur-rich waters around hydrothermal vents.

Microbiology is the study of microscopic organisms. It is true that certain microbes are associated with various sicknesses. However, most microbes are responsible for beneficial processes. Microbes demonstrate the cognitive abilities of decision-making, group communication, and group behavior. Microbes can communicate with each other in order to form structures and function as a multicellular creature. Microbes use an elaborate language of signals which elicit a wide range of other behaviors. Some microbes use secreted chemicals as messages. One chemical message tells others that there is a lack of food in a particular location. The microbes that receive this message then go in other directions.

Individual microbes send out signals that communicate their presence, and when a certain number have signaled they launch various group activities. This is called "quorum sensing." For example, some colonies of bacteria light up when enough bacteria are present. Similarly, they defend each other from antibiotics, grow food together, and eat each other's waste. Microbes can send signals that determine the numbers of an adversary. In this way, the microbes find out if they are stronger than the defense system of the adversary. When a critical juncture is reached, microbes launch an attack. The attack can take many different forms.

Microbes are usually in constant communication with other microbes inside or outside their colony. They can intercept communication from other microbes and larger creatures. Microbes can change their behavior to defeat the larger creature or to help a comrade. Microbes can interpret the signals of other species and then send return signals to change the behavior of the other organism. Some microbes send signals to trick a rival into lowering its defenses. The signal can stop a yeast cell from growing into a more powerful multicellular fungus organism. In humans, some microbes increase the tendency of children to touch their mouths and thereby aid transmission of the microbe.

In a similar manner, human cells send signals to the bacteria and intercept their communications. A well-known example is the use of yogurt and other probiotics to send helpful signals in the human gut. Natural probiotics are colonies of microbes living in the gut that help the cells to maintain normal function and avoid infections. Incredibly complex communications occur all the time, as countless colonies of bacteria live in and around us. In fact, while a human has about 10 trillion of its own cells, it also has ten to a hundred times more bacterial cells and a thousand times more virus cells at any given time. The vast intercellular communication of microbes determines much of what happens in people.

Quantum mechanics and the uncertainty principle

by Enders A. Robinson

Interference or interaction patterns

Let us explain the Uncertainty Principle as it would apply to students. Every measurement has this characteristic: If one quantity is measured with more precision, another related quantity is measured with less precision. Interference on interaction patterns show how it is impossible to devise a method to classify students as to achievements that will not at the same time disturb the students to change their interaction pattern. Suppose that a first-grade class is divided into two groups; namely, high-achievers in athletics and low-achievers in athletics. At eighth-grade they might have the two separate distributions

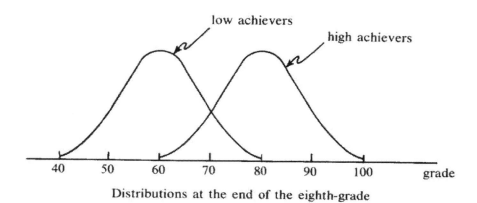

Distributions at the end of the eighth-grade

In the diagram below, the dashed curve is the sum of the distributions given in the above diagram. On the other hand suppose that we did not separate first grade class, but let them continue as one class. At eighth grade their distribution, for example, might be the solid curve in the diagram below.

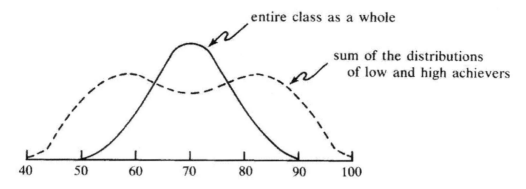

As we see, the solid curve is different from the dashed curve. In other words, the distribution for the entire class as a whole is not simply the sum of the two distributions for the split class. The reason is that there is an *interference* or *interaction effect* between high and low achievers when the entire class is together, and that there is no interference effect when the class has been separated into two distinct groups. In our diagrams we see that in this case the interaction effect resulted in pulling more students in toward the mean. When the class was not separated some low achievers in athletics did better and some high achievers in athletics did worse than they would have done if they were separated. This result obtains for this particular case. Every case is different, so no general statement can be made. The various distributions have to be found before any conclusions can be drawn.

Introduction of quantum mechanics

The science of physics springs from the work of Galileo and Isaac Newton in the seventeenth century. Physics became an exact science. The laws of physics gave exact answers. Unfortunately, sciences dealing with living things (such as biology, education, and economics) are not predisposed to exact answers. In answer, the disciplines of probability and statistics were developed. We can never know the exact makeup of school children. All we can do is find probability distributions as we have discussed above.

In the year 1900, a significant turning point came in physics. It was the introduction of quantum mechanics. The exact Newtonian mechanics worked well for objects on the human scale of things. In a baseball game, the person at bat can see the pitched baseball in motion coming at him. Otherwise he could not hit the baseball. However, Newtonian mechanics does not work for very tiny objects. In those regions quantum mechanics must be used. Quantum mechanics tells us that we cannot see an election in motion no matter what we do.

When one uses the phrase "a bridge too far," the implication is that the goal or mission being described is not going to happen, or is going to wind up being unsuccessful. For example, a company with an overreaching goal might end up going out of business. The bridge between a baseball and an electron is a bridge too far. We can never reach such a bridge. Except for probability distributions, we can never see what is really going on in the quantum world. A teacher in a classroom can see the students and know what is going on. On the other hand, we see electrons essentially as statistics governed by probability distributions and we can never know what is really going on.

Einstein, as a unifier, believed the large and small of the universe could be abstracted into a single unified theory. Emil Johann Wiechert (1861–1928) was a German physicist and geophysicist who made many contributions to both fields, including being among the first to discover the electron and presenting the first verifiable model of a layered structure of the earth. Wiechert exposed a diversity of details in the earth and created tools for the discovery of those details. Wiechert was a diversifier. He believed that the universe is inexhaustible and potentially incomprehensible to the human mind—that no matter how long or far we look into the misty distances, the universe will not conform to abstractions. In 1896 Wiechert said:

> "So far as modern science is concerned, we have to abandon completely the idea that, by going into the realm of the small, we shall reach the ultimate foundations of the universe. I believe we can abandon this idea without any regret. The universe is infinite in all directions, not only above us in the large but also below us in the small. If we start from our human scale of existence and explore the content of the universe further and further, we finally arrive, both in the large and in the small, at misty distances where first our senses and then even our concepts fail us." Emil Wiechert, "Die Theorie der Elektrodynamik und die Röntgen'sche Entdeckung," Schriften der Physikalisch-Ökonomischen Gesellschaft zu Königsberg 37, 1–48 (1896))

Where is the misty distance in the small? It is the distance given by the size of an atom. For particles smaller than an atom, our senses and even our concepts fail us. Let us explain. A chemical element (such as sulfur) is made up of identical sulfur atoms. Atoms are extremely small; typical sizes are around 100 picometers. Subatomic particles are particles much smaller than an atom. Subatomic particles are so small that any attempt to predict their behavior using classical physics (as if they were baseballs) gives noticeably incorrect predictions due to quantum effects. In other words, in the subatomic world, our senses fail us.

Matter waves

In 1674 in Delft, Antoni van Leeuwenhoek (1632–1723) looked through the microscope that he had carefully constructed. The specimen was a small glass tube containing water from a nearby lake. Leeuwenhoek did not see pure clear water. Instead he saw another world, a world unknown up to that time. It was an aquarium filled with minuscule little animals swimming in all directions, each about one thousand times as small as a tiny cheese mite. Some were shaped like spiral serpents, some were globular, and some were elongated ovals. Leeuwenhoek had discovered the microscopic world inhabited by microorganisms (also known as microbes. The biological world was much more diversified than previously believed.

In 1924, Louis de Broglie (1892–1987) maintained that, just as light has wave and particle properties, all microscopic material particles (e.g., electrons, protons, atoms, molecules) also have dual character. They behave as a particle as well as wave. Such a wave is called a *matter wave*, a *de Broglie wave*, or a *probability wave.* (A probability wave is a wave whose amplitude at a given region and over a given time interval corresponds to the probability of observing a given particle within that region in that time.) In fact, the concept that matter behaves like a wave is referred to as the de Broglie hypothesis. This means that an electron which has been regarded as a particle also behaves like a wave. Thus, according to de Broglie, all of the material particles in motion possess wave characteristics. However, the dual nature is significant for only microscopic bodies. For large bodies, the wavelengths are too small to be measured. Probability waves play a central role in the theory of quantum mechanics.

The wave-particle duality refers to the exhibition of both wave-like and particle-like properties by a single entity. For example, electrons undergo diffraction and can interfere with each other as waves, but they also act as point-like masses and electric charges. The measurement of the wave function will randomly "collapse," or rather "decohere," the probability wave into a sharply peaked function at a well-defined position, (subject to uncertainty), a property traditionally associated with particles. More precisely, a wave function collapse is said to occur when a wave function (initially in a superposition of several eigenstates) appears to reduce to a single eigenstate (by observation). Such a collapse is the essence of measurement in quantum mechanics and connects the probability-wave function with classical observables such as position and momentum. In simple words, the measurement of a probability wave yields a particle. We can observe the interference of mechanical waves whenever we throw stones into a pond. We can never observe the interference of probability waves because the very act of observation collapses the waves into particles, which in turn are subject to the Heisenberg Uncertainty Principle.

Quantum mechanics solves the problems of the stability of atoms and the nature of spectral lines. It also brings chemistry into the framework of physics. Quantum electrodynamics (i.e., the quantum field theory of photons, electrons, and positrons) has led to the Standard Model. This model unifies physics, except for gravitation, dark matter, and many unexplained numerical quantities. The Standard Model is a set of equations that can fit onto a single sheet of paper. This sheet of paper arguably represents the greatest intellectual achievement of mankind up to the present. It is a major step toward the Holy Grail, i.e. a unified field theory (UFT). It is a theory that allows all that is usually thought of as fundamental forces and elementary particles to be written in terms of a single field. There is currently no accepted unified field theory, and thus it remains an open line of research.

So, when it comes to "seeing" our research, an additional aspect we should discuss involves sight, resolution, and probability. The resolution of a microscope, for example, refers to the shortest distance between two points that a user can still see as separate images. The resolution of Leeuwenhoek's microscope, which uses light as its illumination source, is sufficient to see microbes. In comparison, an electron microscope uses a beam of accelerated electrons as a source of illumination. Because the wavelength of an electron can be up to 100,000 times shorter than that of visible light photons, the electron microscope has a higher resolving power than a light microscope and can reveal the structure of smaller objects. Can atoms be seen under an electron microscope? The answer is partially yes. In certain situations, the images can be interpreted as representations of atoms or even atomic nuclei. Has anyone ever seen electrons and protons under an electron microscope? Electrons and protons are subatomic particles that travel as waves. A subatomic particle is smaller than an atom. When we talk about waves at the atomic level, we are referring to matter waves, i.e., probability waves which are 3D graphs that describe the probability of finding an electron at a certain point around a nucleus. Electrons are much smaller than most atomic nuclei, so we are able to use them as a medium to view the features of atoms. Electrons are incredibly tiny and have extremely low mass. They move extremely fast and, due to the Heisenberg Uncertainty Principle, their exact position is practically unknowable. We can only approximate their position to within a certain uncertainty. Without being able to acquire an exact position makes it impossible to view an electron. That aside, their mass is so low that even the smallest interaction with them (involving another electron or photon) will send them flying off so that we cannot view them. Because there is no way to see electrons, we use the electron cloud model of the atom, which indicates where electrons are likely to be, but never where they actually are. The electron cloud is, in fact, a probability field.

Gravity and magnetic methods are an essential part of oil exploration. Despite being comparatively low-resolution, gravity and magnetic methods have some very big advantages. These geophysical methods passively measure natural variations in the earth's gravity and magnetic fields over a map area and then attempt to relate these variations to geologic features in the subsurface. Lacking a controlled source, such surveys are usually environmentally unobjectionable. At a comparatively low cost, airborne potential field surveys can provide coverage of large areas. Magnetic surveys are used to determine magnetic anomalies associated with iron formations which contain magnetite.

Magnetic surveys have been conducted by geophysicists for the past 100 years, and magnetic compasses have been used for a much longer period than that. So, although scientific research has made greater progress since, for example, the magnetic compass of Christopher Columbus, a few words should be said about how much more could be learned from the natural world about the use of magnetic information.

Indeed, geophysical methods that employ magnetic reference points are crude in comparison to the high-resolution procedures used by a bird or turtle, a butterfly or a fish. Animals have the ability to navigate and find their way accurately without maps or instruments. In particular, an ant continuously determines its position relative to a known starting point (e.g., its nest) while traveling on a crooked path. At every point along its journey, the ant can always return directly in a straight line to its nest. A specific example is the Sahara Desert ant, which forages for insects that have died of heat stress. These ants can sustain surface temperatures of up to 70°C (178°F). The ant will venture out a distance as much as a half of a kilometer on a tortuous path that continually meanders and twists in all directions. The ant completes its journey when it finds a dead insect. The ant then goes in a straight-line path back to its nest. It is the shortest route. This skill is necessary to its survival under the harsh desert conditions.

With respect to size, this ant travels farther from its nest than any other animal that lives on the Sahara. There are no landmarks on a desert. It is all sand. An ant does not know where or when it will find a dead insect. As a result, at each point along its path, the ant computes the distance and direction to its nest. How does the ant do this? Ants can do this in the dark, so they do not need the sunlight. At the same time the ant must correct for terrain. It takes more steps to traverse a fixed horizontal distance on a bumpy terrain than on a flat terrain. However, the ant gets the correct value in either case. It seems that ants have a "mental integrator" which allows them to accumulate changes in direction, and from there to keep track of their location. The same seems to apply to moles when they dig their underground tunnels. The "mental integrator" is a form of dead reckoning (as used by Columbus) which requires a magnetic compass to determine direction. It is generally accepted that many animals obtain their orientation or navigational behavior by magnetic field variations. They have internal compasses just as real as the compass that Columbus used. What kind of compass within an ant or a mole can sense and amplify something as weak as earth's magnetic field?

Magnetoception is the ability of an animal to perceive earth's magnetic field. The earth's magnetic field can have a decisive effect on living things. By magnetoception, animals can find food, return their nests, and meet each other. Bats and geese use magnetoception for navigational, altitude, and location purposes. Magnetoception allows honeybees to possess the extraordinary ability to create a map of their surroundings. Invertebrates with magnetoception include fruit flies, lobsters, and certain bacteria. Vertebrates with magnetoception include many species of birds, turtles, sharks, and stingrays. The type of magnetoception present in sea creatures such as sharks, stingrays, and chimaeras is called *inductive sensing*. The mollusks (*Tochuina tetraquetra*) orient themselves between magnetic north and east before a full moon. The evidence is that magnetite in the beak of pigeons accounts for their ability to navigate using magnetoception.

The use of magnetic fields to navigate is found in magnetotactic bacteria. They are crucial for understanding other forms of magnetoception in animals. Magnetotactic bacteria move according to the direction of the North Pole, and hence they are magnetosensitive bacteria. The sensitivity of magnetotactic bacterium to the earth's magnetic field arises from the fact the bacterium precipitates chains of crystals of magnetic minerals within its interior. These crystals, and sometimes the chains of crystals, can be preserved in the geological record as magnetofossils. Reports of magnetofossils extend to 1.9 billion years ago.

Magnetism is an effect of quantum mechanics. At the subatomic level, an electron acts as a tiny magnet. It is a rotating electrically charged particle. Thus, to obtain a fine representation of the magnetic field, one must go beyond geophysical prospecting, and descend into the subatomic level, which is the realm of quantum mechanics. In that domain, traveling electrons and other subatomic entities exist as matter waves (probability waves), not as individual particles. Probability waves within the magnetotactic bacterium interfere and entangle in a state that is affected by the earth's magnetic field. Then, the resulting probability wave can influence a chemical reaction at the molecular level. Such chemical reactions provide the bacterium with the ability to navigate. The same type of behavior is present in all animals that use magnetic navigation. As expressed by Shakespeare, "In nature's infinite book of secrecy, A little I can read."

Every atom is composed of a nucleus and one or more electrons bound to the nucleus. Atoms can attach to one or more other atoms by chemical bonds to form molecules. The electron is a subatomic particle with negative electric charge. Like all elementary particles, electrons exhibit properties of both particles and waves. However, particles like a baseball are quite different from waves like ocean waves. In other words, in the subatomic world, even our concepts fail us. Electrons play an essential role in numerous physical phenomena, such as electricity, magnetism, and chemistry. Since an electron has charge, it has a surrounding electric field, and if that electron is moving relative to an observer, it will generate a magnetic field.

The resolution of microscope is sufficient to see microbes (for example, bacteria). An electron microscope is a microscope that uses a beam of accelerated electrons as a source of illumination. The electron microscope has a higher resolving power than a regular microscope and can reveal the structure of smaller objects. Can atoms be seen under an electron microscope? The answer is partially yes. In certain situations, the images can be interpreted as representations of atoms or even atomic nuclei.

A subatomic particle is smaller than an atom. When we talk about waves at the atomic level, it is about probability waves which are 3D graphs that describe the probability of finding an electron at a certain point around a nucleus. Electrons are incredibly tiny and have extremely low mass. Electrons move extremely fast, and due to the Heisenberg Uncertainty Principle, their exact position is practically unknowable. We can only approximate their position within a region of uncertainty. Without being able to acquire an exact position makes it impossible to view an electron.

The smallest thing that can be seen using an electron microscope is about the size of an atom. The electron microscope cannot resolve anything smaller than an atom. Scientists must turn to other tools to study subatomic objects, such as the Large Hadron Collider (LHC). The LHC hurls beams of protons and ions at a velocity approaching the speed of light. The LHC causes the beams to collide with each other, and then records the results of the collision. As an analogy, the LHC is like a race track where the cars are going so fast that you cannot see them. You can only see an accident. In the same way we cannot see an election in its natural state. We can only see the results of a crash. We can only infer what was happening before the crash in terms of probability.

The planetary model of an atom depicts electrons orbiting the nucleus in a way similar to the planets orbiting the Sun. Unfortunately elementary particles behave in ways that defy classical physics. As a result, the planetary model fails us. Fortunately, Erwin Schrodinger proposed the Electron Cloud Model. In this model, electrons are not depicted as particles moving around a central nucleus in a fixed orbit. Instead, electrons are depicted as 'clouds' around the nucleus. In other words, in the electron cloud model, elections are represented by probability waves. The absolute value of a probability wave gives the probability density of where the electron may likely be found. In conclusion, an electron is both a probability wave and a particle. We cannot see the probability wave which is described as a cloud, and we can only see particles as the ruins of a crash. The examination of the subatomic world is limited to methods of remote sensing as done by the LHC. For purposes of examination and experimentation, the subatomic world is forbidden territory. In the subatomic world, our senses and then even our concepts fail us.

Preface

In quantum mechanics, Heisenberg's uncertainty principle asserts a fundamental limit to the precision with which certain pairs of physical properties of a particle such as position and momentum can be known simultaneously. The *interference* or *interaction effect* is the heart Heisenberg's uncertainty principle. It asserts a fundamental limit to the precision with which certain pairs of physical properties of a subatomic particle (such as position and momentum of an electron) can be known simultaneously.

Trees

Fungi are microorganisms such as yeasts and molds, as well as mushrooms. Roots of trees in the wild are interconnected by extensive and complex networks of fungi. When connected by these fungal threads, known as mycelium, trees and other plants are able to communicate, help their neighbors by sharing nutrients, or even sabotage unwelcome plants by spreading toxic chemicals. This partnership of plants and fungi, which is especially prevalent in old-growth forests, is symbiotic in nature, with the trees providing carbohydrates to the fungi, which in turn gathers water and nutrients such as phosphorus and nitrogen for its benefactors. An estimated 90 per cent of land plants participate in this mutually beneficial relationship.

When we look at a forest, we see a lot of individual trees and bushes. Their branches and leaves intertwine, but do not connect. It seems like it is survival of the fittest. We cannot see underground. In the underground, their roots intertwine. However, the roots are joined by fungi. Here the trees and bushes are cooperating to keep the entire forest healthy and strong. We are in a position to dig up the roots and closely examine their interconnections. In such a study our senses and even our concepts do not fail us.

All things are made of atoms and molecules, so they have roots in the subatomic domain. Molecular chemistry and molecular biology deal with molecules without delving into their subatomic roots. Quantum chemistry and quantum biology deal with molecules without delving into their subatomic roots. Unlike a forest, the subatomic roots cannot ever be examined in their natural state. At best we can sometimes see the ruins of a crash.

Bacteria

Living cells are of two basic types: prokaryotic and eukaryotic. "Prokaryotic" means "before a nucleus," and "eukaryotic" means "possessing a true nucleus." A eukaryote is an organism with complex cells, or a single cell with a complex structure. Specialized compartments called organelles exist within eukaryotic cells and they play different roles in the cell. For instance, mitochondria generate energy from food molecules. Prokaryotes have horizontal gene transfer (HGT). HGT refers to the transfer of genes between organisms in a manner other than traditional reproduction. Eukaryotes have vertical gene transfer (VGT). VGT is the transmission of genes from the parental generation to offspring via sexual or asexual reproduction.

When we look at bacteria, we see a lot of individual cells. They are close together, but do not connect. It seems like it is survival of the fittest. We cannot see the subatomic world. In the underground, the bacteria intertwine and connect. The bacteria are cooperating to keep the entire community healthy and strong. We are not in a position to dig up the roots and closely examine their interconnections. In such a study our senses and even our concepts fail us.

Bacteria are prokaryotes, for they lack a membrane-bound nucleus. Bacteria are the dominant living creatures on Earth, having been present for perhaps three-quarters of Earth history and having adapted to almost all available ecological habitats. Typically a few micrometers in length, bacteria have a number of shapes, ranging from spheres to rods and spirals. Bacteria were among the first life forms to appear on Earth, and are present in most of its habitats. Bacteria inhabit soil, water, acidic hot springs, radioactive waste, and the deep portions of Earth's crust. Bacteria also live in symbiotic and parasitic relationships with plants and animals.

The human body contains about 100 trillion cells, but only maybe one in 10 of those cells is actually — human. The rest are from bacteria, viruses and other microorganisms. However the average person could be composed of about 40 trillion bacteria and 30 trillion human cells, according to researchers at the Weizmann Institute

Levels of smallness
The Non-life Level deals with molecules. The mystery of life cannot be explained at this level. Molecules embrace inanimate objects. They can be observed by chemical and optical experiments. We can observe the properties of non-life at this level.

The level dealing with atoms is the boundary level.

The Life Level deals with electrons and other subatomic particles. The mystery of life resides at this level. Electrons and other subatomic particles embrace animate objects. Electrons and other subatomic particles (probability waves) cannot be observed. We cannot observe the properties of life at this level. The mystery of life can never be solved.

Chromosome is a linear strand of DNA and associated proteins in the nucleus of eukaryotic cells that carries the genes and functions in the transmission of hereditary information. Superposition refers to the fact that a particle exists in many possible states simultaneously. When we observe the particle it takes one particular state.

Photosynthesis is the staggeringly efficient process by which plants and some bacteria build the molecules they need, using energy from sunlight. Photosynthesis seems to use what is called "superposition" - being seemingly in more than one place at one time.

Watch the process closely enough and it appears there are little packets of energy simultaneously "trying" all of the possible paths to get where they need to go, and then settling on the most efficient.

Entanglement refers to the fact that two particles can become entangled so that their properties depend on each other, no matter how far apart they get. A measurement of one seems to affect the measurement of the other instantaneously. This was something Einstein once called "spooky action at a distance." It helps birds navigate

Tunnelling refers to the fact that a particle can break through an energy barrier, seeming to disappear on one side of it and reappear on the other. Lots of modern electronics and imaging depends on this effect.

The deepest divisions are very old. The ancestors of all life were single-celled and prokaryotic. Prokaryotes were preset 3.5 billion years ago and ruled the planet for about 2 billion years. Eukaryotes appeared about 1.25 billion years ago.

Bacteria are almost everywhere on earth. They are found in air, water, and land. They are found in solid rock 30 000 feet deep in the earth. Neither bacteria nor archaea evolved into complex life forms as did the eukaryotes. Bacteria are essentially the same today as when they first appeared 3.5 billon years ago. Bacteria have extraordinary genetic and biochemical versatility.

Magneto-reception

Magneto-reception is a sense which allows an organism to detect a magnetic field to perceive direction, altitude or location. This sensory modality is used by a range of animals for orientation and navigation, and as a method for animals to develop regional maps. For the purpose of navigation, magneto-reception deals with the detection of the Earth's magnetic field. Columbus had a magnetic compass, but it was crude in comparison to the high-resolution procedures used by a bird or turtle. Many animals can find their way accurately without maps or instruments. Birds such as the Arctic tern, insects such as the monarch butterfly and fish such as the salmon regularly migrate thousands of miles to and from their breeding grounds, and many other species navigate effectively over shorter distances.

At every point along its journey, the ant can always return directly in a straight line to its nest. At each point along its path, the ant computes the distance and direction to its nest. How does the ant do this? Ants have a "mental integrator" which allows them to accumulate changes in direction, and from there to keep track of their location. The same applies to moles when they dig their underground tunnels.

It is generally accepted that many animals obtain their orientation or navigational behavior by magnetic field variations. They have internal compasses just as real as the compass that Columbus used. How can the compass in an ant or a mole sense and amplify something as weak as Earth's magnetic field? Our best instruments cannot ever come close to an ant's ability.

The use of magnetic fields to navigate is found in magneto-tactic bacteria. They are crucial for understanding other forms of magneto reception in animals. Magneto-tactic bacteria move according to the direction of the North Pole, and hence they are magneto-sensitive bacteria. Reports of magneto-fossils extend to 1.9 billion years in the past.

Magnetism is an effect of quantum mechanics. At the subatomic level an electron acts as a tiny magnet. It is a rotating electrically charged particle. Thus, to obtain a fine representation of the magnetic field, one must descend down into the subatomic level, which is the realm of quantum mechanics. In that domain, traveling electrons exist as probability waves, not as individual particles.

Probability waves within the magneto-tactic bacterium interfere and entangle in a state that is affected by the earth's magnetic field. The resulting probability wave can then influence a chemical reaction at the molecular level. Such chemical reactions provide the bacterium with the ability to navigate. The same type of behavior is present in all animals that use magnetic navigation

We do know that animals have systems of intelligence that operate at the quantum level where it is impossible to directly observe the interference of probability waves. We have the theory of probability waves but we cannot observe them. At present it is impossible to conceive of any artificial system that could match the subatomic intelligence of a bacterium, much less than that of an ant.

Many animals including birds like European Robins exploit a very fragile quantum property, called entanglement, for long-distance navigation based on the relative orientation with respect to the Earth's magnetic field direction. More surprisingly, they are able to keep such entanglement in their eyes, at room temperature. In particular, this feature does trigger different chemical products inside a protein, hence providing a chemical compass. Then, this allows the bird to create a map of the Earth's magnetic field.

Conclusion
An inertial navigation system (INS) uses a computer, motion sensors (accelerometers), rotation sensors (gyroscopes), and occasionally magnetic sensors (magnetometers) to continuously calculate by dead reckoning the position, the orientation, and the velocity (direction and speed of movement) of a moving object without the need for external references. Inertial navigation systems are heavy and bulky. They are used on ships,

aircraft, submarines, guided missiles, and spacecraft. In contrast, bacteria, insects, and other animals have natural navigation systems that put to shame any man-made equipment in size and accuracy. The purpose of magneto-reception in birds and other animals may be varied, but has proved difficult to understand. For 50 years animal magneto-reception has been studied and yet no sensory receptor has been identified. It is difficult to discern the parts of the animal brain where this information is processed. The precise use of magneto-reception in animal navigation is unclear. One explanation is that the processing in the animal's brain is done at the subatomic level, in which case the precise mechanism can never be identified, much less understood. Then the LORD answered Job out of the whirlwind and said: "You may come this far, but no farther." (Job 38:11)

Remote sensing

Active and passive

Remote sensing refers to the acquisition of information about an object by the use of sensing devices that are not in physical contact with the object. Remote sensing is characterized by an intelligent use of signals that penetrate the unknown. There are two kinds of remote sensing: *passive* and *active*. In passive remote sensing, the observer waits for signals from unknown and unreachable regions. In active remote sensing, the observer emits signals into such regions and then records the resulting reflected, refracted, or scattered signals. Remote sensing depends on the use of signals that allow communication between the observer and the remote object. The most important type of signal is the traveling wave, whether mechanical (as in sound) or electromagnetic (as in light).

Many methods of remote sensing have been developed over the years. The development of the telescope and microscope in the early seventeenth century provided means to obtain images that could not be seen by the unaided eye. With telescopes, the astronomer can look outward to the stars and galaxies. With microscopes, the biologist can look inward to the microorganisms (microbes) that exist throughout the biosphere. An echocardiogram lets a doctor see the internal movements of the heart and blood without penetrating the skin. A satellite can monitor the features on the earth's surface and determine the environmental status of land cover, land use, and natural resources. Nondestructive testing finds hidden defects without taking the airplane apart.

If we could see the earth in cross section, we would find a sharp division between the core, or central part, and the mantle, or outer part. We would also find that the outer surface of the mantle has a very shallow skin layer of different composition, known as the crust. How did we obtain such knowledge? Earthquakes generate seismic waves. The seismic waves serve as the signals required for remote sensing. Because we must wait for earthquakes to occur, earthquake seismology represents passive remote sensing. In seismic exploration, source signals are transmitted into the ground, and the reflected seismic waves are recorded and processed. Exploration seismology represents active remote sensing.

Active remote sensing provides the basis for nondestructive testing. By comparing known input signals to measured output signals, the condition of a system can be determined without the use of invasive approaches such as disassembly or failure testing. For example, the system might be an aircraft wing whose trustworthiness must be routinely tested. Nondestructive testing does not require the disabling or sacrifice of the aircraft wing.

Noninvasive medical procedures, which involve no break in the skin, represent forms of remote sensing. Examples are magnetic resonance imaging (MRI), electrocardiography (EKG), electroencephalography (EEG), electrical impedance tomography (EIT), electroneuronography, magnetoencephalography, nuclear magnetic resonance spectroscopy, and diagnostic sonography (ultrasonography).

Remote sensing provides a way to search for the beginning of time. By the late 1920s, Edward Hubble had established that the universe was organized into galaxies of various sizes and shapes, each one consisting of billions of stars. It was found that most galaxies had light that shifted toward the red. The simplest interpretation of the red shift is that the galaxies are moving away from us. This conclusion fitted in well with Einstein's general theory of relativity.

Remote sensing makes it possible to collect data on dangerous or inaccessible areas. Remote sensing applications include monitoring areas such as the Amazon Basin and the Arctic and Antarctic regions, and the depth sounding of coastal and ocean depths. Remote sensing also replaces costly and slow data collection on the ground, ensuring in the process that areas or objects are not disturbed. Orbital platforms collect and transmit data from different parts of the electromagnetic spectrum, which in conjunction with large-scale aerial or ground-based sensing, provides researchers with enough information to monitor trends such as El Niño and other natural long and short term phenomena. Other uses include different areas of the earth sciences such as natural resource management and land usage and conservation.

A hologram creates a three-dimensional image of an object that we can see with our eyes. How can we create a three-dimensional of an object that we cannot see at all? Many ingenious methods of remote sensing have been developed for this purpose. These methods have opened up whole new worlds to us. The explorers of old traversed the seven seas to find new lands and then sailed home with their discoveries. We cannot travel to the stars to find out what they are made of. Instead, we must seek this information indirectly by analyzing starlight. We cannot travel underground to determine what is inside the earth. Instead, we must seek this information indirectly by sending seismic signals into the ground and interpreting their echoes.

Echolocation in animals

Several species of animals use echolocation for navigation and for foraging or hunting. The animal determines orientation to other objects through interpretation of reflected sound. Bats and dolphins are good examples of such animals. They emit calls and listen to the echoes of these calls. They use these echoes to locate, range, and identify objects. Echolocation works like active sonar. Ranging is done by measuring the time delay between the animal's own sound emission and any echoes that return from the environment. Unlike some sonar that relies on an extremely narrow beam to localize a target, animal echolocation relies on multiple receivers. Echolocating animals have two ears positioned slightly apart. The echoes returning to the two ears arrive at different times and at different loudness levels, depending on the position of the object generating the echoes. The time and loudness differences are used by the animals to perceive direction.

With echolocation, a bat can see not only where it is going but also how big another animal is, what kind of animal it is, and other features. Some moths have developed a protection against bats. They are able to hear the bat's ultrasounds and flee as soon as they notice these sounds, or stop beating their wings for a period of time to deprive the bat of the characteristic echo signature of moving wings which it may home in on. To counteract this, the bat may cease producing the ultrasound bursts as it nears its prey, and can thus avoid detection..

Echolocation is used by dolphins and most whales. It guides them through darkness of the deep and helps them to identify prey. Toothed whales emit a focused beam of high-frequency clicks in the direction that their head is pointing. Sounds are generated by passing air from the bony nares through the phonic lips. These sounds are reflected by the dense concave bone of the cranium and an air sac at its base. The focused beam is modulated by a large fatty organ known as the "melon." This acts like an acoustic lens because it is composed of lipids of differing densities. Most toothed whales use clicks in a series, or click train, for echolocation, while the sperm whale may produce clicks individually.

A reverberation is a special kind of multiple reflection. The category "multiple reflections" includes both reverberations and other types of multiple reflections. A reverberation in a multiple reflection that makes many repetitive turns between the same two interfaces. For example, in exploration at sea, the water layer acts like a drumhead. A drumhead is a membrane stretched over one or both of the open ends of a drum. The drumhead is struck with sticks, mallets, or hands, so that it vibrates and the sound reverberates through the drum. Because water reverberations generally overwhelm the primary reflections from depth, exploration at sea was not possible (except in rare instances) in the days before digital signal processing.

In music we like reverberations. Composers of sacred music made use of the complex natural reverberations inside cathedrals. This knowledge was later used in the design of opera houses and concert halls. They were built to create reverberations that would enhance sound in the days before electrical amplification.

In seismic analysis, we do not like reverberations because they hide the primary reflections. We need to remove the reverberations (and other multiple reflections) in order to detect the primary reflections. The primary reflections represent the signal.

Remember that we have assumed that the ambient noise is so small that we can rule it out. As a result the reverberations (and other multiple reflections) represent the noise. If there were no primary reflections, there would be no multiple reflections. In other words, if there were no signal, there would be no noise. That is why reverberations (and other multiple reflections) are called signal-generated noise. We need to deconvolve the received seismic trace to take away the signal-generated noise so that we obtain the signal.

Most of the underground structure of the earth's near crust is like a vast and elaborate cathedral, even more multifarious than Chartres. In such complex situations, the reverberations would so overwhelm and hide the primary reflections that analog seismic method would not work. In 1950, such regions of the earth were not explorable. In a relatively few areas the underground structure was like a plain unadorned colonial New England meeting house. In such situations, the analog seismic method did work but at the cost many dry holes.

Biological clocks

Biological clocks are natural devices existing in living things that keep track of time. Every organ and even every cell seems to have some sort of clock. The clocks preserve the daily patterns of activity when the organism is removed from daily light or temperature changes. It is not known how biological clocks work. Does the organism have a physicochemical timing system that generates periods of the same duration as those of the earth and moon? When deprived of the usual environmental variations such as those in light and temperature, can the organism detect related variations in such forces as the earth's magnetic and electric fields?

Biological clocks in humans keep the daily rhythm of sleep and wakefulness. Such rhythms are called circadian (i.e., about a day). Circadian rhythms can vary widely among living things. Underlying this rhythm are other timed variations. There are daily variations in blood sugar, kidney excretion, cell-divisions, body temperature, and hormone secretion. When humans are confined in rooms without clocks or windows, they try to keep their daily patterns of sleep and wake. However they systematically drift to progressively earlier or later times of day. The resulting rhythmic periods will deviate somewhat from 24 hours.

Biological clocks occur throughout the animal kingdom, from single-celled forms to mammals. Animal clocks adjust activities to the day-night cycles or to the ebb and flow of the tides. They also time monthly and annual migratory and reproductive activity. The annual return of the swallows to Capistrano, California, occurs on the same day each. The annual breeding of the palolo worms of the South Pacific follows a timed rhythm. These worms rise to the surface of the water for breeding each year at dawn exactly one week after the November full moon. Plants also possess clocks. Bean seedlings raise their leaves in the morning and lower them at night. The brown alga *Dictyota* has a monthly reproductive rhythm. Daily variations in respiration, photosynthetic capacity, and growth rate are governed by internal biological clocks.

A clock has three main components: an oscillating system, such as a pendulum, spring, or electrical circuit; a source of energy; and a trigger mechanism or escapement that connects the energy source to the oscillator. A clock's face presents the oscillator's output in some useful way. Biological clocks have the same three components. For example, a nerve cell's membrane is an oscillator, the energy is supplied by the cell's metabolism, and the trigger mechanisms are controlled ionic channels in the membrane. The result is a cycle of membrane voltage whose phase can be viewed as a hand moving on a clock face.

Chapter 5. The relationship between analog and digital systems

5.1 **Mathematical description of the uniform-rate sampling process**

Up to now, our discussions have been primarily concerned with the digital signal, i.e. an ordered sequence of numbers. However, many physical systems are characterized by processes which change continuously with time. For example, the sound output of a stereo system represents a continuous variation of sound presure waves with time. Signals that vary in this fashion are called *analog* signals. An example of an analog signal is shown in Figure 5-1.

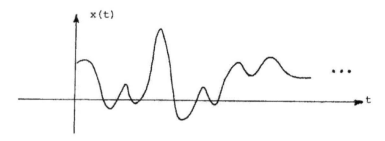

Figure 5-1

An analog signal

Now suppose we wish to process this signal in some fashion by using a digital computer. We must put the analog signal in a different form, since the computer cannot store such a continuously changing function. This analog-to-digital conversion process is called *sampling*.

Sampling is the act of examining a continuous function of time, or some other independent variable, at selected values of the independent variable. The value of the function at the instant of examination is the "sampled" value of the function. Thus, the sampling process generates a numerical sequence or digital signal. However, we note that sampled signals are only a subclass of the general catagory of digital signals.

Mathematically, the sampled signal may be described by a sampling operation which is carried out by a sampler. In general, the sampler converts a continuous-time signal into a discrete-time signal according to one of the many possible sampling schemes. Some of the well-known sampling schemes are:

1. Uniform-rate sampling
2. Multirate sampling

Chapter 5. The relationship between analog and digital systems

3. Skip sampling
4. Cyclic sampling
5. Finite pulsewidth sampling
6. Pulsewidth modulation
7. Random sampling

In almost all cases, a sampled signal is derived from a continuous signal (either actually or mathematically) by observing its value at a set of equally spaced time instants. In this mode of operation, the sampler is classified as a periodic or *uniform-rate sampler*. For the sake of simplicity, only uniform-rate sampling is discussed in this Article.

Since the sampler is described as a device which converts a continuous-time signal into a signal in digital or pulse form, we can interpret the sampling operation as a modulator which generally operates on two inputs, the signal and the carrier. For the uniform-rate sampler shown in Figure 5-2, the signal is a continuous-time function $x(t)$, and the carrier is a unit pulse train with a period T. If we designate the unit pulse train by

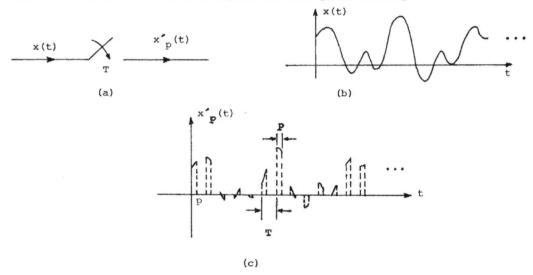

Figure 5-2

The uniform-rate sampling process

(a) A uniform-rate sampler with finite sampling duration p and period T.
(b) continuous-time input $x(t)$
(c) digital output $x'_p(t)$

$p(t)$, then

$$p(t) = \sum_{k=-\infty}^{\infty} [u(t-kT) - u(t-kT-p)] \quad (p<T) \qquad (1)$$

where u(t) is the unit-step function defined by

$$u(t) = \begin{cases} 0 & \text{for } t<0 \\ 1 & \text{for } t \geq 0 \end{cases}$$

and it is assumed that the sampling operation starts at $t=-\infty$. The constant k in equation (1) takes on only integer values, and p is the sampling duration of the sampler. Thus, the action of the uniform-rate sampler with finite sampler duration can be described by

$$x'_p(t) = x(t) \cdot p(t) \qquad (2)$$

or

$$x'_p(t) = x(t) \sum_{k=-\infty}^{\infty} [u(t-kT) - u(t-kT-p)] \quad (p<T) \qquad (3)$$

where the carrier signal p(t) is shown in Figure 5-3.

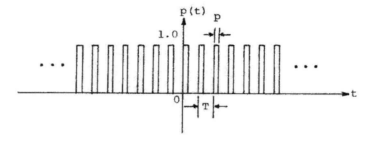

Figure 5-3

The unit pulse train p(t)

One can interpret the sampling operation as a pulse modulation process. A schematic diagram of a pulse modulator is shown in Figure 5-4.

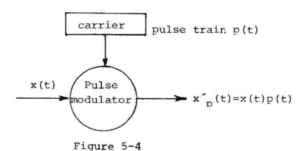

Figure 5-4

The pulse modulator as a sampling device.

Chapter 5. The relationship between analog and digital systems

The pulse modulator representation of a sampler is actually applicable to many other types of sampling operations, and only the carrier signal p(t) need be changed accordingly.

Thus far, the output of a sampler has been described by the time domain characteristics of the input and output signals. It is also of interest to investigate the spectrum of the sampler output $x_p^*(t)$. Hence, given knowledge of the frequency content of the sampler input $x(t)$, let us investigate what frequency components are contained in $x_p^*(t)$.

For a uniform-rate sampler, p(t) is a periodic function with period T and has the Fourier series expansion

$$p(t) = \sum_{n=-\infty}^{\infty} \alpha_n e^{in\omega_s t} \qquad (4)$$

where ω_s is the *sampling frequency* in radians per second, and is related to the *sampling period* T by

$$\omega_s = \frac{2\pi}{T} \qquad (5)$$

The complex Fourier coefficients α_n are given by

$$\alpha_n = \frac{1}{T} \int_0^T p(t) e^{-in\omega_s t} \, dt \qquad (6)$$

Since p(t) = 1 for $0 \leq t \leq p$, equation (6) becomes

$$\alpha_n = \frac{1}{T} \int_0^p e^{-in\omega_s t} \, dt \qquad (7)$$

$$= \frac{1}{in\omega_s T} (1 - e^{in\omega_s p})$$

$$= \frac{p}{T} \frac{\sin(\frac{n\omega_s p}{2})}{\frac{n\omega_s p}{2}} e^{-\frac{in\omega_s p}{2}}$$

Using equation (4), the pulse train p(t) can be written

$$p(t) = \sum_{n=-\infty}^{\infty} \frac{p}{T} \frac{\sin(\frac{n\omega_s p}{2})}{n\omega_s p/2} e^{-\frac{in\omega_s p}{2}} e^{in\omega_s t} \qquad (8)$$

From equation (2), the output of a uniform-rate sampler is now written as

$$\hat{x}_p(t) = \sum_{n=-\infty}^{\infty} \alpha_n x(t) e^{in\omega_s t} \quad (9)$$

where α_n is given by equation (7).

Taking the Fourier transform of equation (9) yields

$$\hat{X}_p(\omega) = \sum_{n=-\infty}^{\infty} \alpha_n X(\omega - n\omega_s) \quad (10)$$

Equation (10) shows the important result that the frequency components contained in the original continuous-time input x(t) are still present in the sampler output $\hat{x}_p(t)$. However, the spectrum of the sampler output $\hat{X}_p(\omega)$ is equal to the spectrum of the sampler input $X(\omega)$ weighted by the Fourier coefficients α_n and shifted in accordance with the sampling frequency ω_s.

In deriving equation (10), we have assumed that the spectrum of x(t) was somewhat arbitrary, the only restriction being that its Fourier transform $X(\omega)$ exist. We shall now consider a special class of signals known as *band-limited* signals.

A bandlimited signal is one for which the Fourier transform (i.e. the magnitude spectrum) is identically zero everywhere except for a finite range of frequencies. If the region in which the non-zero spectrum exists includes zero frequency, then the band-limited signal is said to be *low-pass*. If it does not include zero frequency, then the band-limited signal is said to be *bandpass*. In any case, however, a bandlimited signal must exist for all time, although it may contain only finite energy. The concept of band-limited signals is a convenient one in practical system design as well as theoretical calculations, even though such signals cannot exist in actuality. In almost all cases of practical interest there is some range of frequencies outside of which the spectrum is so small that it can be assumed to be zero with negligible error. Thus, the magnitude spectrum $|X(\omega)|$ of the continuous input x(t) will be considered as a bandlimited signal.

From equation (10), the magnitude spectrum $|\hat{X}_p(\omega)|$ of the sampler output $\hat{x}_p(t)$ may be written

$$|\hat{X}_p(\omega)| = \left| \sum_{n=-\infty}^{\infty} \alpha_n X(\omega - n\omega_s) \right| \quad (11)$$

$$\leq \sum_{n=-\infty}^{\infty} |\alpha_n| |X(\omega - n\omega_s)|$$

Figure 5-5 illustrates a low-pass bandlimited magnitude spectrum $|X(\omega)|$ and its relationship to the sampler output magnitude spectrum $|\hat{X}_p(\omega)|$.

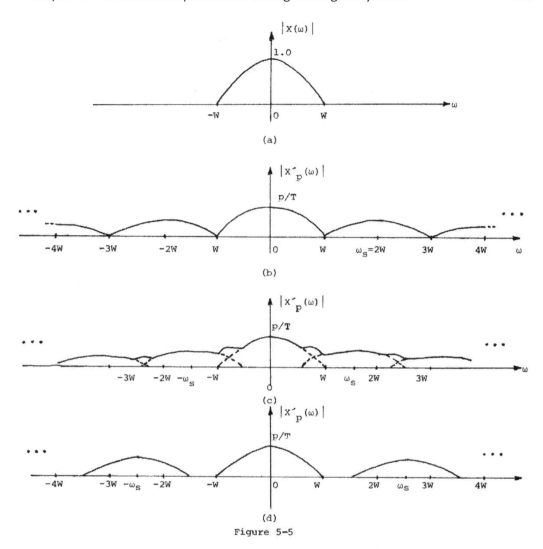

Figure 5-5

magnitude spectrum of sampled function $x'_p(t)$

    (a) magnitude spectrum of low-pass band-limited signal $x(t)$
    (b) $\omega_s = 2W$
    (c) $\omega_s < 2W$
    (d) $\omega_s > 2W$

It is interesting to note that $|X^\sim_p(\omega)|$ contains not only the fundamental component of $X(\omega)$ but also the harmonic components $X(\omega-n\omega_s)$ $n=\pm 1, \pm 2, \ldots$. The nth harmonic component in the output magnitude spectrum $|X^\sim_p(\omega)|$ is obtained by multiplying $|X(\omega)|$ by its corresponding Fourier coefficient $|\alpha_n|$ and shifting it by $n\omega_s$, $n=\pm 1, \pm 2, \ldots$. Therefore, the sampler may be visualized as a harmonic generator whose output contains the weighted fundamental components, plus all the weighted harmonic components at all frequencies separated by the sampling frequency ω_s. The band around zero frequency still carries essentially all the information contained in the continuous input signal, but the same information also repeats along the frequency axis; the amplitude of each component weighted by the magnitude of its corresponding Fourier coefficient $|\alpha_n|$.

PROBLEMS FOR ARTICLE 5.1

1. Show that if the sampling duration p is very very small, the output of a finite-pulse-width sampler can be approximated by

$$x^\sim_p(t) \approx p \sum_{k=-\infty}^{\infty} x(t)\delta(t-kT)$$

Thus, the finite-pulsewidth sampler can be approximated by an *ideal sampler* connected in series with an attenuator with attenuation p as shown below.

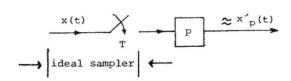

2. Plot the magnitude spectrum $|X^\sim_p(\omega)|$ of an ideal sampler when the input x(t) has the following spectrum:

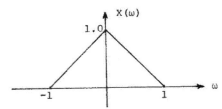

Assume a sampling frequency $\omega_s = 5$ radians/sec.

3. With regard to Figure 5-5, under what conditions can one successfully recover the original spectrum $X(\omega)$ from the sampled spectrum $X^\sim_p(\omega)$? Discuss a procedure for doing this.

Chapter 5. The relationship between analog and digital systems 239

4. Obtain an expression for the phase spectrum $\theta\hat{}_p(\omega)$ of the output of a finite-pulsewidth sampler where

$$X\hat{}_p(\omega) = |X\hat{}_p(\omega)| e^{i\theta\hat{}_p(\omega)}$$

5. Let $x(t)$ be a low-pass, band-limited time function whose spectrum is zero for $|f|>W$, where f and W are in Hertz. This function is ideally sampled at a rate $1/T=2W$ samples per second and the samples are designated as $x(k/2W)$, where $k=0,\pm 1,\pm 2, \ldots$ This procedure assumes that

$$x\hat{}_p(t) = \sum_{k=-\infty}^{\infty} x(kT)\delta(t-kT)$$

(a) Prove that

$$\frac{1}{2W} \sum_{k=-\infty}^{\infty} [x(k/2W)]^2 = \int_{-\infty}^{\infty} x^2(t)\, dt$$

(b) Discuss the significance of this result.

5.2 The sampling theorem

It should be pointed out that the magnitude spectrum $|X\hat{}_p(\omega)|$ in Figures 5-5 (b) and (d) are plotted for $\omega_s=2W$ and $\omega_s>2W$ respectively. Under these conditions, the harmonic components of $|X\hat{}_p(\omega)|$ are nonoverlapping. Therefore, theoretically the original signal $x(t)$ can be recovered from these spectra by means of an ideal low-pass filter with cutoff frequency W. However, Figure 5-5 (c) shows $X\hat{}_p(\omega)$ for $\omega_s<2W$. In this case, $|X\hat{}_p(\omega)|$ becomes distorted due to the overlapping harmonic components and bears little resemblence to the original low-pass magnitude spectrum $|X(\omega)|$. In fact, the upper frequencies in $X(\omega)$ get reflected into the lower frequencies in $X\hat{}_p(\omega)$. This effect, where a high frequency component in $X(\omega)$ takes on the identity of low frequency component, is called *aliasing*. Figure 5-6 demonstrates the aliasing concept by showing a relatively high frequency and a relatively low frequency that share identical sample points. When aliasing occurs, we say that the analog waveform is *undersampled*.

Figure 5-6

The concept of "aliasing"; a high frequency impersonating a low frequency.

The foregoing argument leads directly to a statement of the *sampling theorem* for low-pass, band-limited signals:

A low pass, band-limited function having no frequency components outside of the frequency interval from -W to W radians/sec. may be described uniquely and completely for all time, by a set of sample values taken at time instants separated by π/W seconds or less.

Thus, proper sampling requires that the samples be taken at a rate at least twice the highest frequency present in x(t), that is $\omega_s=2W$. This sampling rate is generally referred to as the *Nyquist rate*. Further, the highest frequency present in x(t) is called the *Nyquist frequency*. The Nyquist frequency is sometimes called the *folding* frequency which has the value $\omega_s/2$. The term "folding" frequency is appropriate, for the low-pass magnitude spectrum $|X(\omega)|$ can be obtained by folding the first harmonic component $|X(\omega-\omega_s)|$ about the frequency $\omega_s/2$.

In practice, certain factors dictate the choice of the sampling frequency ω_s and may make it necessary to sample at a rate much higher than the theoretical minimum $\omega_s=2W$. Furthermore, strictly speaking, a band-limited signal does not exist in many physical systems. All physical signals found in the real world do contain components covering a wide frequency range. It is because the amplitudes of the higher frequency components are greatly diminished that a bandlimited signal is assumed. Therefore, in practice, these factors plus the unrealizeability of an ideal low-pass filter make impossible the exact reproduction of a continuous signal from the sampled signal even if the sampling theorem is satisfied.

Let the time function x(t) have a spectrum X(ω) that is limited to the band ±W. Assume that x(t) is known at discrete times $t_n = \frac{n\pi}{W}$, n=0,±1,±2,... . The value $x(t_n)=x_n$ can be found in terms of the spectrum X(ω) as follows:

$$x_n = x\left(\frac{n\pi}{W}\right) = \frac{1}{2\pi} \int_{-W}^{W} X(\omega) e^{i\omega\frac{n\pi}{W}} d\omega \tag{1}$$

This can be written as

$$x_n = \frac{W}{\pi} \left[\frac{1}{2W} \int_{-W}^{W} X(\omega) e^{-i\left(-\frac{n\omega\pi}{W}\right)} d\omega \right] \tag{2}$$

which is just W/π times the -nth coefficient of the complex exponential Fourier series expansion for X(ω) over the interval -W≤ω≤W. In view of this, X(ω) can be expressed in terms of x_n as

$$X(\omega) = \sum_{n=-\infty}^{\infty} \frac{x_n \pi}{W} e^{-j\frac{n\omega\pi}{W}} \tag{3}$$

Chapter 5. The relationship between analog and digital systems

king the inverse transform of equation (3) gives

$$x(t) = \frac{1}{2\pi} \int_{-W}^{W} X(\omega) e^{i\omega t} d\omega \qquad (4)$$

$$= \sum_{n=-\infty}^{\infty} \frac{x_n}{2W} \int_{-W}^{W} e^{i\omega(t-\frac{n\pi}{W})} d\omega$$

aluating the integral in equation (4) yields

$$x(t) = \sum_{n=-\infty}^{\infty} x_n \frac{\sin W(t-\frac{n\pi}{W})}{W(t-\frac{n\pi}{W})}$$

$$= \sum_{n=-\infty}^{\infty} x(\frac{n\pi}{W}) \frac{\sin W(t-\frac{n\pi}{W})}{W(t-\frac{n\pi}{W})} \qquad (5)$$

From equation (5) it is seen that $x(t)$ can be recovered from x_n by umming over the properly weighted values of x_n. Thus, equation (5) pro-.des an interpolation formula for recovering the continuous-time signal [(t) from its sampled values x_n.

It is also possible to obtain a sampling theorem for bandpass, band-.mited signals. However, we should keep in mind that our sampling theorem ; applicable to low-pass bandlimited signals.

PROBLEMS FOR ARTICLE 5.2

. A signal $x(t)$ can still be defined completely by sampling it at a rate less than 2W rad/sec provided that the derivatives of the signal are known at the sampling instants as well as the amplitude information.

Prove that if a signal $x(t)$ contains no frequency components higher than W rad/sec, it is completely characterized by the values $x^{(k)}(nT)$, $x^{(k-1)}(nT)$, ..., $x^{(1)}(nT)$, and $x(nT)$ $(n=0,1,2,...)$, of the signal measured at instants of time separated by $T=(k+1)\frac{\pi}{W}$ seconds, where

$$x^{(k)}(nT) = \left.\frac{d^k x(t)}{dt^k}\right|_{t=nT}$$

(Note: This means that when the values of the first derivative $x^{(1)}(nT)$ for $n=0,1,2,...$, are known in addition to the values of $x(nT)$, the maximum allowable sampling time is $T=2\pi/W$, which is twice the time required when $x(nT)$ alone is measured.)

2. A bandpass bandlimited signal x(t) is to be sampled and then reconstructed by passing the samples through a bandpass filter. If the samples are to be taken every T seconds by a uniform-rate sampler with duration p seconds, determine the minimum sampling rate if $X(\omega)$ only exists for $100 \leq \omega \leq 120$ and $-120 \leq \omega \leq -100$. Does there exist a maximum sampling rate?

3. A low-pass bandlimited waveform x(t) has a maximum frequency content of 10 Hz. After sampling, the signal is to be reconstructed by passing the samples through a low-pass filter whose spectrum $H(\omega)$ is given by

$$H(\omega) = \frac{b}{b + i\omega}$$

Specify appropriate sampling rates and filter bandwidth, as well as the relationship of these parameters to the distortion of the recovered signal.

4. Determine the minimum sampling rate required and suggest a value for the bandwidth of a low-pass filter to be used to reconstruct the output of a microphone into which a female vocalist is singing a particular song. Her song could be preserved on a record, tape, and so on, or it could be stored as a set of numbers. Approximately how many numbers (samples) would have to be stored in order that her song can be reproduced without distortion for a 3 minute recording? Would the numbers have to be kept in order? What would she sou d like if you lost half her numbers?

5. The time function $x(t) = 10 \cos(2\pi \cdot 500t) \cos^2(2\pi \cdot 1000t)$ is to be sampled 4500 times each second.

   (a) If reconstruction is to be accomplished by passing the sampled signal through an ideal low-pass filter of bandwidth 2600 Hz, determine the output time function, assuming the filter has zero phase shift and unity gain over its passband.

   (b) Compute the mean-squared error of the output time function.

   (c) What is the minimum sampling rate that permits the signal to be uniquely reconstructed.

6. Given the signal

$$x(t) = \cos^3 2\omega_0 t + \frac{3}{2}\sin^2 \omega_0 t - \frac{3}{2}$$

   (a) What is the folding frequency?

   (b) What is the Nyquist sampling rate?

   (c) Sketch the spectrum of this signal before and after an *ideal* sampling operation.

Chapter 5. The relationship between analog and digital systems

7. The sinusoidal time function $\cos\omega_1 t$ is sampled at regular intervals defined by $t=nT$, $n=0,\pm 1,\pm 2,\ldots$. Determine and sketch the resulting spectrum for each of the following conditions:

   (a) $\omega_1 = \dfrac{\omega_o}{3}$ (b) $\omega_1 = -\dfrac{\omega_o}{2}$ (c) $\omega_1 = \dfrac{2}{3}\omega_o$ (d) $\omega_1 = \omega_o$

   where $\omega_o = \dfrac{2\pi}{T}$.

   If the sampled sequence is passed through an ideal low-pass filter whose output is expected to be the continuous function $\cos\omega_1 t$, find the particular ω_1-values in the above set for which this expectation is realized, and specify the appropriate cut-off frequency in each case.

Chapter 6. Design of digital filters

6.1 Design of moving average (MA) filters

FIR is an acronym for "finite-length impulse response". A FIR filter is a digital filter with a finite-duration impulse response. Such filters can be causal or noncausal. The impulse response of a causal FIR filter is of the form $h_0, h_1, h_2, \ldots, h_{N-1}$; that is, a causal FIR filter is a moving average (MA) filter (see Article 3.6). As a result, the transfer function of a causal FIR filter (i.e. a MA filter) is a polynomial in z; that is,

$$H(z) = h_0 + h_1 z + h_2 z^2 + \cdots + h_{N-1} z^{N-1}$$

Provided the last coefficient h_{N-1} is not zero, this polynomial is of degree N-1. In such a case, the polynomial H(z) has N-1 zeroes that can be located anywhere in the finite z-plane. If we represent these zeroes by the symbols $z_1, z_2 \ldots, z_{N-1}$ then we can write the transfer function in factored form as

$$H(z) = h_{N-1}(z-z_1)(z-z_2)\cdots(z-z_{N-1})$$

The frequency spectrum $H(\omega)$ is the trigonometric polynomial resulting by letting $z=e^{-i\omega}$ in the transfer function H(z); that is,

$$H(\omega) = h_0 + h_1 e^{-i\omega} + h_2 e^{-i2\omega} + \cdots + h_{N-1} e^{-i\omega(N-1)}$$

As we have seen, any finite-duration sequence $h_0, h_1, \ldots, h_{N-1}$ of length N is completely specified by N samples $H_0, H_1, H_2, \ldots, H_{N-1}$ of its frequency spectrum, where

$$H_k = H\left(\frac{2\pi k}{N}\right), \quad k=0,1,2,\ldots,N-1$$

Thus, the design of a MA filter may be carried out by finding either its impulse response coefficients or N samples of its frequency spectrum.

An important subclass of MA (i.e. causal FIR) filters consists of the symmetric filters. The impulse response of a symmetric filter satisfies the condition

$$h_n = h_{N-1-n}$$

This symmetry condition means that the MA filter has a linear phase spectrum, as we now will show. The point of symmetry is

$$M = \frac{N-1}{2}$$

Chapter 6. Design of digital filters

The point of symmetry is an integer if N is odd, and is an integer minus one-half if N is even. As a result, we must distinguish between odd and even values of N. Examples of symmetric MA filters are shown in Figure 6-1. For a symmetric filter it is convenient to define new coefficients g_n as follows. First, let us treat the case of N odd. We let g_0 be the coefficient at the point of symmetry M, that is,

$$g_0 = h_M$$

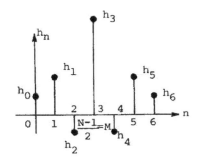
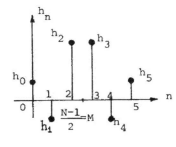

(a) N=7 (odd)   (b) N=6 (even)

FIGURE 6-1

Typical impulse responses h_n for symmetric MA filters (a) N odd (b) N even

Then we let g_1 be the sum of the next coefficients on each side of the point of symmetry, that is,

$$g_1 = h_{M-1} + h_{M+1} = 2h_{M-1}$$

Similarly, we define g_2 as

$$g_2 = h_{M-2} + h_{M+2} = 2h_{M-2}$$

and so on, until we define

$$g_M = h_0 + h_{N-1} = 2h_0$$

Next, let us treat the case of N even. We let g_0 be the sum of the coefficients on each side of the point of symmetry, that is,

$$g_0 = h_{M-\frac{1}{2}} + h_{M+\frac{1}{2}} = 2h_{M-\frac{1}{2}}$$

Similarly, we define g_1 as

$$g_1 = h_{M-\frac{3}{2}} + h_{M+\frac{3}{2}} = 2h_{M-\frac{3}{2}}$$

and so on, until we define

$$g_{M-\frac{1}{2}} = h_0 + h_{N-1} = 2h_0$$

In summary, these new coefficients are defined as

$$\left. \begin{array}{l} g_0 = h_M \\ g_n = 2h_{M-n}, \; n=1,2,\ldots M \end{array} \right\} \; M=\frac{N-1}{2}, \; N \text{ odd} \quad (1)$$

and

$$g_n = 2h_{M-\frac{1}{2}-n}, \; n=0,1,2,\ldots M-\frac{1}{2} \; \Big\} \; M=\frac{N-1}{2}, \; N \text{ even} \quad (2)$$

Figure 6-2 shows the new coefficients g_n for the symmetric MA filters of Figure 6-1.

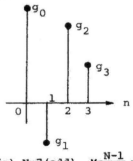
(a) N=7 (odd), $M=\frac{N-1}{2} = 3$

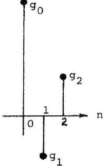
(b) N=6 (even), $M=\frac{N-1}{2} = 2.5$

FIGURE 6-2

Impulse responses g_n derived from symmetric MA filters of Figure 6-1.

The transfer function of a symmetric MA filter can be written as

$$H(z) = z^M(h_0 z^{-M} + h_1 z^{-M+1} + \cdots + h_{N-2} z^{N-2-M} + h_{N-1} z^{N-1-M})$$

$$= z^M(h_0 z^{-M} + h_1 z^{-M+1} + \cdots + h_{N-2} z^{M-1} + h_{N-1} z^M)$$

Chapter 6. Design of digital filters

where $M = (N-1)/2$. In case N is odd, this equation becomes

$$H(z) = z^M[g_0 + g_1(\frac{z^{-1}+z}{2}) + g_2(\frac{z^{-2}+z^2}{2}) + \cdots + g_M(\frac{z^{-M}+z^M}{2})]$$

and in case N is even, it becomes

$$H(z) = z^M[g_0(\frac{z^{-\frac{1}{2}}+z^{\frac{1}{2}}}{2}) + g_1(\frac{z^{-\frac{3}{2}}+z^{\frac{3}{2}}}{2}) + \cdots + g_{M-\frac{1}{2}}(\frac{z^{-M}+z^M}{2})]$$

Because

$$\frac{e^{in\omega} + e^{-in\omega}}{2} = \cos n\omega$$

The above equations become, upon letting $z=e^{-i\omega}$, the following:

For N odd, $M = (N-1)/2$, the frequency spectrum is

$$H(\omega) = e^{-i\omega M}(g_0 + g_1\cos\omega + g_2\cos 2\omega + \cdots + g_M\cos M\omega) \tag{3}$$

and for N even, $M = (N-1)/2$, the frequency spectrum is

$$H(\omega) = e^{-i\omega M}(g_0\cos\frac{\omega}{2} + g_1\cos\frac{3\omega}{2} + \cdots + g_{M-\frac{1}{2}}\cos M\omega) \tag{4}$$

Equations (3) and (4) show that $H(\omega)$ has a linear phase spectrum corresponding to a delay of M, that is, a delay of $(N-1)/2$ time units. We note that for the case of N odd, the delay is an integer, whereas for N even the delay is an integer minus one-half. We have thus shown that a symmetric MA filter has linear phase. Conversely, it can be shown that a causal filter with linear phase is a symmetric MA filter. (See Problem 1).

Since causal linear-phase filters, or what is the same thing, symmetric filters, are often required in signal processing, let us now discuss the design of such filters.

Suppose that the desired filter has an infinite-duration impulse response sequence f_n. The simplest method of MA filter design is to truncate the sequence f_n; that is, let the MA filter have the impulse response

$$h_n = \begin{cases} f_n, & n=0,1,2,\ldots,N-1 \\ 0 & \text{otherwise} \end{cases}$$

More generally, we can design the MA filter by letting h_n be the product of the desired impulse response f_n and a finite-duration window w_n, as given by

$$h_n = f_n w_n$$

In the case of truncation, the window is the box-car sequence

$$w_n = \begin{cases} 1, & n=0,1,2,\ldots,N-1 \\ 0, & \text{otherwise} \end{cases}$$

However, other more desireable windows are usually used. Let $W(\omega)$ be the frequency spectrum of the window w_n; that is,

$$W(\omega) = \sum_{n=-\infty}^{\infty} w_n e^{-in\omega}$$

The spectrum of h_n is

$$H(\omega) = \sum_{n=-\infty}^{\infty} h_n e^{-in\omega} = \sum_{n=-\infty}^{\infty} f_n w_n e^{-in\omega}$$

However, the complex convolution theorem gives

$$H(\omega) = \frac{1}{2\pi} \int_{-\pi}^{\pi} F(\theta) W(\omega-\theta) d\theta \qquad (5)$$

which says that $H(\omega)$ is the convolution of the desired frequency spectrum $F(\omega)$ with the window frequency spectrum $W(\omega)$. In other words, the frequency spectrum $H(\omega)$ is a smeared version of the desired frequency spectrum $F(\omega)$. The smearing is done by the window frequency spectrum $W(\omega)$. The more narrow and spike-like the window spectrum $W(\omega)$ the less the smearing. Figure 6-3 shows the smearing process in the case of a real box-car spectrum $F(\omega)$ and a typical window spectrum.

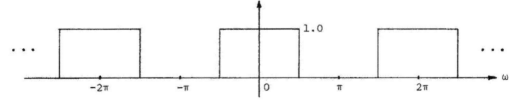

(a) Desired spectrum corresponding to the sequence

$$f_n = \frac{\sin\omega_c n}{\pi n} \text{ for all } n; \quad \omega_c = \pi/2.$$

Chapter 6. Design of digital filters

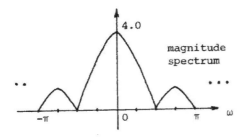
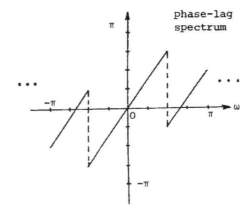

(b) Window spectrum of the even box-car $W_n = u_n - u_{n-N}$ where u_n is the unit step sequence: $N = 4$.

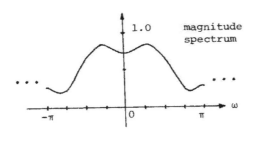
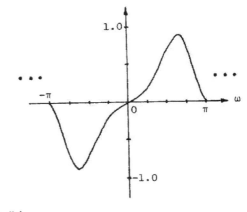

(c) The convolution of (a) and (b).

FIGURE 6-3

The spectrum of a windowed sequence
(a) desired spectrum (b) window spectrum
(c) "smeared" spectrum of windowed sequence

The choice of window sequence w_n is governed by the desire to have the duration of w_n as short as possible in time while having $W(\omega)$ as narrow as possible in frequency. In this way the length of the impulse response of the MA filter is as small as possible in keeping with a faithful reproduction of the desired frequency spectrum. However, these two requirements are necessarily conflicting, so some compromise has to be reached. The many different windows in use represent different compromises.

Let us illustrate these points in the case of some well-known windows. As we have seen simple truncation is the same as making use of the box-car sequence with frequency spectrum

$$W(\omega) = \sum_{n=0}^{N-1} e^{-in\omega} = \frac{1-e^{-i\omega N}}{1-e^{-i\omega}}$$

$$= \frac{\sin(\omega N/2)}{\sin(\omega/2)} e^{-i\omega(\frac{N-1}{2})} \tag{6}$$

Of course, the box-car sequence is symmetric, so the phase is linear, as we see in equation (6). The magnitude spectrum $|W(\omega)|$ is shown in Figure 6-4.

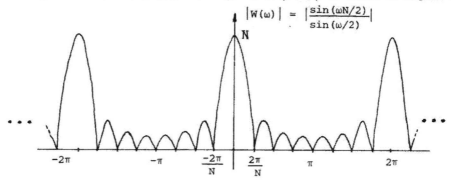

FIGURE 6-4

Magnitude spectrum of the box-car sequence for N=8.

The main lobe occurs in the interval between $\omega=-2\pi/N$ and $2\pi/N$. As N increases, we see that the width of the main lobe decreases. However, the magnitude spectrum of the box-car window has the following property. Whereas the widths of the lobes decrease with increasing N, the heights of the lobes increase with increasing N. As a result, the effect of the side lobes is not insignificant, and gives rise to oscillations in the frequency spectrum of the MA filter.

Other window sequences have magnitude spectra with smaller side-lobes and therefore, these windows result in smaller oscillations in the frequency spectra of the MA filters. Such window sequences are tapered smoothly to zero at each end, so they are called tapered windows. The tapering diminishes the height of the side lobes with respect to the main lobe. However, this reduction of the side lobes is achieved at the expense of a wider main lobe. As a result, the oscillations in the frequency spectrum of the MA filter are less, but the smearing effect is greater, than in the case of a box-car window sequence.

Let us list some well-known window sequences for the discrete points $n=0,1,2,\ldots,N-1$. The values of the windows are zero for $n<0$ and $n \geq N$. Each

Chapter 6. Design of digital filters

of these windows are symmetric, so each has a linear phase spectrum.

Box-car or rectangular window

$$w_n = 1, \quad 0 \le n \le N-1$$

Bartlett or triangular window (convolution of a rectangle with itself)

$$w_n = \begin{cases} \dfrac{2n}{N-1}, & 0 \le n \le \dfrac{N-1}{2} \\ \\ 2 - \dfrac{2n}{N-1}, & \dfrac{N-1}{2} \le n \le N-1 \end{cases}$$

Binomial window (digital counterpart of the continuous-time Parzen window; convolution of a two-point rectangle with itself N-1 times.)

$$w_n = \dfrac{B(N-1)!}{(N-1-n)!\, n!}, \quad 0 \le n \le N-1$$

where

$$B = \begin{cases} \dfrac{\left(\dfrac{N-1}{2}\right)! \left(\dfrac{N-1}{2}\right)!}{(N-1)!}, & N \text{ odd} \\ \\ \dfrac{\left(\dfrac{N-2}{2}\right)! \left(\dfrac{N}{2}\right)!}{(N-1)!}, & N \text{ even} \end{cases}$$

Hanning or sine-squared window

$$w_n = \sin^2\left(\dfrac{\pi n}{N-1}\right) = 0.5 - 0.5 \cos\left(\dfrac{2\pi n}{N-1}\right), \quad 0 \le n \le N-1$$

Hamming window

$$w_n = 0.54 - 0.46 \cos\left(\dfrac{2\pi n}{N-1}\right), \quad 0 \le n \le N-1$$

These windows for N=21 and their magnitude spectra are plotted in Figures 6-5 and 6-6.

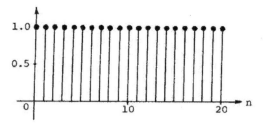

(a) Box-car or rectangular window

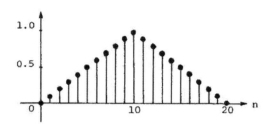

(b) Bartlett or triangular window

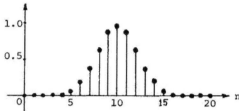

(c) Binomial window

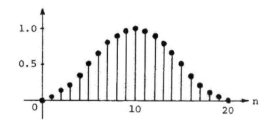

(d) Hanning or sine-squared window

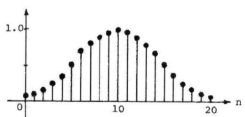

(e) Hamming window

FIGURE 6-5

Some well-known window sequences. Graphs are for N=21.

Chapter 6. Design of digital filters

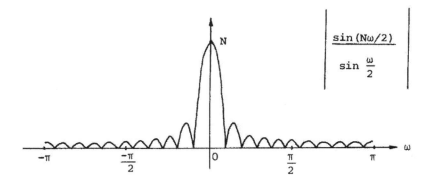

(a) Box-car or rectangular window

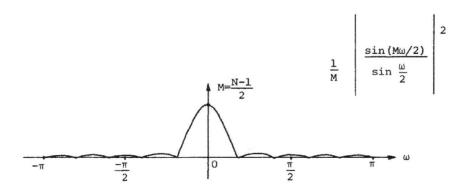

(b) Bartlett or triangular window

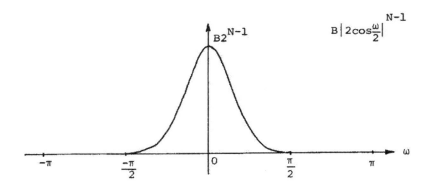

(c) Binomial window

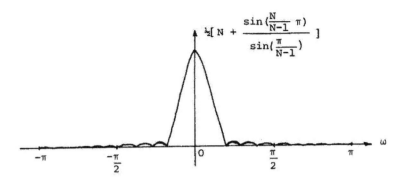

(d) Hanning or sine-squared window

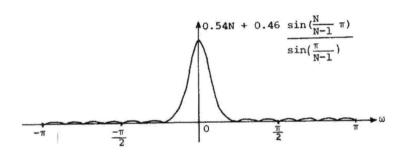

(e) Hamming window

FIGURE 6-6

The corresponding magnitude spectra of the various windows in Figure 6-5. Graphs are for N=21.

The rectangular window has the narrowest main lobe but the first side lobe is only 13 db below the main lobe. All the other windows are tapered. This tapering results in a wider main lobe but the peaks of the side lobes are greatly reduced.

The magnitude spectrum for the Bartlett window is equal to the square of the magnitude spectrum of the box-car (with frequency scale doubled), because the Bartlett window is the convolution of two box-cars (with time scale halved). The binomial window results in no side lobes and can be obtained by convolving a two-point rectangle with itself N-1 times. Both the Hanning and Hamming windows yield a narrower main lobe than the Bartlett or Binomial windows and their side lobes are greatly reduced.

Chapter 6. Design of digital filters

Let us now design a low-pass filter. We want the MA filter so designed to be a symmetric filter of duration N, which we suppose is odd. As a result, the delay is $M=(N-1)/2$, so we define the desired frequency spectrum as

$$F(\omega) = \begin{cases} e^{-i\omega M}, & |\omega| \le |\omega_c| \\ 0 & \text{otherwise} \end{cases}$$

where ω_c is the cut-off frequency. The impulse response of the desired low-pass filter is

$$f_n = \frac{1}{2\pi} \int_{-\omega_c}^{\omega_c} e^{i\omega(n-M)} d\omega = \frac{\sin[\omega_c(n-M)]}{\pi(n-M)},$$

which is infinitely long. To design a MA filter we define

$$h_n = f_n w_n$$

Since f_n is symmetrical about the point M, the MA filter h_n will also be symmetrical, provided that we use a symmetrical window. Figures 6-7 and 6-8 show the impulse responses and corresponding magnitude spectra for low-pass FIR filters designed by the use of the various windows listed in Figure 6-5.

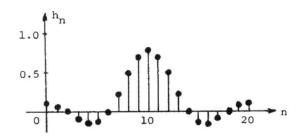

(a) rectangular-weighted impulse response

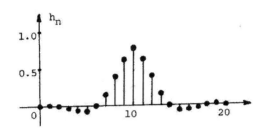
(b) Bartlett-weighted impulse response

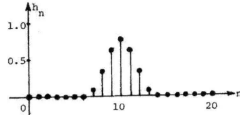
(c) binomial-weighted impulse response

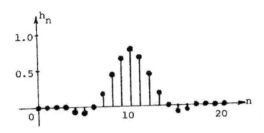
(d) Hanning-weighted impulse response

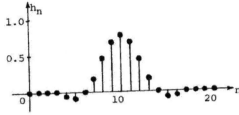
(e) Hamming-weighted impulse response

Figure 6-7

Impulse responses for low-pass FIR filters designed by the use of the various windows listed in Figure 6-5.

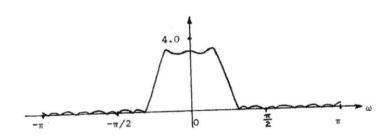
(a) magnitude spectrum of the rectangular-seighted impulse response

Chapter 6. Design of digital filters

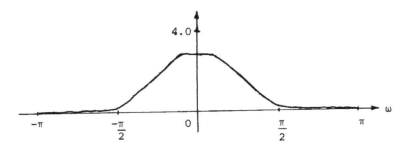

(b) magnitude spectrum of Bartlett-weighted impulse response

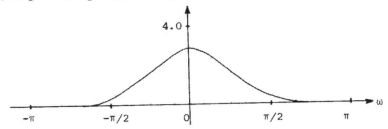

(c) magnitude spectrum of binomial-weighted impulse response

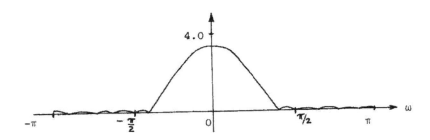

(d) magnitude spectrum of Hanning-weighted impulse response

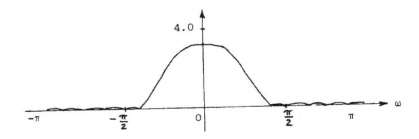

(e) magnitude spectrum of Hamming-weighted impulse response

Figure 6-8

Magnitude spectra of the corresponding impulse responses in Figure 6-7.

1. Show that a causal MA filter with a linear phase-lag spectrum is a symmetric MA filter.

2. Consider a MA filter with transfer function

$$H(z) = h_0 + h_1 z + \cdots + h_{M-1} z^{M-1} - h_{M-1} z^{M+1} - \cdots - h_1 z^{N-2} - h_0 z^{N-1}$$

    Note that the filter is antisymmetric about the point $M=(N-1)\frac{1}{2}$ and $h_M=0$.

    (a) Derive the frequency spectrum of this filter for N odd.

    (b) Does this filter have a linear phase-lag spectrum? Explain.

3. The impulse response of a MA filter is

$$h_n = \binom{N-1}{n} = \frac{(N-1)!}{(N-1-n)!\, n!}, \quad n=0,1,\ldots,N-1$$

    where $\binom{N-1}{n}$ are the binomial coefficients.

    (a) Derive the frequency spectrum of this filter.

    (b) Plot the magnitude and phase-lag spectra over the range $0 \leq \omega \leq \pi$ for N=9.

4. Consider the minimum-delay MA system

$$H_{min}(z) = h_0 + h_1 z + \cdots + h_{N-1} z^{N-1}$$

    and the corresponding minimum-advance system $H_{min}(z^{-1})$, that is,

$$H_{min}(z^{-1}) = h_{N-1} z^{-N+1} + h_{N-2} z^{-N+2} + \cdots + h_0$$

    (a) Determine the appropriate transfer function $A(z)$ such that the cascaded system

$$H(z) = A(z) H_{min}(z) H_{min}(z^{-1})$$

    is a symmetric MA filter.

    (b) Plot the phase-lag spectrum of the filter $A(z)$ over the range $0 \leq \omega \leq \pi$ for the case N=20.

    (c) What is the contribution of the phase-lag spectrum of the system $H_{min}(z) H_{min}(z^{-1})$ to the overall phase-lag spectrum associated with $H(z)$?

Chapter 6. Design of digital filters

5. The impulse response of a desired low-pass filter is

$$f_n = \frac{\sin[0.25\pi(n-4)]}{\pi(n-4)}$$

(a) Design a symmetric MA filter of duration N=9 using a Hanning window. Plot the magnitude spectrum of the MA filter over the range $0 \leq \omega \leq \pi$.

(b) Repeat part (a) using a Bartlett window.

6. Consider the window sequence

$$w_n = a - b \cos \frac{2\pi n}{N-1}, \quad n=0,1,\ldots,N-1$$

where $a \geq b > 0$.

(a) Derive the frequency spectrum of this sequence.

(b) What effect does the ratio a/b have on the side lobes of the magnitude spectrum of w_n?

6.2 Design of recursive (ARMA) filters

The design of a recursive (or ARMA) filter involves the determination of a transfer function which is a rational function in the complex variable z. We recall that a recursive filter is defined as one with a rational transfer function (Article 3.7). The transfer function must meet certain performance specifications. Also, the principle of parsimony applies in that in most design problems we want a transfer function of minimal complexity. A number of design methods for digital filters have been developed. In many applications a frequency selective filter is required. Such a filter is designed to allow certain frequency components to pass through but to attenuate others. The design specification for this type of filter is given in the frequency domain.

In this Article we will treat the design of a low-pass recursive filter. The ideal magnitude spectrum of a low-pass digital filter has the brick-wall shape shown in Figure 6-9.

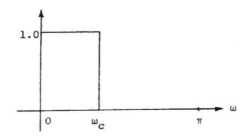

FIGURE 6-9

Magnitude spectrum of an ideal low-pass filter.

The design problem reduces to that of finding a particular function from general classes of functions. The particular function is chosen so as to approximate the ideal magnitude spectrum in a prescribed sense.

One general class of digital filters are the so-called polynomial filters. The squared magnitude spectrum of a member of this class can be expressed in the form

$$|H(\omega)|^2 = \frac{1}{1 + \varepsilon^2 P^2(\omega)} \qquad (1)$$

where ε is a real constant and $P^2(\omega)$ is a real polynomial in $\tan^2(\omega/2)$. More specifically, the function $P^2(\omega)$ can be expressed in the general form

$$P^2(\omega) = \sum_{k=0}^{N} p_k \tan^{2k}\left(\frac{\omega}{2}\right) \qquad (2)$$

where the coefficients p_k are real.

We want $|H(\omega)|^2$ as given in the above polynomial filter form (equation (1)) to approximate the brick-wall or low-pass magnitude spectrum in Figure 6-9. Let us first examine this general form before proceeding to evaluate specific parameters.

At the Nyquist frequency $\omega=\pi$ we have

$$\tan\left(\frac{\pi}{2}\right) = \infty$$

so $P^2(\omega)$ is infinite there and therefore the magnitude spectrum there is zero. At frequency $\omega=0$, we see that $P^2(\omega)$ is zero, so the magnitude spectrum there is unity. When the function $\tan(\omega/2)$ is large, then the polynomial $P^2(\omega)$ behaves as its largest term, namely $\tan^{2N}(\omega/2)$. Since $\tan(\omega/2)$ is a monotonic increasing function of ω, it follows that above a certain frequency ω_c the polynomial $P^2(\omega)$ will increase monotonically to infinity and hence $|H(\omega)|^2$ will decrease monotonically to zero at the Nyquist frequency π. Of course, the function $|H(\omega)|^2$ is periodic with a period of 2π.

Chapter 6. Design of digital filters

In summary, within the baseband $0 \leq \omega \leq \pi$, the squared magnitude spectrum $|H(\omega)|^2$ of the polynomial filter in equation (1) decreases monotonically to zero in the range $\omega_c \leq \omega \leq \pi$. Thus, $|H(\omega)|^2$ has the proper form for a low-pass filter.

If we divide the baseband $0 \leq \omega \leq \pi$ into a passband $0 \leq \omega \leq \omega_c$ (corresponding to the location of the brick wall) and a stopband $\omega_c \leq \omega \leq \pi$, it is seen that the choice of $|H(\omega)|^2$ as given above makes the magnitude spectrum of the required low-pass digital filter monotonic in the stopband. The variation within the passband, however, must be determined from the prescribed values of the polynomial coefficients.

The so-called Butterworth low-pass digital filter can be obtained by letting $P^2(\omega)$ take its simplest nontrivial form, namely

$$\varepsilon^2 P^2(\omega) = a \tan^{2N}(\tfrac{\omega}{2})$$

where a is a real constant. The resulting function

$$|H(\omega)|^2 = \frac{1}{1 + a \tan^{2N}(\omega/2)} \qquad (3)$$

is monotonically decreasing in the passband as well as the stopband. If the magnitude spectrum $|H(\omega)|$ is to fall by 3 db at the cutoff frequency ω_c, then the constant a becomes

$$a = [\tan^{2N}(\tfrac{\omega_c}{2})]^{-1}$$

and therefore equation (3) becomes

$$|H(\omega)|^2 = \left[1 + \left(\frac{\tan(\omega/2)}{\tan(\omega_c/2)}\right)^{2N}\right]^{-1} \qquad (4)$$

From equation (4) we see that

$$|H(0)| = 1$$

$$|H(\omega_c)| = \frac{1}{\sqrt{2}}$$

$$|H(\pi)| = 0$$

We see that the magnitude spectrum decreases monotonically from unity to zero within the baseband in a sense similar to the Butterworth low-pass analog filter.

To synthesize the low-pass digital filter we must locate the position of its poles and zeroes. We let

$$w = u + iv = \frac{1-z}{1+z}$$

When $z = e^{-i\omega}$ we have

$$w = \frac{1 - e^{-i\omega}}{1 + e^{-i\omega}} = i\tan(\omega/2)$$

so $u=0$ and $v=\tan(\omega/2)$. In the w-plane, the poles of $|H(\omega)|^2$ will be located at the roots of the equation

$$1 + \left(\frac{-iw}{v_c}\right)^{2N} = 0 \tag{5}$$

where $v_c = \tan(\omega_c/2)$. Equation (5) becomes

$$1 + (-1)^N \left(\frac{w}{v_c}\right)^{2N} = 0$$

Thus, for N even

$$w_k = v_c e^{i\frac{\pi(2k+1)}{2N}}, \quad k=0,1,2,\ldots,2N-1$$

or for N odd

$$w_k = v_c e^{i\frac{\pi k}{N}}, \quad k=0,1,2,\ldots,N-1$$

Hence, for even N

$$\left.\begin{array}{l} u_k = v_c\cos\left(\frac{2k+1}{2N}\right)\pi \\ \\ v_k = v_c\sin\left(\frac{2k+1}{2N}\right)\pi \end{array}\right\} k=0,1,2,\ldots,2N-1 \tag{6}$$

and for odd N

$$\left.\begin{array}{l} u_k = v_c\cos\frac{\pi k}{N} \\ \\ v_k = v_c\sin\frac{\pi k}{N} \end{array}\right\} k=0,1,2,\ldots,N-1 \tag{7}$$

Equations (6) and (7) are the parametric equations for a circle at the origin of radius v_c in the w-plane. This circle in the z-plane through the transformation $w=(1-z)/(1+z)$ becomes the following curve:

Chapter 6. Design of digital filters

We have

$$z = x + iy = \frac{1-w}{1+w} = \frac{1-(u+iv)}{1+(u+iv)}$$

so

$$x = \frac{1-(u^2+v^2)}{(1+u)^2+v^2} \quad, \quad y = \frac{-2v}{(1+u)^2+v^2}$$

Since

$$u^2+v^2 = v_c^2 \quad,$$

we have

$$x = \frac{1-v_c^2}{1+2u+v_c^2} \quad, \quad y = \frac{-2v}{1+2u+v_c^2}$$

so the required curve is

$$y^2 + \left[x - \frac{1+v_c^2}{1-v_c^2} \right] = \frac{4v_c^2}{(1-v_c^2)^2} \tag{8}$$

Thus, this curve is a circle of radius

$$\rho = \frac{2v_c}{1-v_c^2} = \tan\omega_c$$

and center

$$\left(\frac{1+v_c^2}{1-v_c^2} , 0 \right) = (\sec\omega_c, 0)$$

because

$$v_c = -\tan(\omega_c/2)$$

Hence, the pole positions are given by

$$x_k = \frac{1-\tan^2(\omega_c/2)}{1-2\tan(\omega_c/2)\cos(\frac{2k+1}{N}\pi) + \tan^2(\omega_c/2)} \quad, \quad y_k = \frac{2\tan(\omega_c/2)\sin(\frac{2k+1}{N}\pi)}{1-2\tan(\omega_c/2)\cos(\frac{2k+1}{N}\pi) + \tan^2(\omega_c/2)} \tag{9}$$

for the range k=0,1,2,...,2N-1 for N even. If N is odd, replace (2k+1)/2N by k/N in equation (9) and the range by k=0,1,2,...,N-1.
In summary, the synthesis procedure is

(1) Evaluate the order of the filter N from the given specifications

(2) Determine the pole locations in the z-plane and choose those that lie outside the unit circle.
(3) There exists an Nth order zero at $z=-1$
(4) From the zeroes and poles construct the required transfer function.

Example 1. A low-pass digital filter is to have a cutoff frequency of 4.5 kHz. The transition ratio is required to be 0.9 and the attenuation at the transition frequency better than 60 dB. The sampling frequency is 18 kHz.

Solution. First we change the time unit from one second to one sample spacing. Thus, we define

$$\Delta t = \frac{1}{18 \text{ kHz}}$$

as one time unit. Then ω_c in radians per time unit is

$$\omega_c = 2\pi \left(\frac{4.5 \text{ kHz}}{18 \text{ kHz}} \right) = 0.5\pi$$

The transition frequency is 4.5 kHz/0.9 = 5 kHz whith in radians per time unit is

$$\omega_1 = 2\pi \left(\frac{5 \text{ kHz}}{18 \text{ kHz}} \right) = 0.55\pi$$

Now

$$\tan(\omega_c/2) = \tan(0.25\pi) = 1$$

and

$$\tan(\omega_1/2) = \tan(5\pi/18) = 1.18$$

so at the transition frequency we have

$$10 \log_{10}(1+1.18^{2N}) = 60$$

which gives

$$N = \frac{6}{2(0.79)} = 3.8 \approx 4$$

Because $\tan(\omega_c/2) = 1$, the poles in the w-plane lie on a unit circle. The coordinates of the poles are

$$u_k = \cos\left(\frac{2k+1}{8}\pi\right) \;,\; v_k = \sin\left(\frac{2k+1}{8}\pi\right) \;,\; k=0,1,2,\ldots,7$$

Chapter 6. Design of digital filters

which gives

u_k	v_k
± 0.92388	± 0.38268
± 0.38268	± 0.92388

In the z-plane these poles lie on the imaginary axis; that is, the z-plane poles have coordinates

x_k	y_k	Position
0	± 0.19891	Inside unit circle
0	± 5.02732	Outside unit circle
0	± 0.66818	Inside unit circle
0	± 1.49660	Outside unit circle

Thus, four poles lie inside the unit circle in the z-plane and four poles lie outside. The poles outside the unit circle yield the stable transfer function; the polynomial corresponding to these poles is

$$A(z) = (z-5.02732i)(z+5.02732i)(z-1.49660i)(z+1.49660i)$$

$$= (2.76536 + 1.23464z^2)(3.84776 + 0.15224z^2)$$

Since the filter is for N=4, there is a 4th order zero at z= -1. Thus, the required transfer function is

$$H(z) = \Upsilon \frac{(1+z)^4}{A(z)}$$

where Υ is a gain constant. Letting the gain be zero at $\omega=0$ (corresponds to z=1) we have

$$H(1) = 1 = \frac{\Upsilon\, 2^4}{(4)(4)} = \Upsilon$$

so $\Upsilon = 1$. The magnitude spectrum $|H(\omega)|$ is shown in Figure 6-10.

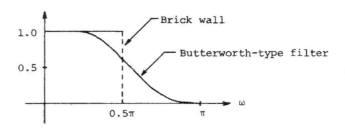

FIGURE 6-10

Magnitude spectrum of Butterworth filter for N=4, $\omega_c = \frac{\pi}{2}$

High-pass, bandpass, and bandstop filters may be designed from low-pass filters by means of frequency transformations. The following table gives the necessary transformations needed to transform a given low-pass digital filter to other forms, whose cutoff frequency is β.

Filter type	Transformation (w)	Associated design formula
Lowpass	$\dfrac{z-\alpha}{1-\alpha z}$	$\alpha = \dfrac{\sin(\frac{\beta-\omega_c}{2})}{\sin(\frac{\beta+\omega_c}{2})}$
Highpass	$\dfrac{z+\alpha}{1+\alpha z}$	$\alpha = -\dfrac{\cos(\frac{\beta-\omega_c}{2})}{\cos(\frac{\beta+\omega_c}{2})}$
Bandpass	$-\dfrac{\frac{\beta-1}{\beta+1} - \frac{2\alpha\beta}{\beta+1}z + z^2}{1 - \frac{2\alpha\beta}{\beta+1}z + \frac{\beta-1}{\beta+1}z^2}$	$\alpha = \cos\omega_0 = \dfrac{\cos(\frac{\omega_2+\omega_1}{2})}{\cos(\frac{\omega_2-\omega_1}{2})}$ $\beta = \cot(\frac{\omega_2-\omega_1}{2})\tan\frac{\omega_0}{2}$
Bandstop	$\dfrac{\frac{1-\beta}{1+\beta} - \frac{2\alpha}{1+\beta}z + z^2}{1 - \frac{2\alpha}{1+\beta}z + \frac{1-\beta}{1+\beta}z^2}$	$\alpha = \cos\omega_0 = \dfrac{\cos(\frac{\omega_2+\omega_1}{2})}{\cos(\frac{\omega_2-\omega_1}{2})}$ $\beta = \tan(\frac{\omega_2-\omega_1}{2})\tan\frac{\omega_0}{2}$

PROBLEMS FOR ARTICLE 6.2

1. A recursive (ARMA) filter can be represented by the difference equation

Chapter 6. Design of digital filters

$$y_n = \sum_{k=1}^{M} f_k y_{n-k} + \sum_{k=0}^{N} g_k x_{n-k}$$

(a) Show that the squared magnitude spectrum can be written as

$$|H(\omega)|^2 = \frac{\sum_{k=0}^{N} g'_k \cos^{2k} \frac{\omega}{2}}{\sum_{k=0}^{M} f'_k \cos^{2k} \frac{\omega}{2}}$$

where the g'_k and f'_k coefficients are respectively dependent on the real coefficients g_k and f_k.

(b) Using the trigonometric identity $\cos^2 \frac{\omega}{2} = 1 - \sin^2 \frac{\omega}{2}$, develop an expression for the squared magnitude spectrum of the ARMA filter in terms of even powers of $\sin \frac{\omega}{2}$.

(c) Alternatively, ARMA filters could be posed in the form

$$|H(\omega)|^2 = \frac{\sum_{k=0}^{N} q_k \tan^{2k} \frac{\omega}{2}}{\sum_{k=0}^{M} p_k \tan^{2k} \frac{\omega}{2}}$$

Show how this representation reduces to the low-pass Butterworth filter discussed in this Article.

2. The Butterworth low-pass filter studied in this Article is sometimes referred to as the *tangent* Butterworth low-pass filter. Another type of low-pass filter is the *sine* Butterworth low-pass filter whose squared magnitude spectrum is

$$|H(\omega)|^2 = \frac{1}{1 + a \sin^{2N}(\omega/2)}$$

(a) Determine the value of a such that the magnitude spectrum $|H(\omega)|$ is down by 3 db at the cutoff frequency ω_c.

(b) Evaluate the squared magnitude spectrum at the frequency $\omega=\pi-\omega_c$, where ω_c is the 3 db-cutoff frequency.

(c) Under the conditions that $10\log|H(\omega)|^2 = -120$ db at $\omega=\pi-\omega_c$ and $\omega_c=\pi/50$ ($\frac{\omega_c}{2}\ll 1$), determine the order of the filter N.

3. Write down an expression for the transfer function of the Butterworth low-pass filter discussed in this Article.

(a) Determine whether or not the filter is invertible.

(b) Determine an expression for the impulse response of this filter.

4. Letting $\phi(\omega)$ denote the phase-lag spectrum of the Butterworth low-pass filter in this Article, determine the quantity $\Delta\phi=\phi(\pi)-\phi(-\pi)$. Is this filter minimum-delay? Explain.

5. A low-pass digital filter is to have a cutoff frequency of 1 kHz. The transition ratio is required to be 0.9 and the attenuation at the transition frequency better than 60 db. If the sampling frequency is 2.5 kHz, design a Butterworth low-pass digital filter that meets these specifications.

6.3 Least-squares design of moving average (MA) filters

In the two preceding Articles, the characteristics of digital filters have been developed, independent of assumptions as to the nature of the input data. However, in order to evaluate the usefulness of a digital filter, it is often necessary to consider the characteristics of the signal and noise to which the digital filter will be applied. Also, these characteristics of the signal and noise will in a large part determine the criterion by which the digital filter should be optimized. It is apparent from the above discussion that the criterion of optimization depends upon the nature of the input signal and also upon the desired output. There are various approaches to determining the best criterion. In Chapter 8, we will consider the design of digital filters in the case when the signals and noise

Chapter 6. Design of digital filters

are random processes. In this Article we want to consider the case where the forms of the input signal and the desired output signals are known.

The design problem to be considered may be formulated as follows. Given a signal x_n we want to operate on x_n in some manner so as to obtain the best approximation to the signal s_n. That is, let $T(x_n)$ be the best approximation to s_n. More generally, we may let $T(x_n)$ be the best approximation to the shifted signal $s_{n+\alpha}$, where α is a time shift. At this point, the criterion of best approximation and the form of the operator are unspecified.

Let us now consider an ideal system f_n. An ideal system would transform the input into the desired output. If the ideal system is a linear shift—invariant system, then

$$s_{n+\alpha} = f_n * x_n \tag{1}$$

In terms of Fourier transforms, equation (1) becomes

$$S(\omega)e^{i\omega\alpha} = F(\omega)X(\omega) \tag{2}$$

The solution of equation (2) gives the filter characteristics of the *ideal filter* as

$$F(\omega) = \frac{S(\omega)e^{i\omega\alpha}}{X(\omega)} \tag{3}$$

Equation (3) represents the formal solution to the problem. However, for actual computations this equation is of no help, because the impulse response f_n of the ideal system $F(\omega)$ will generally be an infinitely-long two-sided operator. For practical purposes, a digital filter with a finite number of coefficients is required, so let us try to approximate the ideal filter f_n by a moving average (MA) filter h_n where

$$h_n = 0 \text{ for } n<0 \text{ and for } n>M \tag{4}$$

(We recall that an MA filter is defined as a causal linear shift-invariant filter with a finite-length impulse response. Alternatively, a MA filter can be defined as a linear shift-invariant filter that has a transfer function equal to a polynomial in z.) Thus, we want to approximate the frequency response $F(\omega)$ of the ideal filter by the frequency response

$$H(\omega) = \sum_{n=0}^{M} h_n e^{-i\omega n} \tag{5}$$

of the required MA filter.

Such an approximation procedure means that a certain amount of information contained in the infinite-length impulse response f_n be lost in order to obtain the approximate finite-length impulse response h_n. Consequently, we shall need some sort of averaging process to carry out this approximation. We want the difference

$$F(\omega) - H(\omega) \tag{6}$$

to be small in some sense. For example, we might choose the coefficients h_n so that the mean-squared difference

$$\frac{1}{2\pi} \int_{-\pi}^{\pi} |F(\omega) - H(\omega)|^2 d\omega \qquad (7)$$

is a minimum. However, in expression (7) we see that the squared difference $|F(\omega) - H(\omega)|^2$ is given a uniform weighting for all frequencies. It would make more sense to weight the squared difference according to the energy spectrum $|X(\omega)|^2$ of the input signal. Thus, let us choose the MA coefficients h_n so that the mean-weighted-squared-difference, or mean-square-error,

$$I = \frac{1}{2\pi} \int_{-\pi}^{\pi} |F(\omega) - H(\omega)|^2 |X(\omega)|^2 d\omega \qquad (8)$$

is a minimum. Equation (8) can be written as

$$I = \frac{1}{2\pi} \int_{-\pi}^{\pi} |F(\omega)X(\omega) - H(\omega)X(\omega)|^2 d\omega \qquad (9)$$

If we make use of equation (2) we obtain

$$I = \frac{1}{2\pi} \int_{-\pi}^{\pi} |S(\omega)e^{i\omega\alpha} - H(\omega)X(\omega)|^2 d\omega \qquad (10)$$

Now $S(\omega)$ is the spectrum of the desired output signal s_n and $H(\omega)X(\omega)$ is the spectrum of the actual output signal $h_n * x_n$. If we apply Parseval's equality (see Article 4.2) to equation (10) we obtain

$$I = \sum_{n=-\infty}^{\infty} |s_{n+\alpha} - h_n * x_n|^2 \qquad (11)$$

Because we are dealing with real signals, equation (11) becomes

$$I = \sum_{n=-\infty}^{\infty} (s_{n+\alpha} - \sum_{k=0}^{M} h_k x_{n-k})^2 \qquad (12)$$

In order to minimize I, we set its partial derivatives with respect to each of $h_0, h_1, \ldots, h_M$ equal to zero. We obtain

$$\frac{\partial I}{\partial h_j} = -2 \sum_{n=-\infty}^{\infty} (s_{n+\alpha} - \sum_{k=0}^{M} h_k x_{n-k}) x_{n-j} = 0 \qquad (13)$$

Chapter 6. Design of digital filters

for $j=0,1,2,\ldots,M$. The set of equations (13) are

$$\sum_{k=0}^{M} h_k \left[\sum_{n=-\infty}^{\infty} x_{n-k} x_{n-j} \right] = \sum_{n=-\infty}^{\infty} s_{n+\alpha} x_{n-j} \qquad (14)$$

for $j=0,1,2,\ldots,M$. We recognize the serial correlation coefficient

$$r_{j-k} = \sum_{n=-\infty}^{\infty} x_{n-k} x_{n-j} \qquad (15)$$

Also, we define the cross-correlation coefficient

$$g_{j+\alpha} = \sum_{n=-\infty}^{\infty} s_{n+\alpha} x_{n-j} \qquad (16)$$

Then the set of equations (14) becomes

$$\sum_{k=0}^{M} h_k r_{j-k} = g_{j+\alpha} \qquad (17)$$

for $j=0,1,2,\ldots,M$. This set of equations are called the *Toeplitz normal equations*. The serial correlation coefficients (15) and the cross-correlation coefficients (16) can be computed from the known input signal x_n and desired output signal s_n. Then the Toeplitz normal equations (17) can be solved to find the required filter coefficients h_n. Because the output $h_n * x_n$ of this filter approximates the desired output signal s_n in a least squares sense, this filter is called the *least-squares shaping filter*.

Because of the special form of the simultaneous equations (17), called the Toeplitz form, the equations may be solved by an efficient recursive procedure called the Toeplitz recursion. The Toeplitz recursion is described in Appendix A of this book.

In computer applications, the input signal will be a finite-length wavelet

$$(x_0, x_1, x_2, \ldots, x_N) \qquad (18)$$

The actual output y_n of the shaping filter will therefore be a finite-length wavelet

$$(y_0, y_1, y_2, \ldots, y_{M+N}) \qquad (19)$$

where

$$y_n = \sum_{k=0}^{M} h_k x_{n-k} \qquad (20)$$

Also, we shall assume the desired signal is a finite-length wavelet

$$(s_0, s_1, s_2, \ldots, s_K) \qquad (21)$$

In our development of the shaping filter we have allowed the desired output to be a time-shifted version of this desired signal, where the time-shift is α. Clearly, this time shift is an important parameter in the shaping operation. If α is positive, then the desired output $s_{n+\alpha}$ is an advanced version of the signal wavelet (21). If α is negative, then the desired output $s_{n+\alpha}$ is a delayed version of the signal wavelet (21). When $\alpha=K$, then the signal wavelet (21) has been advanced to such an extent that the coefficient s_K occurs at time-index 0; that is,

$$\text{Desired output:} \quad (s_0, s_1, s_2, \ldots, \overset{n=0}{\underset{\downarrow}{s_K}}) \tag{22}$$

$$\text{Actual output:} \quad (\underset{\underset{n=0}{\uparrow}}{y_0}, y_1, y_2, \ldots, y_{M+N})$$

Thus, when $\alpha=K$, the coefficient s_K occurs at the same time point (i.e. $n=0$) as the coefficient y_0 in the actual output, but otherwise the desired output s_{n+K} and actual output y_n have no other non-zero coefficients occurring at the same time. When $\alpha=K-1$, the desired output s_{n+K-1} and actual output y_n have two non-zero coefficients in common:

$$\text{Desired output:} \quad (s_0, s_1, s_2, \ldots, \overset{n=0}{\underset{\downarrow}{s_{K-1}}}, s_K)$$

$$\text{Actual output:} \quad (\underset{\underset{n=0}{\uparrow}}{y_0}, y_1, y_2, \ldots, y_{M+N})$$

Of course when $\alpha=0$, the desired and actual outputs line up, that is,

$$\text{Desired output:} \quad (\overset{n=0}{\underset{\downarrow}{s_0}}, s_1, s_2, \ldots, s_K)$$

$$\text{Actual output:} \quad (\underset{\underset{n=0}{\uparrow}}{y_0}, y_1, y_2, \ldots, y_K, \ldots, y_{M+N})$$

When α becomes negative, then the desired output lags the actual output. When $\alpha = -M-N$, then only one point is in common:

Chapter 6. Design of digital filters

$$\text{Desired output:} \quad (0,0,\ldots,\underset{\underset{n=0}{\uparrow}}{s_0},s_1,s_2,\ldots,\underset{\underset{n=M+N}{\uparrow}}{s_K})$$

$$\text{Actual output:} \quad (\underset{\underset{n=0}{\uparrow}}{y_0},y_1,\ldots,y_{M+N})$$

In conclusion, there is overlap between desired and actual outputs for values of the shift α in the range $-M-N \leq \alpha \leq K$. When α is outside of this range, there is no overlap and consequently all the coefficients in the desired output represent irreducible error; that is, the cross-correlation

$$g_{j+\alpha} = 0 \text{ for } j=1,2,\ldots,M$$

so $h_n=0$ for $n=0,1,2,\ldots,M$ and equation (12) for the mean-square error becomes

$$I = \sum_{n=-\alpha}^{K-\alpha} s_{n+\alpha}^2 = \sum_{n=0}^{K} s_n^2 \tag{23}$$

However, for some or all α within the range $-M-N \leq \alpha \leq K$, the mean-square error (12) will be smaller than that given by equation (23). Hence, for each value of α in this range, the value of the mean-square error (12) can be computed. The value of α that gives the smallest value of I represents the *optimum-shift least-squares shaping filter*.

A special case of the least-squares shaping filter is the *least-squares spiking filter*. A spiking filter is a shaping filter for which the desired output signal is a spike. Thus, the signal s_n is the unit impulse

$$s_n = \delta_n = \begin{cases} 1, & n=0 \\ 0, & n \neq 0 \end{cases}$$

The length of the desired wavelet s_n is 1 (since there is only one non-zero coefficient) so the parameter K is K=0. Thus, the α range of interest is $-M-N \leq \alpha \leq 0$. The spiking filter for $\alpha=0$ is called the zero-lag spiking filter, for $\alpha=-1$ the one-lag spiking filter, for $\alpha=-2$ the two-lag spiking filter, and so on. The value of α which gives the smallest mean-square error is called the optimum-lag, and the corresponding spiking filter the *optimum-lag least-squares spiking filter*.

PROBLEMS FOR ARTICLE 6.3

1. Determine an expression for the *minimum* mean-square error I_{min} associated with a least-squares shaping filter. Interpret your result for the case when $\alpha=0$ and the cross-correlation coefficients are zero.

2. Given the input sequence $x_n=(x_0,x_1)=(1,0.5)$, determine the least-squares shaping filter h_n that best shapes this input into the desired wavelet $s_n=(1,0.5,0.25)$. Repeat this procedure when the input wavelet is $x_n=(x_0,x_1)=(0.5,1)$. Is it more difficult to shape the maximum-delay input $(0.5,1)$ into this particular desired output than the minimum-delay input $(1,0.5)$? Explain.

3. The signal $x_n=(x_0,x_1)=(0.5,1)$ does not have a stable causal inverse, that is, it is not invertible. However, x_n does have a *least squares inverse* if we employ the idea of a least-squares spiking filter. Discuss a procedure for making the given input invertible, that is, determine a least-squares inverse for x_n.

4. Determine the least-squares spiking filter that shapes the minimum-delay input $x_n=(x_0,x_1)=(1,0.5)$ into the desired output $s_n=(1,0,0)$. Repeat this procedure for the input $x_n=(x_0,x_1)=(0.5,1)$. Is it more difficult to "spike" the maximum-delay input than the minimum-delay input? Explain. Suppose the desired output was the delayed spike $s_n=(0,0,1)$. Repeat the above procedure for both the minimum-delay and maximum-delay inputs and explain your results.

5. Consider the least-squares normal equations

$$\sum_{k=0}^{M+1} h_k^{(M+1)} r_{j-k} = g_{j+\alpha} \text{ for } j=0,1,2,\cdots,M+1$$

Assuming that the filter coefficients satisfy the relation

$$h_k^{(M+1)} = h_k^{(M)} - a_{M+1-k}^{(M+1)} h_{M+1}^{(M+1)} \text{ for } k=0,1,\cdots,M$$

where $a_k^{(M+1)}$ is an auxillary sequence,

(a) Show that

$$h_{M+1}^{(M+1)} = \frac{g_{M+1+\alpha} - \sum_{k=0}^{M} h_k^{(M)} r_{M+1-k}}{r_0 - \sum_{k=1}^{M+1} a_k^{(M+1)} r_k}$$

Chapter 6. Design of digital filters

where $h_0^{(0)} = \dfrac{g_\alpha}{r_0}$

(Hint: Consider the case j=M+1 when expanding the normal equations.)

(b) Assuming that the auxilary sequence $a_k^{(M+1)}$ of part (a) satisfies the relation

$$a_k^{(M+1)} = a_k^{(M)} - a_{M+1-k}^{(M)} a_{M+1}^{(M+1)} \quad \text{for } k=1,2,\ldots,M$$

show that

$$a_{M+1}^{(M+1)} = \dfrac{r_{M+1} - \sum_{k=1}^{M} a_k^{(M)} r_{M+1-k}}{r_0 - \sum_{k=1}^{M} a_k^{(M)} r_k}$$

where $a_1^{(1)} = \dfrac{r_1}{r_0}$

(Hint: Consider the case j=0,1,...,M when expanding the normal equations. After some manipulation, there results a new set of simultaneous equations. Expand this new set of equations to obtain the desired result.)

(c) Combining the results of parts (a) and (b), indicate a recursive procedure for solving the normal equations for the filter coefficients $h_k^{(M+1)}$ at stage M+1 based on the coefficients $h_k^{(M)}$ at stage M. Refer to Appendix A.

Chapter 7. The kepstrum

7.1 Even-odd and real-imaginary relationships for causal systems

An even sequence e_n and an odd sequence o_n are defined by the relations

$$e_n = e^*_{-n} \quad \text{for all } n \tag{1}$$
$$o_n = -o^*_{-n} \quad \text{for all } n$$

In this definition we have allowed for the possibility of complex sequences.
Any sequence can be expressed as a sum of an even sequence and an odd sequence. In particular, let the sequence h_n be a (possibly complex-valued) *causal* sequence. Define its even part as

$$e_n = \begin{cases} \dfrac{h_n}{2} & , n > 0 \\ \operatorname{Re}(h_0) & , n = 0 \\ \dfrac{h^*_{-n}}{2} & , n < 0 \end{cases} \tag{2}$$

and its odd part as

$$o_n = \begin{cases} \dfrac{h_n}{2} & , n > 0 \\ i\operatorname{Im}(h_0) & , n = 0 \\ \dfrac{-h^*_{-n}}{2} & , n < 0 \end{cases} \tag{3}$$

From now on we shall consider only those complex-valued sequences for which $\operatorname{Im}(h_0)=0$.
We see that the e_n and o_n given by equations (2) and (3) do in fact satisfy definition (1), so the sequence e_n is indeed even and the sequence o_n is indeed odd. Also from equations (2) and (3), we can immediately verify that h_n is causal; that is,

$$h_n = e_n + o_n = \begin{cases} h_n & , n \geq 0 \\ 0 & , n < 0 \end{cases} \tag{4}$$

The decomposition of the real exponential sequence $h_n = a^n u_n$ into its even and odd parts is shown in Figure 7-1 for the case $0 < a < 1$.

Chapter 7. The kepstrum

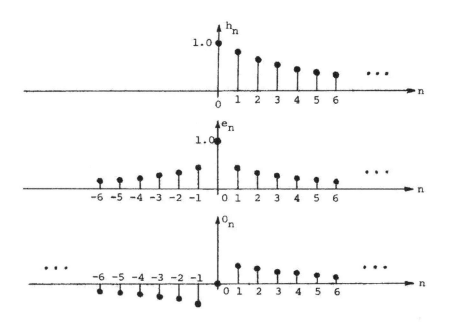

FIGURE 7-1

A real-valued causal sequence h_n, its even part e_n and its odd part o_n.

Let us consider the implication of equation (4). If we define

$$u_n^+ = \begin{cases} 2, & n>0 \\ 1, & n=0 \\ 0, & n<0 \end{cases} \quad (5)$$

then

$$h_n = e_n u_n^+ \quad \text{(for all n)} \quad (6)$$

and

$$h_n = o_n u_n^+ + h_0 \delta_n \quad \text{(for all n)} \quad (7)$$

We see that h_n can be completely recovered from e_n. However, h_n can be recovered from o_n only for $n \neq 0$; that is, h_n can be recovered from o_n and h_0.

The Laplace z-transform of the causal sequence is the power series

$$H(z) = \sum_{n=0}^{\infty} h_n z^n \tag{8}$$

We assume that the sequence h_n is stable (Definition 1 in Article 2.3); as a result, the power series converges on the unit circle. The power series evaluated on the unit circle becomes the Fourier series

$$H(\omega) = \sum_{n=0}^{\infty} h_n e^{-in\omega} \tag{9}$$

Because $h_n = 0$ for $n < 0$, we can just as well write the limits on the summation in (9) from $n = -\infty$ to $n = \infty$. Using equation (4), the Fourier series (9) becomes

$$H(\omega) = \sum_{n=-\infty}^{\infty} (e_n + o_n) e^{-in\omega}$$

$$= \sum_{n=-\infty}^{\infty} e_n e^{-in\omega} + \sum_{n=-\infty}^{\infty} o_n e^{-in\omega} \tag{10}$$

If the complex conjugate of a number is equal to the number, then we can conclude that the number is real. Let us check to see if the first term on the right-hand side of equation (10) is real. We write

$$\left(\sum_{n=-\infty}^{\infty} e_n e^{-in\omega} \right)^* = \sum_{n=-\infty}^{\infty} e_n^* e^{in\omega} = \sum_{n=-\infty}^{\infty} e_{-n} e^{in\omega} = \sum_{k=-\infty}^{\infty} e_k e^{-ik\omega}$$

where we have used equation (1) and where $k = -n$. This shows that the term is indeed real. If the complex conjugate of a number is equal to minus the number, then we can conclude that the number is imaginary. Let us now check to see if the second term on the right-hand side of equation (10) is imaginary. We write

$$\left(\sum_{n=-\infty}^{\infty} o_n e^{-in\omega} \right)^* = \sum_{n=-\infty}^{\infty} o_n^* e^{in\omega} = -\sum_{n=-\infty}^{\infty} o_{-n} e^{in\omega} = -\sum_{k=-\infty}^{\infty} o_k e^{-ik\omega}$$

where we have used equation (1) and where $k = -n$. This shows that the term is indeed imaginary. Hence, equation (10) represents a breakdown of the spectrum $H(\omega)$ into its real and imaginary parts; that is,

$$\text{Re}[H(\omega)] = \sum_{n=-\infty}^{\infty} e_n e^{-in\omega}, \quad e_n = e_{-n}^* \tag{11}$$

$$i\,\text{Im}[H(\omega)] = \sum_{n=-\infty}^{\infty} o_n e^{-in\omega}, \quad o_n = -o_{-n}^* \tag{12}$$

$$o_0 = 0$$

Chapter 7. The kepstrum

What we have done so far in this Article can be interpreted in terms of the classical complex methods in the theory of Fourier series. We can regard equation (11) as the complex form of the Fourier series of the real function $\text{Re}[H(\omega)]$. The Fourier series (11) is the real part of the power series (8) evaluated on the unit circle $z=e^{-i\omega}$. The Fourier series (12), with vanishing constant term, when added to (11) gives the power series (8) on the unit circle. The Fourier series (12) divided by i gives

$$\text{Im}[H(\omega)] = -i \sum_{n=-\infty}^{\infty} o_n e^{-in\omega} \quad , \quad o_n = -o_{-n}^* \qquad (13)$$

$$o_0 = 0$$

which is called the *conjugate Fourier series* to (11).

A consequence of equation (11) is that the Fourier transform $H(\omega)$, given by equation (9), of a stable causal sequence is completely known if we know its real part $\text{Re}[H(\omega)]$. This is because according to (11), we can compute the e_n as the Fourier coefficients of $\text{Re}[H(\omega)]$, i.e.

$$e_n = \frac{1}{2\pi} \int_{-\pi}^{\pi} \text{Re}[H(\omega)] e^{in\omega} d\omega \text{ (for all integers n)} \qquad (14)$$

Then using equation (6), we can compute the h_n, from which we can compute $H(\omega)$. From the theory of Fourier series (Article 4.1) we know that the minimum requirement needed is that the function $\text{Re}[H(\omega)]$ be integrable.

The fact that Fourier series are the real parts of power series on the circle $z=re^{-i\omega}$ facilitates in many cases the finding of the sums of the Fourier series. For example, the Fourier series

$$P_r(\omega) = 1 + 2 \sum_{n=1}^{\infty} r^n \cos n\omega$$

$$Q_r(\omega) = - \sum_{n=1}^{\infty} r^n \sin n\omega$$

where $0 \leq r \leq 1$, are the real and imaginary parts of the power series

$$1 + 2z + 2z^2 + 2z^3 + \cdots$$

where $z = re^{-i\omega}$. Because the sum of this power series is

$$\frac{1+z}{1-z} \quad \text{for} \quad |z| < 1 \quad ,$$

we obtain without difficulty

$$P_r(\omega) = \text{Re}\left(\frac{1+re^{-i\omega}}{1-re^{-i\omega}}\right) = \frac{1-r^2}{1-2r\cos\omega + r^2} \quad \text{for } r<1 \qquad (15)$$

and

$$Q_r(\omega) = \text{Im}\left(\frac{1+re^{-i\omega}}{1-re^{-i\omega}}\right) = \frac{-2r\sin\omega}{1-2r\cos\omega + r^2} \quad \text{for } r<1 \qquad (16)$$

The functions $P_r(\omega)$ and $Q_r(\omega)$ are called for historical reasons *Poisson's kernel* and *Poisson's conjugate kernel*.

Similarly, from the power series

$$\log\left(\frac{1}{1-z}\right) = z + \frac{z^2}{2} + \frac{z^3}{3} + \cdots$$

where $|z|<1$, we obtain (for $r<1$)

$$\sum_{n=1}^{\infty} \frac{\cos n\omega}{n} r^n = \text{Re}\left[\log\left(\frac{1}{1-re^{-i\omega}}\right)\right] = \frac{1}{2}\log\left(\frac{1}{1-2r\cos\omega + r^2}\right)$$

$$\sum_{n=1}^{\infty} \frac{\sin n\omega}{n} r^n = \text{Im}\left[\log\left(\frac{1}{1-re^{-i\omega}}\right)\right] = \tan^{-1}\left(\frac{-r\sin\omega}{1-r\cos\omega}\right)$$

Let us now show that if h_n is a stable causal sequence, then its transfer function $H(z)$ can be determined anywhere within the unit circle from knowledge of only $\text{Re}[H(\omega)]$ (i.e. from knowledge of the real part of $H(z)$ on the unit circle $z=e^{-i\omega}$). For any point z within the unit circle we write $z=re^{-i\omega}$, and using equations (6) and (8) we obtain

$$H(z) = \sum_{n=0}^{\infty} h_n z^n = \sum_{n=-\infty}^{\infty} e_n u_n^+ z^n$$

which is, by equation (5),

$$H(z) = e_0 + 2\sum_{n=1}^{\infty} e_n z^n$$

Using equation (14) for e_n we obtain

$$H(z) = \frac{1}{2\pi}\int_{-\pi}^{\pi} \text{Re}[H(\omega')]\,d\omega' + 2\sum_{n=1}^{\infty}\left[\frac{1}{2\pi}\int_{-\pi}^{\pi} \text{Re}[H(\omega')]e^{in\omega'}d\omega'\right]z^n$$

which is

$$H(z) = \frac{1}{2\pi}\int_{-\pi}^{\pi}\left[1 + 2\sum_{n=1}^{\infty} e^{in\omega'}z^n\right]\text{Re}[H(\omega')]\,d\omega'$$

The expression in square brackets contains a geometric series and can be summed as

$$1 + 2\sum_{n=1}^{\infty}(e^{i\omega'}z)^n = \frac{1+e^{i\omega'}z}{1-e^{i\omega'}z} \quad \text{for } |z|<1$$

Chapter 7. The kepstrum

Thus, we have

$$H(z) = \frac{1}{2\pi} \int_{-\pi}^{\pi} \left(\frac{1 + ze^{i\omega'}}{1 - ze^{i\omega'}} \right) \text{Re}[H(\omega')] d\omega' \quad , \quad |z| < 1$$

or

$$H(re^{-i\omega}) = \frac{1}{2\pi} \int_{-\pi}^{\pi} \left(\frac{1 + re^{-i(\omega-\omega')}}{1 - re^{-i(\omega-\omega')}} \right) \text{Re}[H(\omega')] d\omega' \quad , \quad r < 1$$

This equation expresses $H(z)$ for z within the unit circle in terms of its real part $\text{Re}[H(\omega)]$ on the unit circle. However, it is also useful to break this equation down into its real and imaginary parts. If we make use of Poisson's kernel (15) and Poisson's conjugate kernel (16) we obtain

$$\text{Re}[H(re^{-i\omega})] = \frac{1}{2\pi} \int_{-\pi}^{\pi} P_r(\omega - \omega') \text{Re}[H(\omega')] d\omega' \tag{17}$$

and

$$\text{Im}[H(re^{-i\omega})] = \frac{1}{2\pi} \int_{-\pi}^{\pi} Q_r(\omega - \omega') \text{Re}[H(\omega')] d\omega' \tag{18}$$

These are *real* integral relations for the real and imaginary parts of the transfer function (of a stable causal system) for $z = re^{-i\omega}$ inside the unit circle in terms of the real part of the transfer function on the unit circle.

In order to obtain a direct relationship between the real part on the unit circle and the imaginary part on the unit circle, it is necessary to take the limit as $r \to 1$ in equations (18). If we bring the limiting operation within the integral sign, we obtain an improper integral, since the function

$$\lim_{r \to 1} Q_r(\omega - \omega') = \lim_{r \to 1} \frac{-2r\sin(\omega - \omega')}{1 - 2r\cos(\omega - \omega') + r^2}$$

$$= \frac{-2\sin(\omega - \omega')}{2 - 2\cos(\omega - \omega')} = -\cot\left(\frac{\omega - \omega'}{2}\right)$$

has a singularity at $\omega - \omega' = 0$. However, this difficulty can be avoided by interpreting the resulting integral as the *Cauchy principal value*. Thus, equation (18) becomes as $r \to 1$

$$\text{Im}[H(e^{-i\omega})] = -\frac{1}{2\pi} P \int_{-\pi}^{\pi} \cot\left(\frac{\omega - \omega'}{2}\right) \text{Re}[H(\omega')] d\omega' \tag{19}$$

where the symbol P denotes the Cauchy principal value of the integral. In words, $\text{Im}[H(\omega)]$ is equal to the periodic convolution of $\cot\frac{\omega}{2}$ with $\text{Re}[H(\omega)]$. These two functions involved in the convolution are shown in Figure 7-2.

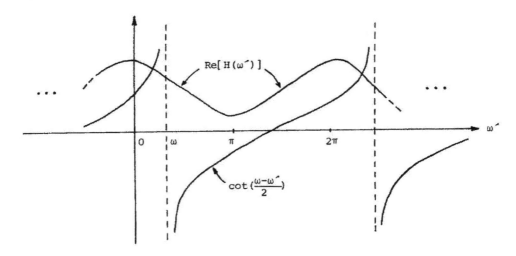

FIGURE 7-2

The functions $\text{Re}[H(\omega')]$ and $\cot\left(\frac{\omega-\omega'}{2}\right)$ involved in the periodic convolution of equation (19).

Equation (19) is a classic result in the theory of Fourier series. It gives the relationship between the sum $\text{Im}[H(\omega)]$ of the conjugate Fourier series (13) and the sum $\text{Re}[H(\omega)]$ of the Fourier series (11). Equation (19) may be described in words by saying that $\text{Im}[H(\omega)]$ is the *Hilbert transform* of $\text{Re}[H(\omega)]$. Given the real part of the spectrum of a stable causal signal h_n, equation (19) shows how the imaginary part of the spectrum may be obtained from it. In other words, given the real part of the spectrum, the imaginary part of the spectrum cannot be arbitrarily assigned. We say that $\text{Im}[H(\omega)]$ and $\text{Re}[H(\omega)]$ in equation (19) form a *Hilbert transform pair*.

PROBLEMS FOR ARTICLE 7.1

1. Given $\text{Re}[H(\omega)] = 1 + a\cos\omega$, find $|H(\omega)|$.

2. Consider the minimum-delay sequence h_n with spectrum $H(\omega)$. Given $\log|H(\omega)|$, determine a procedure for obtaining the phase-lag spectrum $\phi(\omega)$.

3. Discuss the meaning of the "Cauchy principal value" of an integral.

Chapter 7. The kepstrum

7.2 Relationship between gain and phase-lag

The word "gain" is sometimes used rather loosely as a synonym for "voltage amplification" or "current amplification". In more precise usage the term "gain" has a specific meaning: the logarithm of the magnitude of the spectrum. Let the spectrum $H(\omega)$ be written in complex polar form

$$H(\omega) = |H(\omega)|e^{-i\phi(\omega)} \tag{1}$$

where $|H(\omega)|$ is the magnitude spectrum and $\phi(\omega) = -\arg H(\omega)$ is the phase-lag spectrum. The gain is defined as

$$G(\omega) = \log|H(\omega)| \tag{2}$$

Thus, the logarithm of the spectrum can be written in terms of the gain and phase-lag as

$$\log H(\omega) = G(\omega) - i\phi(\omega) \tag{3}$$

In other words, the gain is the real part of the logarithm of the spectrum, i.e.

$$G(\omega) = \text{Re}[\log H(\omega)] \tag{4}$$

and phase-lag is the negative of the imaginary part of the logarithm of the spectrum, i.e.

$$\phi(\omega) = -\text{Im}[\log H(\omega)] \tag{5}$$

When an overall system is represented as the cascade of two or more individual systems, the gain and phase-lag curves of the overall system is obtainable by simple addition of the gain and phase-lag curves respectively of the individual systems. Specifically, if

$$H(\omega) = H_1(\omega)H_2(\omega)$$

then

$$G(\omega) = G_1(\omega) + G_2(\omega)$$

$$\phi(\omega) = \phi_1(\omega) + \phi_2(\omega)$$

Before we proceed to a more detailed discussion of gain and phase-lag curves a word about units is in order. The expression (2) for gain implies the use of natural logarithms. The unit of the natural logarithmic scale is the *neper*. If for a certain frequency ω_1 we have $G(\omega_1) = 4$, then we say that the gain is 4 nepers at that frequency. If $X(\omega)$ denotes the spectrum of the input and $Y(\omega)$ the spectrum of the output, then

$$\log\left|\frac{Y(\omega_1)}{X(\omega_1)}\right| = 4$$

or

$$|Y(\omega_1)| = e^4 |X(\omega_1)|$$

That is, a gain of 4 nepers means that the output magnitude is e^4 times the input magnitude. In practice, the logarithmic scales are often used; the most popular being the "decibel" scale. However, the neper scale is the most appealing from a mathematical point of view.

Figure 7-3 shows the gain and phase-lag curves corresponding to various basic systems for the range $-\pi \leq \omega \leq \pi$.

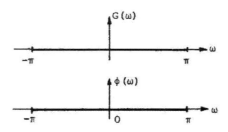

(a) Trivial all-pass system; $H(z) = 1$

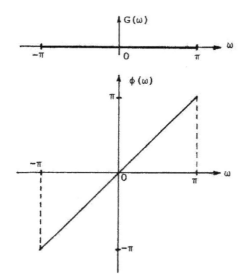

(b) Unit-delay all-pass system; $H(z) = z$

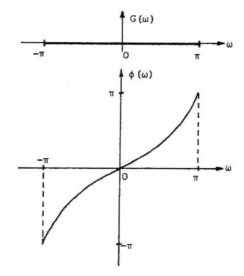

(c) Dispersive all-pass system;

$$H(z) = \frac{0.5 + z}{1 + 0.5z}$$

Chapter 7. The kepstrum

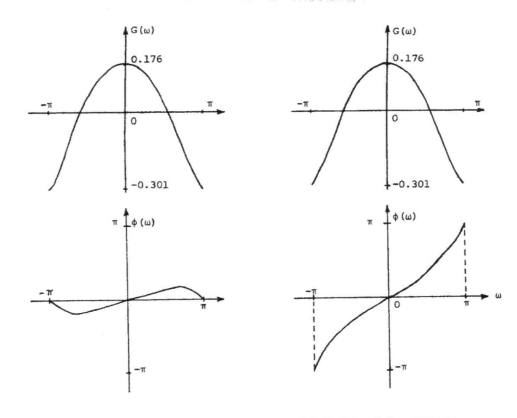

(d) Minimum-delay system;
    H(z) = 1 + 0.5z

(e) Maximum-delay system;
    H(z) = 0.5 + z

FIGURE 7-3

Typical gain and phase-lag curves corresponding
to various basic systems

As we know (Article 4.3) the spectrum of a real signal is conjugate-symmetric; that is,

$$H(\omega) = H^*(-\omega) \text{ for real } h_n.$$

Thus, for real signals, it follows that the gain curve is symmetric and the phase curve is anti-symmetric, that is,

$$\left. \begin{array}{l} G(\omega) = G(-\omega) \\ \phi(\omega) = -\phi(-\omega) \end{array} \right\} \text{ for real } h_n.$$

Suppose now that we are given a gain curve $G(\omega)$. This curve is a real function of frequency ω in the range $-\pi$ to π. We would like to represent the function $G(\omega)$ by a Fourier series, so we must at least impose the condition on $G(\omega)$ that it be integrable, that is, we require the condition

$$\frac{1}{2\pi} \int_{-\pi}^{\pi} G(\omega) d\omega < \infty \tag{6}$$

(This condition is called the Paley-Wiener condition.) Under this condition, the Fourier coefficients

$$e_n = \frac{1}{2\pi} \int_{-\pi}^{\pi} G(\omega) e^{in\omega} d\omega \quad \text{(for all integers n)}$$

exist. Thus, the Fourier series is

$$G(\omega) = \sum_{n=-\infty}^{\infty} e_n e^{-in\omega}$$

We have used the symbol e_n for the Fourier coefficients because e_n is an even function, i.e. $e_n = e_{-n}^*$. This evenness of e_n follows from the fact that $G(\omega)$ is real.

Example 1. Let the gain curve be

$$G(\omega) = \log(1 - 2a\cos\omega + a^2)^{1/2}, \quad 0 < a < 1$$

The Fourier coefficients are

$$e_n = \frac{1}{2\pi} \int_{-\pi}^{\pi} \log(1 - 2a\cos\omega + a^2)^{1/2} e^{i\omega n} d\omega$$

or

$$e_0 = 0$$
$$e_n = \frac{-a^{|n|}}{2|n|}$$

Thus, the Fourier series is

$$G(\omega) = \sum_{n=-\infty}^{-1} \frac{-a^{-n}}{2(-n)} e^{-in\omega} + \sum_{n=1}^{\infty} \frac{-a^n}{2n} e^{-in\omega}$$

$$= \sum_{n=1}^{\infty} \frac{-a^n}{n} \cos n\omega$$

Because $G(\omega)$ is a real even function of ω, we see that its Fourier series is a Fourier cosine series.

Thus, given an integrable gain function $G(\omega)$, we are able to find its Fourier coefficients e_n (for all integers n). Because the gain is real,

Chapter 7. The kepstrum

these Fourier coefficients e_n are an even sequence, that is, $e_n = e^*_{-n}$. Now let us refer back to Article 7.1. Given an even sequence e_n we know how to construct a stable causal sequence f_n whose even part is the given even sequence; that is, given the even sequence e_n we can construct the stable causal sequence

$$f_n = e_n u_n^+ = \begin{cases} 2e_n , & n>0 \\ e_n , & n=0 \\ 0 , & n<0 \end{cases} \qquad (7)$$

where f_n can be expressed as

$$f_n = e_n + o_n \qquad (8)$$

and o_n is odd (i.e. $o_n = -o^*_{-n}$). As a result the spectrum $F(\omega)$ has the decomposition

$$F(\omega) = \mathrm{Re}[F(\omega)] + i\,\mathrm{Im}[F(\omega)]$$

$$= \sum_{n=-\infty}^{\infty} e_n e^{-in\omega} + i \sum_{n=-\infty}^{\infty} o_n e^{-in\omega} \qquad (9)$$

$$= G(\omega) - i\phi(\omega)$$

Thus the real part of $F(\omega)$ is the gain and the imaginary part of $F(\omega)$ is the negative of the phase-lag. The system $F(z)$

$$F(z) = \sum_{n=0}^{\infty} f_n z^n \qquad (10)$$

so constructed is causal and stable, so it has the properties of a stable causal system, that is, $F(z)$ is analytic in the unit disc $|z|<1$. If we define $H_{min}(z)$ as

$$F(z) = \log H_{min}(z) \qquad (11)$$

then it follows that $H_{min}(z)$ is the exponential function of $F(z)$, i.e.

$$H_{min}(z) = e^{F(z)} \qquad (12)$$

and the inverse of $H_{min}(z)$ is the exponential function of $-F(z)$; i.e.

$$H_{min}^{-1} = \frac{1}{H_{min}(z)} = e^{-F(z)} \qquad (13)$$

Since the exponential function preserves the property of being analytic, it follows that $H_{min}(z)$ and $H_{min}^{-1}(z)$ both must be analytic in the unit disc.

As a result, both $H_{min}(z)$ and $H_{min}^{-1}(z)$ are stable causal systems, so $H_{min}(z)$ and $H_{min}^{-1}(z)$ are each invertible. In summary, if $F(z)$ is causal and stable, then $H_{min}(z) = \exp[F(z)]$ is minimum-delay. (We recall that the terms minimum-delay and invertible are equivalent.)

Example 2. Let us continue Example 1. The conjugate Fourier series to the Fourier cosine series

$$G(\omega) = \sum_{n=1}^{\infty} -\frac{a^n}{n} \cos n\omega, \quad 0<a<1$$

is the negative of the corresponding Fourier sine series, that is,

$$G_{conj}(\omega) = -\sum_{n=1}^{\infty} -\frac{a^n}{n} \sin n\omega, \quad 0<a<1$$

From equations (11) and (13) of Article 7.1 we know that the spectrum of a causal stable system is given by

$$F(\omega) = G(\omega) + i\, G_{conj}(\omega)$$

$$= \sum_{n=1}^{\infty} -\frac{a^n}{n} \cos n\omega - i \sum_{n=1}^{\infty} -\frac{a^n}{n} \sin n\omega$$

$$= \sum_{n=1}^{\infty} -\frac{a^n}{n} e^{-in\omega}$$

Thus, the Laplace z-transform of the causal stable system is

$$F(z) = \sum_{n=1}^{\infty} -\frac{a^n}{n} z^n = \log(1-az), \quad 0<a<1$$

It follows that $H_{min}(z) = 1-az$ is minimum-delay with the given gain $G(\omega) = \log(1 - 2a\cos\omega + a^2)^{1/2}$, $0<a<1$.

We can summarize our results to this point as follows. Given a real gain function $G(\omega)$ with the condition that it be integrable, we can find a stable causal system $F(z)$ with spectrum $F(\omega)$ whose real part is this gain; i.e. $\text{Re}[F(\omega)] = G(\omega)$. If we exponentiate the system $F(z)$ we obtain the system

$$H_{min}(z) = e^{F(z)}$$

which is minimum-delay with gain equal to the given gain function, i.e.

$$\log|H_{min}(\omega)| = G(\omega).$$

Let us now consider the phase-lag. We know that

$$F(\omega) = \log H_{min}(\omega) = \log |H_{min}(\omega)| - i\, \phi_{min}(\omega)$$

Chapter 7. The kepstrum

where $\phi_{min}(\omega)$ is the phase-lag spectrum or phase-lag. Since the system $H_{min}(z)$ is minimum-delay, then $\phi_{min}(\omega)$ is the minimum-phase-lag spectrum. Since

$$\text{Re}[F(\omega)] = \log|H_{min}(\omega)| = G(\omega)$$

and

$$\text{Im}[F(\omega)] = -\phi_{min}(\omega)$$

we can use the Hilbert transform (equation (19) of Article 7.1) to compute the phase-lag from the gain; that is,

$$\phi_{min}(\omega) = \frac{1}{2\pi} P \int_{-\pi}^{\pi} \cot\left(\frac{\omega-\omega'}{2}\right) G(\omega') d\omega'$$

This equation expresses the minimum-phase-lag $\phi_{min}(\omega)$ of the minimum-delay system $H_{min}(\omega)$ in terms of its gain $G(\omega) = \log|H_{min}(\omega)|$.

Example 3. Given the gain $G(\omega) = \log(1-2a\cos\omega+a^2)^{1/2}$ where $0<a<1$, find the corresponding minimum-phase-lag spectrum. We have

$$\phi_{min}(\omega) = \frac{1}{2\pi} P \int_{-\pi}^{\pi} \cot\left(\frac{\omega-\omega'}{2}\right) \log(1 - 2a\cos\omega' + a^2)^{1/2} d\omega'$$

$$= \tan^{-1}\left(\frac{-a\sin\omega}{1 - a\cos\omega}\right)$$

Given a real function $G(\omega)$, the Paley-Wiener condition (6) is necessary and sufficient to insure the existence of the causal system h_n with gain $G(\omega)$. A stable system whose gain function violates the Paley-Wiener condition must have an impulse response extending into the past; that is, it is noncausal.

Given a real function $G(\omega)$ that does satisfy the Paley-Wiener condition (6) we have shown how to construct a stable causal system with this gain. The system so constructed, as we have seen, is minimum-delay. The Hilbert transform fixes $\phi_{min}(\omega)$ and thereby determines the spectrum

$$H_{min}(\omega) = \exp[G(\omega) - i\phi_{min}(\omega)]$$

However, there are other causal (or realizeable) systems, say h_n, having the same gain $G(\omega)$ but with a phase-lag different from $\phi_{min}(\omega)$. To see this, we must consider causal systems whose magnitude spectra are constant. We have treated such systems in Article 4.5 under the name of all-pass systems. Some simple examples of all-pass systems are given in Figure 7-3.

Let us now review the canonical representation of a stable causal system $H(z)$ (see Article 4.5). Let $H_{min}(z)$ be a transfer function determined by a Hilbert transformation of a gain function. Let $H(z)$ be any other transfer function having the same gain. Then the quotient

$$H_{ap}(z) = \frac{H(z)}{H_{min}(z)}$$

gives a system with zero gain (i.e. $|H_{ap}(\omega)| = 1$). Also $H_{ap}(z)$ will certainly be causal, because $\log H_{min}(z)$, and consequently $H_{min}(z)$ and $1/H_{min}(z)$ are causal (i.e. $H_{min}(z)$ is minimum-delay), and hence $H(z)/H_{min}(z)$ is causal (since the product of two causal systems is likewise causal). Thus, the canonical representation of $H(z)$ is

$$H(z) = H_{ap}(z) H_{min}(z)$$

where $H_{ap}(z)$ is an all-pass system and $H_{min}(z)$ is a minimum-delay system with the same gain as $H(z)$. That is,

$$G(\omega) = G_{ap}(\omega) + G_{min}(\omega)$$

$$= G_{min}(\omega) \quad \text{(since } G_{ap}(\omega) = 0\text{)}$$

and

$$\phi(\omega) = \phi_{ap}(\omega) + \phi_{min}(\omega)$$

where $\dfrac{d\phi_{ap}(\omega)}{d\omega} > 0$.

It may appear contradictory that the Hilbert transformation gives a unique $\text{Im}[H(\omega)]$ from $\text{Re}[H(\omega)]$ for any stable causal system $H(z)$ whether it is minimum-delay or not, whereas the determination of $\phi(\omega)$ from $G(\omega)$ is not unique unless $H(z)$ is minimum-delay. The key lies in the following observation. Although possession by $\log H(z)$ of the properties of a stable causal system makes $H(z)$ and $1/H(z)$ each stable and causal, the stability and causality of $H(z)$ does not necessarily mean that $\log H(z)$ necessarily has these properties. The all-pass system

$$H_{ap}(z) = \frac{a+z}{1+az} \quad , \quad |a|<1$$

is stable and causal, but its logarithm becomes infinite in the unit disc at the point $z=-a$. Hence $\log H_{ap}(z)$ cannot be both stable and causal, and since stability is understood throughout our discussions, non-causality is the only alternative. Thus we can never obtain a non-trivial all-pass system from Hilbert transformation of a gain. As a result, the only systems obtained from Hilbert transformation of a gain are minimum-delay.

Chapter 7. The kepstrum

PROBLEMS FOR ARTICLE 7.2

1. Given the gain $G(\omega) = (\log a)\cos\omega$, where $|\log a| < 1$, find the corresponding minimum-phase-lag spectrum. Show that this gain satisfies the Paley-Wiener condition.

2. Determine the transfer function $H_{min}(z)$ of the minimum-delay system with gain

$$G(\omega) = \log(1 + 2a\cos\omega + a^2)^{1/2}, \quad |a| < 1$$

3. The transfer function of a system is given by

$$H(z) = \frac{\sin z}{z} = 1 - \frac{1}{3!}z^2 + \frac{1}{5!}z^4 - \frac{1}{7!}z^6 + \cdots \quad (|z| < \pi)$$

   (a) Determine the coefficients f_n in the expansion

$$\log H(z) = \sum_{n=0}^{\infty} f_n z^n$$

   (b) Determine the gain and phase-lag spectrum of this system.

4. In the study of *continuous-time* systems, the Paley-Wiener criterion is

$$\int_{-\infty}^{\infty} \frac{|\log G(\omega')|}{1+\omega'^2} d\omega' < \infty$$

where $G(\omega') = \log|H(\omega')|$ and $H(\omega')$ is given by

$$\int_{-\infty}^{\infty} h(t) e^{-i\omega' t} dt$$

Show that the mapping

$$e^{-i\omega} = \frac{i\omega' - 1}{i\omega' + 1}$$

yields the digital counterpart of the Paley-Wiener criterion.

7.3 The kepstrum

In this Article we wish to introduce the concept of the kepstrum. The kepstrum may be defined for a system $H(z)$ which may or may not be minimum-delay. In Article 7.2 we considered the minimum-delay case, which can be summarized as follows. If $H_{min}(z)$ is minimum-delay then $H_{min}(z)$ is analytic in the unit disc and has no zeroes in the unit disc. Because the logarithm of zero is infinite, it is clear that the logarithm of an analytic function blows up at a zero of the analytic function. Because $H_{min}(z)$ has no zero in the unit disc it is clear that $\log H_{min}(z)$ does not blow up in the unit disc, and as a result $\log H_{min}(z)$ has a Taylor-Maclaurin series expansion in the unit disc:

$$\log H_{min}(z) = \sum_{n=0}^{\infty} f_n z^n, \quad |z| < 1 \tag{1}$$

The coefficients f_n of this Taylor-Maclaurin series are the coefficients of a stable causal system. We call these coefficients the *kepstrum* of the minimum-delay system $H_{min}(z)$.

However, the concept of the kepstrum is not limited to minimum-delay systems. Let us now consider a nonminimum-delay system $H(z)$. If we assume that $H(z)$ has no zeroes or poles in an annular region including the unit circle, then $\log H(z)$ is analytic in this annular region. As a result $\log H(z)$ has a Laurent expansion

$$\log H(z) = \sum_{n=-\infty}^{\infty} f_n z^n \tag{2}$$

in this annular region. The coefficients f_n of this Laurent series are the coefficients of a stable noncausal system. We call these coefficients the *kepstrum* of the nonminimum-delay system $H(z)$.

Let us now return to the case of a minimum-delay system

$$H_{min}(z) = \sum_{n=0}^{\infty} h_n z^n \tag{3}$$

From equations (1) and (3) we obtain

$$H_{min}(z) = e^{F(z)}$$

or

$$\sum_{n=0}^{\infty} h_n z^n = \exp\left[\sum_{n=0}^{\infty} f_n z^n\right] \tag{4}$$

A formula for obtaining the minimum-delay sequence h_n from the kepstrum f_n can be obtained as follows. Taking the derivative of equation (4) yields

$$\frac{d}{dz}\left(\sum_{n=0}^{\infty} h_n z^n\right) = \exp\left[\sum_{n=0}^{\infty} f_n z^n\right] \frac{d}{dz}\left(\sum_{n=0}^{\infty} f_n z^n\right) \tag{5}$$

Dividing equation (5) by equation (4) we get

$$\frac{\frac{d}{dz}(\sum_{n=0}^{\infty} h_n z^n)}{\sum_{n=0}^{\infty} h_n z^n} = \frac{d}{dz}(\sum_{n=0}^{\infty} f_n z^n) \qquad (6)$$

Performing the differentiations in equation (6) we obtain

$$\sum_{n=1}^{\infty} n h_n z^{n-1} = (\sum_{n=0}^{\infty} h_n z^n)(\sum_{n=1}^{\infty} n f_n z^{n-1})$$

which can also be written as

$$\sum_{n=0}^{\infty}(n+1)h_{n+1} z^n = (\sum_{n=0}^{\infty} h_n z^n)(\sum_{n=0}^{\infty}(n+1)f_{n+1} z^n) \qquad (7)$$

The inverse Laplace z-transform of equation (7) gives the recursive relation

$$(n+1)h_{n+1} = \sum_{k=0}^{n} h_k (n+1-k) f_{n+1-k} \quad \text{for } n=0,1,2,3,\ldots \qquad (8)$$

which is useful for extracting the minimum-delay sequence h_n from the kepstrum f_n. For $n=0,1,2,3,\ldots$ equation (8) gives

$$\begin{aligned}
n=0: \quad & h_1 = h_0 f_1 \\
n=1: \quad & h_2 = h_0 f_2 + \frac{h_1}{2} f_1 = h_0(f_2 + \frac{1}{2} f_1^2) \\
n=2: \quad & h_3 = h_0 f_3 + \frac{2}{3} h_1 f_2 + \frac{1}{3} h_2 f_1 = h_0(f_3 + f_1 f_2 + \frac{1}{6} f_1^3) \\
n=3: \quad & h_4 = h_0 f_4 + \frac{3}{4} h_1 f_3 + \frac{1}{2} h_2 f_2 + \frac{1}{4} h_3 f_1 \\
& \quad = h_0(f_4 + f_3 f_1 + \frac{1}{2} f_1^2 f_2 + \frac{1}{2} f_2^2 + \frac{1}{24} f_1^3)
\end{aligned} \qquad (9)$$

Let us now interpret the kepstral coefficient f_0. We have from equation (4) with $z=0$ that

$$h_0 = e^{f_0}$$

Thus the leading kepstral coefficient is the logarithm of the leading impulse response coefficient, i.e.

$$f_0 = \log h_0$$

As a result it is often convenient to normalize an impulse response function h_n so that its leading coefficient is unity; thus the leading kepstral coefficient is zero, i.e. $f_0 = \log 1 = 0$.

Let us now examine some of the properties of the kepstrum. At this point it is convenient to introduce the symbols a_n and b_n for impulse response functions and the corresponding Greek symbols α_n and β_n for their respective kepstra. Thus, the kepstrum of a minimum-delay sequence b_n with leading coefficient $b_0 = 1$ is the causal sequence $\beta_1, \beta_2, \beta_3, \ldots$ with leading term $\beta_0 = 0$. If we let $L(b_n)$ denote the Laplace z-transform of b_n, then the kepstrum can be described by the composition of transformations L, log and L^{-1} given by

$$\beta_n = L^{-1} \{\log[L(b_n)]\}$$

Hence to find the kepstrum of a minimum-delay sequence b_n whose leading coefficient is unity, we compute the Laplace z-transform of the sequence, take the natural logarithm of this transform, and find the inverse Laplace z-transform of the quantity $\log B(z)$.

For convenience, we shall define the kepstral operator K given by the successive transformations L, log, and L^{-1} such that

$$K(\cdot) = L^{-1}\{\log[L(\cdot)]\} \tag{10}$$

where $\quad K(b_n) = \beta_n$ and $b_0 = 1$

Let us now consider various properties of the kepstrum.

1. <u>convolution</u>

Given the minimum-delay sequences a_n and b_n whose leading coefficients are unity, then

$$K(a_n * b_n) = K(a_n) + K(b_n) \tag{11}$$

where $K(a_n) = \alpha_1, \alpha_2, \alpha_3, \ldots$

$\quad K(b_n) = \beta_1, \beta_2, \beta_3, \ldots$

Hence, the kepstrum maps convolution into addition. To see this, we write

$$L(a_n * b_n) = A(z) B(z)$$

Then

$$\log[L(a_n * b_n)] = \log[A(z) B(z)]$$
$$= \log A(z) + \log B(z)$$

Taking the inverse Laplace z-transform of the above result, we get

$$L^{-1}\{\log[L(a_n * b_n)]\} = L^{-1}[\log A(z)] + L^{-1}[\log B(z)]$$

or

$$K(a_n * b_n) = K(a_n) + K(b_n)$$

Chapter 7. The kepstrum

2. reverse sequence.

Given the minimum-delay sequence b_n with leading coefficient $b_0=1$, we form the reverse sequence b_{-n} by folding b_n about the origin. The resulting sequence is *minimum-advance*.

Hence, $\quad K(b_{-n}) = \beta_{-n}$ \hfill (12)

We can show this result by first noting that

$$L(b_n) = \sum_{n=0}^{\infty} b_n z^n = B(z)$$

and $\quad L(b_{-n}) = \sum_{n=0}^{\infty} b_n z^{-n} = B(z^{-1})$

Recall that $\log B(z) = \beta_1 z + \beta_2 z^2 + \beta_3 z^3 + \cdots$

Thus, $\log B(z^{-1}) = \beta_1 z^{-1} + \beta_2 z^{-2} + \beta_3 z^{-3} + \cdots$

and we observe that given $K(b_n) = \beta_n$, $K(b_{-n})$ is found by folding β_n about the origin.

In words,

minimum-delay sequence $\longleftrightarrow$ causal kepstrum

minimum-advance sequence $\longleftrightarrow$ purely non-causal kepstrum

3. inverse sequence

Given the minimum-delay sequence b_n with leading coefficient $b_0=1$ we define the inverse sequence b_n^{-1} by the relation

$$b_n * b_n^{-1} = \delta_n = \begin{cases} 1, & n=0 \\ 0, & n \neq 0 \end{cases}$$

Since $\quad L(b_n * b_n^{-1}) = 1$,

Then $\quad B(z) L(b_n^{-1}) = 1$

or $\quad L(b_n^{-1}) = 1/B(z)$

$\quad\quad\quad\quad\quad = [B(z)]^{-1}$

Now,

$$\log[L(b_n^{-1})] = \log[B(z)]^{-1}$$

$$= -\log B(z)$$

Thus, it follows that

$$K(b_n^{-1}) = -\beta_n \hfill (13)$$

In words,

<u>minimum-delay</u> sequence ⟷ <u>causal</u> kepstrum

inverse of minimum-delay sequence ⟷ negative of causal kepstrum

4. <u>reverse-inverse sequence</u>.

Given the minimum-delay sequence b_n with leading coefficient $b_0=1$, we define the sequence b_{-n}^{-1} as the inverse of the reverse sequence.

Thus, $$K(b_{-n}^{-1}) = -\beta_{-n} \tag{14}$$

To see this, we can write

$$L(b_{-n}^{-1}) = [B(z^{-1})]^{-1}$$

Then
$$\log[L(b_{-n}^{-1})] = \log[B(z^{-1})]^{-1}$$
$$= -\log[B(z^{-1})]$$

From property 2, we can state

$$K(b_{-n}^{-1}) = -\beta_{-n}$$

In words,

<u>minimum-delay</u> sequence ⟷ <u>causal</u> kepstrum

reverse of inverse of minimum-delay sequence	⟷	reverse of negative of causal kepstrum
(inverse of minimum-advance sequence)	⟷	negative of purely non-causal kepstrum

In our previous discussion, we developed the relation (equation (7))

$$\sum_{n=0}^{\infty} (n+1) h_n z^n = \left(\sum_{n=0}^{\infty} h_n z^n \right) \left(\sum_{n=0}^{\infty} (n+1) f_{n+1} z^n \right)$$

which can be written as

$$\sum_{n=0}^{\infty} (n+1) f_{n+1} z^n = \frac{1}{H(z)} \cdot \sum_{n=0}^{\infty} (n+1) h_n z^n \tag{15}$$

where

$$H(z) = \sum_{n=0}^{\infty} h_n z^n.$$

Chapter 7. The kepstrum

The inverse Laplace z-transform of equation (15) gives the result

$$K(h_n) = f_{n+1} = \sum_{k=0}^{n} \left(\frac{k+1}{n+1}\right) h_{k+1} h_{n-k}^{-1} \quad \text{for } n=0,1,2, \quad h_0 = 1 \tag{16}$$

which *explicitly* gives the kepstrum f_n in terms of the minimum-delay sequence h_n.

PROBLEMS FOR ARTICLE 7.3

1. Determine the kepstrum of the following causal sequences:

   (a) δ_n (b) $a^n u_n$, $|a|<1$ (c) $1/n!$

2. A minimum-delay system with impulse response h_n has a gain $G(\omega) = (\log a)\cos\omega$, $|\log a|<1$. Determine the kepstrum of the impulse response h_n.

3. Determine whether the following statements are true or false:

   (a) The kepstrum of a minimum-delay sequence is always minimum-delay.

   (b) The kepstrum of a minimum-delay sequence is always a causal infinite-duration sequence.

   (c) The kepstra of sequences with relatively "smooth" spectra tend to damp very quickly.

   (d) The concept of the kepstrum is restricted only to causal systems.

7.4 Removal of an echo

One of the main applications of the kepstrum is the removal of an echo and the estimation of the time delay associated with a signal's onset and its first echo. By means of a simple example we shall demonstrate this concept.

Example 1. We shall consider a unit spike $s_n = \delta_n$ with an echo consisting of strength $b=0.1$ and time delay $m=1$. Thus, the signal δ_n and its echo $0.1\delta_{n-1}$ is additively combined to form the sequence

$$x_n = \delta_n + 0.1\delta_{n-1}$$

The Laplace z-transform of the above yields

$$X(z) = 1 + 0.1z$$

which is minimum-delay. Evaluating $X(z)$ on the unit circle ($z=e^{-i\omega}$), we get the *spectrum*

$$X(\omega) = 1 + 0.1e^{-i\omega}$$

If we let $\Phi(\omega) = |X(\omega)|^2$ denote the *power spectrum* of the sequence $\{x_n\}$, then

$$\Phi(\omega) = (1 + 0.1\cos\omega)^2 + (0.1\sin\omega)^2$$

$$= 1 + 0.01 + 0.2\cos\omega$$

which can be approximated by

$$\Phi(\omega) \approx 1 + 0.2\cos\omega$$

where ω is the continuous frequency variable with dimensions of radians/sample interval.

Now the logarithm of the power spectrum $\Phi(\omega)$ or *log power spectrum* is approximately

$$\log[\Phi(\omega)] \approx \log[1 + 0.2\cos\omega] \approx 0.2\cos\omega \qquad (1)$$

We note that the log power spectrum $\log[\Phi(\omega)]$ is a periodic function in the continuous frequency variable ω, although it is usually only considered over one period, i.e. $-\pi \leq \omega \leq \pi$. If we treat the frequency series in equation (1) as a time series, then the autocorrelation of equation (1) is given by $C(\tau)$ where

$$C(\tau) = \frac{(0.2)^2}{2} \cos\tau \qquad (2)$$

where τ is actually a frequency lag although we are treating τ as a time lag. We shall define the Fourier transform of the autocorrelation $C(\tau)$ by

Chapter 7. The kepstrum

$$C(w) = \int_{-\infty}^{\infty} C(\tau) e^{-iw\tau} d\tau \qquad (3)$$

and note that w is the "frequency" continuous variable with dimensions of radians/radians per sample interval or sample interval (time). Substitution of equation (2) in equation (3) yields

$$C(w) = \int_{-\infty}^{\infty} \frac{(0.2)^2}{2} \cos\tau \, e^{-iw\tau} = \int_{\infty}^{\infty} 0.01 e^{-i(w-1)\tau} d\tau + \int_{\infty}^{\infty} 0.01 e^{-i(w+1)\tau} d\tau$$

$$= 0.01\delta(w-1) + 0.01\delta(w+1)$$

where we see that C(w) is actually the *power spectrum of the log power spectrum* $\log[\Phi(\omega)]$, and is similar to the kepstral transformation. We note that the peak (spike) at w=1 corresponds to the time delay of the echo, and thus illustrates the usefulness of the kepstrum in echo determination.

Chapter 8. Random processes

8.1 Stationary random processes

If at a given instant of time we set out to measure a physical quantity such as an elevation of the sea level, a velocity, or a voltage, the measurement will include automatically the effect of other physical processes. We would like to believe in general that the quantity to be measured is expressed by a closed mathematical function of time which has one and only one definite value at each instant of time. The measurement itself, however, incorporates an extra quantity, which represents the effect of a multiplicity of stray phenomena. This additional variable may be called the error or the noise. We may go on to believe too that strict causality prevails in our universe but that the set of physical processes which affect our reading is so large and varied that the disturbance created can be viewed as being related only to pure chance. For instance, a particular reading on the sea level may be perturbed by a storm which is taking place at the moment of sampling; such a storm could or could not have occurred on that day. The probability of occurrence of such a storm could be evaluated from a long series of records so that we could forecast the average value of the influence of the storm on the reading. In practice this is not done in this way. Instead, we take a series of readings and evaluate their *stability* and their *variability* mathematically. The measure of stability will give an approximate value of the unperturbed reading, while the measure of variability will supply ranges of values within which most readings will fall.

Such an approach is still not practicable for the analysis of a phenomenon for which the quantity measured varies with time: we are searching for the explicit time dependence of a function, and its rough average value over a given interval of time is of very little use.

Phenomena which embody a true variation from one measurement to another and which are perturbed as well by unpredictable extraneous factors are known as random processes. It is our task to disentangle from the noise the true time variation of the quantity studied.

Let us think first about a measurement obtained at a given instant of time $t=nT$. We can assume that this measurement is only one of the many others possible for this particular instant. Usually we use the same symbol x_n for the actual measurement as well as for any member in the set of possible values. The set of all possible values of this variable is called an *ensemble* and x_n is called a *random variable*. We take the interval of definition of this variable to be $(-\infty, \infty)$. To each point of this interval there corresponds a function $f(x_n)$, the *probability density function*, which measures the probability of occurrence of the random variable. From a realistic point of view we expect this function f to be a unimodal density function.

Chapter 8. Random processes

The mean μ_n and variance v_n of the random variable x_n at time $t-nT$ are given respectively by

$$\mu_n = E(x_n) = \int_{-\infty}^{\infty} x_n f(x_n) dx_n \tag{1}$$

and

$$v_n = E[(x_n-\mu_n)^2] = \text{Var}(x_n) = \int_{-\infty}^{\infty} (x_n-\mu_n) f(x_n) dx_n \tag{2}$$

where we have used the general definition of the expected value.

Let us now define here the *covariance* of two random variables x and y each with zero mean:

$$\text{cov}(x,y) = E(xy^*) = \int_{-\infty}^{\infty}\int_{-\infty}^{\infty} xy^* f(x,y) dxdy \tag{3}$$

where $f(x,y)$ is the joint probability density function.

A discrete random process is made up of a sequence of random variables x_n associated with the time index n. For simplicity, we shall assume that the random process x_n is real-valued; the generalization to complex-valued processes can readily be made.

A random process is said to be *stationary* if the probabilities involved are not tied down to a specific origin in time; that is, the probability of any event associated with the time index n is equal to the probability of the corresponding event associated with the time index n+k, where n and k are any integer values. In particular, the mean value $\mu = E(x_n)$ and the variance $v = E[(x_n-\mu)^2]$ of a stationary random or stochastic process are independent of the time index n. In what follows we shall assume that the mean value μ is equal to zero which we may do without loss of generality. Likewise, the autocorrelation coefficients

$$\phi_k = E(x_{n+k} x_n) \tag{4}$$

are independent of n.

Example 1. The simplest example of a stationary random process is a sequence ϵ_n, $n=\cdots,-2,-1,0,1,2,\cdots$ of independent random variables with identical probability distributions. Let the mean value of ϵ_n be zero, and let the variance of ϵ_n be equal to one. The autocorrelation of the process is

$$\phi_k = E(\epsilon_{n+k}\epsilon_n) = \delta_k = \begin{cases} 1, & k=0 \\ 0, & k\neq 0 \end{cases} \tag{5}$$

In the general case, the elements x_n of a stationary process with mean value zero and autocorrelation (5) may not be independent. Equation (5) only implies that the random variables ϵ_n are *uncorrelated*. For this reason we refer to a process with zero mean and autocorrelation (5) as a *process of uncorrelated random variables* or a *white noise process*. However, we note that in the special case of Gaussian stationary processes, lack of correlation is equivalent to independence.

Example 2. For all integers n, let

$$x_n = \frac{\varepsilon_n + \varepsilon_{n-1} + \cdots + \varepsilon_{n-M}}{\sqrt{M+1}}$$

where ε_n is a process of uncorrelated random variables; that is, a white noise process. It is clear that x_n is also a stationary process with mean zero and with autocorrelation

$$\phi_k = \begin{cases} 1 - \frac{|k|}{M+1}, & \text{for } |k| \leq M \\ 0, & \text{for } |k| > M \end{cases}$$

Example 3. A generalization of the process of Example 2 is given by

$$x_n = \sum_{j=0}^{M} h_j \varepsilon_{n-j} \tag{6}$$

for all integers n where the h_j are given real coefficients and ε_n is a white noise process. Equation (6) states that the stationary process x_n is the output of a moving average (MA) filter h_n with a white noise input ε_n. Thus, the process x_n defined by equation (6) is called a moving average (MA) process. Its autocorrelation is

$$\begin{aligned}
\phi_k &= E\left(\sum_{j=0}^{M} h_j \varepsilon_{n+k-j} \sum_{\ell=0}^{M} h_\ell \varepsilon_{n-\ell}\right) \\
&= \sum_{j=0}^{M} \sum_{\ell=0}^{M} h_j h_\ell E(\varepsilon_{n+k-j} \varepsilon_{n-\ell}) \\
&= \sum_{j=0}^{M} \sum_{\ell=0}^{M} h_j h_\ell \delta_{k-j+\ell} \\
&= \sum_{j=0}^{M-|k|} h_j h_{|k|+j}
\end{aligned} \tag{7}$$

Equation (7) says that the autocorrelation of a MA process is equal to the serial correlation of the impulse response of the MA filter.

Chapter 8. Random processes

Example 4. A generalization of the MA process of the preceding example is the process

$$x_n = \sum_{j=0}^{\infty} h_j \epsilon_{n-j} \tag{8}$$

Here the filter has an infinitely-long causal impulse response h_n. The process (8) is called a *causal moving summation process*. A moving average process (6) is a special case of a causal moving summation process.

Example 5. A generalization of the process of Example 4 is the process

$$x_n = \sum_{j=-\infty}^{\infty} h_j \epsilon_{n-j} \tag{9}$$

Here the filter has a noncausal impulse response h_n. The process (9) is called a *moving summation process*.

The autocorrelation of each of the processes in Examples 3, 4, and 5 may be written

$$\phi_k = \sum_{j=-\infty}^{\infty} h_{j+k} h_j \tag{10}$$

where in Example 3, h_n is a finite-length causal sequence, in Example 4 h_n is an infinite-length causal sequence, and in Example 5 h_n is a noncausal sequence.

There is another type of average known as a time average in which the averaging process is carried out with respect to all values of time n for a fixed realization x_n ($-\infty < n < \infty$) of the random process. A stationary process is called an *ergodic* process if the ensemble averages and time averages are equal with probability one. As a result the autocorrelation of an ergodic process may be expressed as the time average

$$\phi_k = \lim_{N \to \infty} \frac{1}{2N+1} \sum_{n=-N}^{N} x_{n+k} x_n \tag{11}$$

The autocorrelation function is a nonnegative definite function, that is, the autocorrelation is symmetric:

$$\phi_k = \phi_{-k}$$

and the autocorrelation has a nonnegative quadratic form

$$\sum_{j=1}^{N} \sum_{\ell=1}^{N} \phi_{j-\ell} a_j a_\ell \geq 0, \quad N=1,2,3,\ldots \tag{12}$$

The nonnegative definiteness of the autocorrelation follows from the inequality

$$\sum_{j=1}^{N}\sum_{\ell=1}^{N} \phi_{j-\ell} a_j a_\ell = \sum_{j=1}^{N}\sum_{\ell=1}^{N} \phi_{|j-\ell|} a_j a_\ell$$

$$= \sum_{j=1}^{N}\sum_{\ell=1}^{N} E(a_j a_\ell x_j x_\ell)$$

$$= E\left[\left(\sum_{j=1}^{N} a_j x_j\right)^2\right] \geq 0$$

The property that the autocorrelation function is nonnegative definite is equivalent to the existence of a cumulative distribution function, known as the spectral distribution of the random process. As it is known from mathematical statistics, a cumulative distribution function is a monotonically non-decreasing and bounded function.

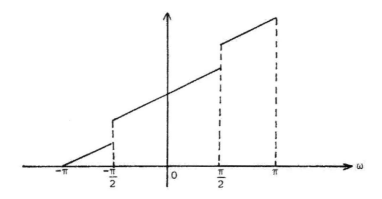

FIGURE 8-1

An example of a cumulative distribution function on the range $-\pi \leq \omega \leq \pi$, with jumps at $-\pi/2$ and $\pi/2$.

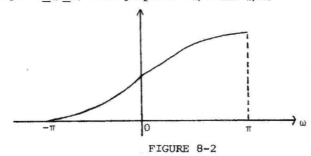

FIGURE 8-2

An example of a cumulative distribution function on the range $-\pi \leq \omega \leq \pi$ with no jumps.

Chapter 8. Random processes

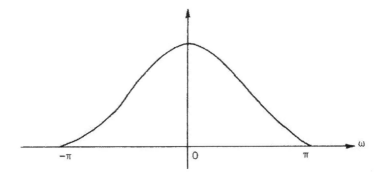

FIGURE 8-3

A density function, namely the derivative of the cumulative distribution function shown in Figure 8-2. The fact that the slope of the cumulative distribution function is nonnegative means that the density function is nonnegative.

Figure 8-1 gives an example of a cumulative distribution function with discontinuities or jumps at certain frequencies. Figure 8-2 gives an example of a smooth cumulative distribution function, and Figure 8-3 gives its derivative. For the purposes of this chapter we only want to consider random processes that have smooth spectral distributions, as in Figure 8-2. As a result, we will be interested in the derivative of the spectral distribution, namely, the spectral density, as in Figure 8-3. The spectral density function is denoted by $\Phi(\omega)$. The autocorrelation and spectral density are Fourier transform pairs:

$$\Phi(\omega) = \sum_{k=-\infty}^{\infty} \phi_k e^{-i\omega k} \tag{13}$$

$$\phi_k = \frac{1}{2\pi} \int_{-\pi}^{\pi} \Phi(\omega) e^{i\omega k} d\omega \tag{14}$$

For real-valued processes x_n the spectral density function is an even function, i.e.

$$\Phi(\omega) = \Phi(-\omega)$$

Example 6. Let $\phi_k = \delta_k$ where

$$\delta_k = \begin{cases} 1, & k=0 \\ 0, & k \neq 0 \end{cases}$$

Then according to formula (13) the spectral density is $\Phi(\omega) = 1$. Since $\Phi(\omega)$ is flat, we call it a white noise spectrum. In fact the process with this autocorrelation and spectrum is the white noise process already considered in Example 1.

We note that if a process has constant spectral density $\Phi(\omega)$ equal to some other value than one, the process will still have $\phi_k = 0$ for $k \neq 0$, and hence the process still consists of uncorrelated random variables. The only difference is that the variance of these random variables is no longer one. Thus white noise processes are characterized by the fact that their spectral densities are constant over the entire interval $-\pi \leq \omega \leq \pi$. However, unless otherwise stated, when we say white noise process we will mean one with variance unity.

Example 7. Suppose that the autocorrelation decays exponentially:

$$\phi_k = a^{|k|} \tag{15}$$

where a is real and $|a| < 1$. The power spectrum is

$$\Phi(\omega) = \sum_{k=-\infty}^{-1} a^{-k} e^{-i\omega k} + \sum_{k=0}^{\infty} a^k e^{-i\omega k}$$

$$= \sum_{k=1}^{\infty} a^k e^{i\omega k} + \sum_{k=0}^{\infty} a^k e^{-i\omega k}$$

$$= \frac{ae^{i\omega}}{1-ae^{i\omega}} + \frac{1}{1-ae^{-i\omega}} = \frac{1-a^2}{|1-ae^{i\omega}|^2} \tag{16}$$

Now let us show that a process x_n with autocorrelation (15) has the causal moving summation representation

$$x_n = \sqrt{1-a^2} \sum_{k=0}^{\infty} a^k \varepsilon_{n-k} \tag{17}$$

If the process (17) has autocorrelation (15), then the autocorrelation according to formula (10) is equal to the serial correlation of the impulse response
$$h_n = \sqrt{1-a^2}\, a^n .$$

Using formula (10) for $k \geq 0$ we obtain

$$\phi_{-k} = \phi_k = (1-a^2) \sum_{j=0}^{\infty} a^{j+k} a^j = (1-a^2) \sum_{j=0}^{\infty} a^{2j+k} = a^k$$

PROBLEMS FOR ARTICLE 8.1

1. Analog-to-digital converters introduce a type of error known as quantization noise denoted by the random variable ε_n. It is reasonable to

assume that ε_n is uniformly distributed, that is, its probability density function is

$$f(\varepsilon_n) = \begin{cases} 1 & , \quad -\tfrac{1}{2} \leq \varepsilon_n \leq \tfrac{1}{2} \\ 0 & , \quad \text{otherwise} \end{cases}$$

(a) Determine the mean and variance of ε_n.

(b) Assuming that ε_n is uncorrelated, find the power spectral density of the quantization noise ε_n.

2. Suppose x_n is a stationary random process with mean η_x and that we form the sequence

$$y_n = (1-\alpha) \sum_{k=-\infty}^{n} x_k \alpha^{n-k}$$

(a) Determine the average value of y_n.

(b) Assume that x_n is also an uncorrelated random variable with variance σ_x^2. Find an expression for the variance of the process y_n.

3. Let us consider the random process

$$x_n = A \cos(n\omega + \theta)$$

where A, ω, and θ are possible random variables.

(a) Determine the autocorrelation of x_n when A and ω are constants and θ is uniformly distributed in $[0, 2\pi]$. Is this process stationary?

(b) Determine the autocorrelation of x_n when ω and θ are constants and A is a random variable. Is this process stationary?

8.2 Signal enhancement and prediction

The possibility of physical prediction depends upon the process having statistical regularity, and on the existence of correlations between past values of the known data and future values of the signal. If the prediction is to be accomplished by a linear operation, then the only type of correlation that can be used is linear correlation. Thus a linear predictor has the disadvantage of not making use of relations contained in the higher moments of the process. It does have the advantage of simplifying the analysis. Moreover, if the process is Gaussian, then all the information is contained in the linear correlations, and so in this case the linear predictor is the absolute optimum.

Many factors ought to be considered when "optimizing" the performance of a filter. An optimization depends upon the purpose of the filter, the nature of the input data, the criterion used for evaluating performance, and allowable tolerances in accuracy.

We will consider the problems involved in preserving or enhancing the waveshape of a signal immersed in noise, and in predicting the future values of the signal. A filter which performs the operation of signal enhancement is called an *enhancement filter* or a *smoothing filter*. The reason for the use of the word "smoothing" is that such a filter generally produces the effect of "smoothing the data" in performing its task of removing the unwanted random roughness caused by the noise. A filter which performs the operation of signal prediction or forecasting is called a *prediction filter*. A filter may combine both operations; a *smoothing and predicting filter* separates the wanted signal from a signal-plus-noise complex and yields future values of the signal.

The simplest case of *prediction* is that in which the pure signal s_n is processed. That is, we suppose that the signal process s_n is available without any contamination. We know the signal s_n for past values of time, and we require a device to yield, as well as possible, the value at a future or advanced time. In other words, we wish to feed the signal process s_n into a filter. The filter is designed so that its actual output y_n is the best approximation to the desired output $s_{n+\alpha}$, which is the signal advanced by the positive time advance α.

Signal enhancement may be described as the problem of separating as well as possible a signal process from an unwanted noise process. The process x_n which we have available is a contaminated process. The contaminated or perturbed process x_n consists of a pure component s_n called the signal, and an impure component p_n called the perturbation or noise; that is, $x_n = s_n + p_n$. We are only interested in the signal, the noise being unwanted. We therefore want to design a filter (h_0, h_1, h_2,...) which will filter out, as well as possible, the noise which is contaminating the signal, thereby enhancing the signal in relation to the noise. The filter should be designed so that its actual output y_n is as close as possible to the desired output s_n, the signal.

The signal enhancement operation may be modified in several ways. For example, the desired output may be the signal s_n delayed by a certain constant time delay β. This is the case of *signal enhancement with delay*. The contaminated process x_n is fed into the filter. The filter is designed so that its actual output y_n is the best approximation to the desired output $s_{n-\beta}$, which is the signal delayed by the positive time delay (or time lag) β.

Another example is the case in which the desired output is the signal advanced by a certain time constant α. The introduction of this time advance α means that the filter is required to predict future values of the signal. This case which incorporates both signal enhancement and prediction is called *signal enhancement with advance*. Here we feed the contaminated process x_n into the filter. The filter is designed so that its actual output y_n is the best approximation to the desired output $s_{n+\alpha}$, which is the signal advanced by the positive time advance α.

Finally, let us formulate the general case, which includes each of the above cases as a special case. The desired output may be any process d_n. We wish to feed a process x_n into a filter. The filter is designed so that its actual output y_n is the best approximation to the desired output d_n.

The basic problem in the theory of signal enhancement and prediction is that of determining the numerical values of the filter coefficients $(h_0, h_1, h_2, \ldots)$. The solution of this problem rests on three main assumptions which determine the range of application of the results. The three assumptions are:

(1) The process representing the input x_n and the desired output d_n are stationary. As we have seen, this means essentially that the statistical properties of the input and desired output do not change with time. The theory as given here cannot properly be applied, for example, to long-term economic effects, for the statistics of economic processes is not the same today as one hundred years ago.

(2) The approximation criterion is taken to be the mean-square-error between the desired output and the actual output. This means that we determine the filter $(h_0, h_1, h_2, \ldots)$ in such a way as to minimize the mean-square-error between the desired output d_n and the actual output y_n. This quantity to be minimized is given by

$$I = E(d_n - y_n)^2 \qquad (1)$$

The average is the ensemble average E, which is taken over all possible inputs and desired outputs with each weighted according to its probability of occurrence. In case the processes are ergodic, the ensemble averages can be replaced by the corresponding time averages.

(3) The operation to be used for signal enhancement and prediction is assumed to be a linear operation on the available information, or in engineering terms, a time-invariant linear digital filter is to be used. The available information consists of the past history of the perturbed signal, i.e. the process x_k with $-\infty < k \leq n$ where n is the present time. A causal filter $(h_0, h_1, h_2, \ldots)$ performs a linear operation on x_k over just this range. For digital computer applications, we want to further restrict ourselves to the case when the operator is of finite length, that is, to a moving average (MA) filter $(h_0, h_1, h_2, \ldots, h_M)$.

The theory may therefore be described as linear least-square smoothing and prediction of stationary processes by means of a causal, time-invariant linear filter. It is recognized that the theory applies only when the above three assumptions are fulfilled, or at least are approximately satisfied. If any one of the conditions is eliminated or changed, then the change must be taken into account, and the problem can become very difficult mathematically.

Linear least-square smoothing and prediction theory is based on statistical regularity. It is on this basis that it is possible to predict, albeat not perfectly, the future behavior of a process when all that is known is a perturbed version of its past history. In general, physical prediction depends fundamentally on the assumption that regularities that have occurred in the past will recur in the future. Such an assumption, of course, can never be proved, but should be regarded as a postulate. The basic assumption that statistical regularities of the past will hold in the future appears in the mathematics as the assumption that the various processes are stationary. This implies that a value of a parameter obtained by averaging a process over the past will be the same as the value obtained by averaging over the future. More specifically, prediction depends essentially on the existence of correlations between the desired output d_n and the input x_n. The assumption that the smoothing and/or prediction is to be done by a linear operation implies that the only type of correlation that can be used is linear correlation, namely the autocorrelation function

$$\phi_k = \phi_{-k} = E(x_n x_{n-k}) \text{ for } k=0,1,2,\ldots \tag{2}$$

of the input, and cross-correlation function

$$\gamma_k = E(d_n x_{n-k}) \text{ for } k=0,1,2,\ldots \tag{3}$$

between desired output and input. If the cross-correlation function between desired output and input (which in the case of pure prediction reduces to the autocorrelation function of the input) were zero, then no significant linear prediction would be possible, and so the best mean-square estimate of the desired output would be its mean value.

For digital computing applications it is important to develop the theory of smoothing and prediction in terms of finite-length filters. The method is, actually, classical least-squares in the context of statistical communication theory.

Let the MA filter be represented by $(h_0, h_1, h_2, \ldots, h_M)$. Let the input process be given by x_n and let the desired output process be given by d_n. We shall now derive the optimum MA filter for smoothing and/or prediction. Without loss of generality, we may assume that the mean values have been removed from the input and desired output, so $E(x_n)=0$ and $E(d_n)=0$. The actual output, which is the convolution of the input with the filter coefficients, is given by the equation

$$y_n = h_0 x_n + h_1 x_{n+1} + \cdots + h_M x_{n-M}$$

Chapter 8. Random processes

The error e_n between desired output and actual output is then

$$e_n = d_n - y_n = d_n - (h_0 x_n + h_1 x_{n-1} + \cdots + h_M x_{n-M})$$

We wish to determine the values of the filter coefficients h_n such that the mean-square-error

$$I = E(e_n^2)$$

is minimum. Now the error e_n may be written as

$$e_n = d_n - y_n = d_n - \sum_{k=0}^{M} h_k x_{n-k}$$

Hence

$$e_n^2 = (d_n - \sum_{k=0}^{M} h_k x_{n-k})(d_n - \sum_{j=0}^{M} h_j x_{n-j})$$

$$= d_n^2 - 2 d_n \sum_{k=0}^{M} h_k x_{n-k} + (\sum_{k=0}^{M} h_k x_{n-k})(\sum_{j=0}^{M} h_j x_{n-j})$$

$$= d_n^2 - 2 \sum_{k=0}^{M} h_k d_n x_{n-k} + \sum_{k=0}^{M} \sum_{j=0}^{M} h_k h_j x_{n-k} x_{n-j}$$

Thus, taking the expected value of e_n^2 we have

$$E(e_n^2) = E(d_n^2) - 2 \sum_{k=0}^{M} h_k E(d_n x_{n-k}) + \sum_{k=0}^{M} \sum_{j=0}^{M} h_k h_j E(x_{n-k} x_{n-j})$$

We see that $E(e_n^2)$ may be written in terms of the correlation functions as

$$I = E(e_n^2) = E(d_n^2) - 2 \sum_{k=0}^{M} h_k \gamma_k + \sum_{k=0}^{M} \sum_{j=0}^{M} h_k h_j \phi_{j-k}$$

Setting the partial derivative of I with respect to each filter coefficient equal to zero, we obtain

$$\frac{\partial I}{\partial h_\ell} = -2 \gamma_\ell + 2 \sum_{k=0}^{M} h_k \phi_{\ell-k} = 0 \quad , \quad \text{for } \ell = 0, 1, 2, \cdots, M$$

or

$$\sum_{k=0}^{M} h_k \phi_{\ell-k} = \gamma_\ell \quad \text{for } \ell=0,1,2,\cdots,M \tag{4}$$

Expanding equation (4) we obtain the set of simultaneous equations given by

$$\begin{aligned} h_0\phi_0 + h_1\phi_{-1} + \cdots + h_M\phi_{-M} &= \gamma_0 \\ h_0\phi_1 + h_1\phi_0 + \cdots + h_M\phi_{1-M} &= \gamma_1 \\ &\cdots \\ h_0\phi_M + h_1\phi_{M-1} + \cdots + h_M\phi_0 &= \gamma_M \end{aligned} \tag{5}$$

which can also be written in matrix form as

$$\begin{bmatrix} \phi_0 & \phi_1 & \cdots & \phi_M \\ \phi_1 & \phi_0 & \cdots & \phi_{M-1} \\ \cdots & & & \\ \phi_M & \phi_{M-1} & & \phi_0 \end{bmatrix} \begin{bmatrix} h_0 \\ h_1 \\ \cdots \\ h_M \end{bmatrix} = \begin{bmatrix} \gamma_0 \\ \gamma_1 \\ \cdots \\ \gamma_M \end{bmatrix} \tag{6}$$

The solution of these equations yields the optimum (M+1)-length operator. These equations ((4), (5), or (6)) are called the *normal equations*. The known quantities are the autocorrelation coefficients ϕ_k of the input x_n and the cross-correlation coefficients γ_k of the desired output d_n with the input x_n. The unknown quantities are the filter coefficients $(h_0, h_1, h_2, \cdots, h_M)$. Because the matrix of this set of equations (refer to equation (6)) is a Toeplitz matrix, the solution may be obtained by making use of the Toeplitz recursion given in Appendix A. In practice one will usually assume that the processes are ergodic, and estimate the required autocorrelation and cross-correlation coefficients as time averages rather than as ensemble averages.

The minimum value of the mean-square-error is

$$I_{min} = \phi_0 - \sum_{k=0}^{M} \gamma_k h_k \tag{7}$$

The value of the minimum I_{min} of the mean-square-error depends upon the parameter M (i.e., depends upon the filter length). If M is increased (i.e., if we use a longer filter) the value of I_{min} must either remain stationary or decrease. In practice one usually computes filters of successively increasing lengths, making use of the Toeplitz recursion. The values of minimum mean-square-error I_{min}, will diminish as the length of the filter

Chapter 8. Random processes

increases. The recursion from M to M+1 can be stopped when one of a set of pre-set conditions is first met, such as:

(1) the filter reaches some maximum pre-set length,

(2) the minimum mean-square-error I_{min} reaches some minimum pre-set value,

(3) the minimum mean-square error curve I_{min} vs. M levels out and shows little probability of further appreciable decrease.

PROBLEMS FOR ARTICLE 8.2

1. We are given infinitely many samples of a stationary zero mean random process x_n, where $\phi_k = E(x_n x_{n+k})$. Form the prediction $\hat{x}_n$ of the nth sample based on the infinite past, that is

$$\hat{x}_n = \sum_{k=1}^{\infty} a_k x_{n-k}$$

(a) Determine the normal equations for the prediction filter $a_1, a_2, a_3, \ldots$ by minimizing the prediction error $\varepsilon_n \equiv x_n - \hat{x}_n$ in the mean-square sense.

(b) What is the autocorrelation of the prediction error?

(c) We now wish to predict the nth sample x_n based on the past N samples, that is, we form the prediction

$$\hat{x}_n = \sum_{n=1}^{N} a_k x_{n-k}$$

Determine the normal equations for the finite-length prediction filter $a_1, a_2, \ldots, a_N$ and the autocorrelation of the prediction error.

8.3 Spectral factorization

Let us now consider a random process x_n with spectral density

$$\Phi(\omega) = \sum_{k=-\infty}^{\infty} \phi_k e^{-ik\omega} \qquad (1)$$

where ϕ_k is the autocorrelation of the process at lag k defined by

$$\phi_k = E(x_{n+k} x_n) \qquad (2)$$

The autocorrelation ϕ_k is related to $\Phi(\omega)$ by the inverse Fourier transform

$$\phi_k = \frac{1}{2\pi} \int_{-\pi}^{\pi} \Phi(\omega) e^{ik\omega} d\omega \qquad (3)$$

In most applications $\Phi(\omega)$ is represented by a rational function, although it does not have to be. However, a power spectral density $\Phi(\omega)$ of a non-deterministic process must satisfy the following conditions:

(1) $\Phi(\omega)$ is nonnegative on the interval $-\pi \leq \omega \leq \pi$

(2) $\Phi(\omega)$ has finite area on the interval $-\pi \leq \omega \leq \pi$

(3) log $\Phi(\omega)$ has finite area on the interval $-\pi \leq \omega \leq \pi$

The problem of spectral factorization is concerned with extracting a causal system $H(\omega)$ whose magnitude spectrum $|H(\omega)|$ is the square root of the power spectrum. In symbols,

$$|H(\omega)| = [\Phi(\omega)]^{\frac{1}{2}} \qquad (4)$$

Hence, $H(\omega)$ has the polar representation

$$H(\omega) = |H(\omega)| e^{-i\phi(\omega)}$$

$$= [\Phi(\omega)]^{\frac{1}{2}} e^{-i\phi(\omega)}$$

and we see that the problem of factorization of the power spectrum is the problem of determining the phase-lag spectrum $\phi(\omega)$ so that the system $H(\omega)$ is causal and stable.

Condition (2) above, called the Paley-Wiener criterion, guarantees that the system $H(\omega)$ is causal. To see this we note that $\log[\Phi(\omega)]^{\frac{1}{2}} = \log|H(\omega)|$. Thus, condition (3) means that $\log|H(\omega)|$ is integrable (i.e. the Paley-Wiener condition in Article 7.2) so there is a causal system with gain $\log[\Phi(\omega)]^{\frac{1}{2}}$.

Chapter 8. Random processes

Recall our discussion on the Hilbert transform in Article 7.2. If $\phi_{min}(\omega)$ represents the minimum-phase-lag (i.e. if the system is the minimum-delay system $H_{min}(z)$) then the phase-lag spectrum is determined by the Hilbert transform

$$\phi_{min}(\omega) = \frac{1}{2\pi} P \int_{-\pi}^{\pi} \cot(\frac{\omega-\omega'}{2}) \log|H_{min}(\omega')| d\omega' \tag{5}$$

$$= \frac{1}{4\pi} P \int_{-\pi}^{\pi} \cot(\frac{\omega-\omega'}{2}) \log\Phi(\omega') d\omega'$$

where P denotes the Cauchy principal value of the integral.

Thus given the power spectrum $\Phi(\omega)$, equations (4) and (5) solve the spectral factorization problem and yield the minimum-delay system $H_{min}(\omega)$. The corresponding minimum-delay sequence h_n can be found from the inverse Fourier transform

$$h_n = \frac{1}{2\pi} \int_{-\pi}^{\pi} H_{min}(\omega) e^{in\omega} d\omega \quad \text{for } n=0,1,2,\ldots \tag{6}$$

Example 1. Consider a zero mean white noise process with unit variance. The autocorrelation ϕ_k is given by

$$\phi_k = \begin{cases} 1, & k=0 \\ 0, & k\neq 0 \end{cases}$$

and the corresponding power spectral density $\Phi(\omega)$ is the Fourier transform

$$\Phi(\omega) = \sum_{k=-\infty}^{\infty} \phi_k e^{-ik\omega}$$

$$= 1 \text{ (for all } \omega)$$

In this case the magnitude spectrum is

$$|H(\omega)| = [\Phi(\omega)]^{\frac{1}{2}} = 1$$

so the gain $\log|H(\omega)| = 0$. Thus, from equation (5) we see that the minimum-phase-lag $\phi_{min}(\omega) = 0$. The corresponding causal stable impulse response is

$$h_n = \begin{cases} 1, & n=0 \\ 0, & n\neq 0 \end{cases}$$

which is the trivial all-pass system of Article 4.5.

Chapter 9. Spectral estimation

9.1 Harmonic analysis

With the advent of the fast Fourier transform the harmonic analysis of discrete-time signals has gained increased importance. We recall that the fast Fourier transform represents a class of efficient algorithms for computing the finite Fourier transform. The finite Fourier transform (FFT) is

$$X_k = \sum_{n=0}^{N-1} x_n W_N^{kn}, \quad k=0,1,\ldots,N-1 \tag{1}$$

where $W_N = e^{-i(2\pi/N)}$. The inverse finite Fourier transform (IFFT) is

$$x_n = \frac{1}{N} \sum_{k=0}^{N-1} X_k W_N^{-kn}, \quad n=0,1,\ldots,N-1 \tag{2}$$

In equations (1) and (2), both x_n and X_k may be complex. The expressions for the FFT and IFFT differ only in the sign of the exponent of W_N and in a scale factor $1/N$. The sequence x_n for $n=0,1,\ldots,N-1$ represents the signal, whereas the sequence X_k for $k=0,1,\ldots,N-1$ represents the finite Fourier transform of the signal. Because n represents time and k represents frequency we call the sequence $x_1, x_2, \ldots, x_{N-1}$ a time series and the sequence $X_1, X_2, \ldots, X_{N-1}$ a frequency series. The frequency series is the FFT of the time series, and the time series is the IFFT of the frequency series.

Let us look at the concepts of time and frequency in more detail. If Δt represents the increment of time, then the time points are $n\Delta t$ where $n=0,1,2,\ldots,N-1$ is the span of the data. It is convenient to choose our time unit such that $\Delta t=1$; that is, one time unit is defined as the time spacing between two consecutive data points. The harmonic frequencies are defined as

$$\omega_k = \frac{2\pi k}{N}, \quad k=0,1,2,\ldots,N-1$$

Thus the kth harmonic frequency has period

$$\frac{2\pi}{\omega_k} = \frac{N}{k}, \quad k=0,1,2,\ldots,N-1.$$

A sine wave with harmonic frequency ω_k executes k complete cycles in the span of the data, thus providing a useful interpretation of the frequency index k. Of course, few of the periods are integers. In summary, the finite Fourier transform provides a harmonic analysis in the form of the frequency series

Chapter 9. Spectral estimation

$$x_0, x_1, x_2, \ldots, x_{N-1}$$

Frequency ω_k: $\quad 0, \dfrac{2\pi}{N}, \dfrac{2(2\pi)}{N}, \ldots, \dfrac{(N-1)2\pi}{N}$

Period $\dfrac{N}{k}$: $\quad \infty, N, \dfrac{N}{2}, \ldots, \dfrac{N}{N-1}$

The time series and the frequency series contain the same information, as one can be obtained from the other by Fourier transformation. Also, each series contains the same total energy, that is,

$$\text{Energy} = \sum_{n=0}^{N-1} |x_n|^2 = \frac{1}{N} \sum_{k=0}^{N-1} |X_k|^2 \qquad (3)$$

Equation (3) is called *Bessel's equality*.

Each frequency component X_k is generally a complex number which can be denoted as

$$X_k = A_k + i B_k = R_k e^{i\theta_k}, \quad k=0,1,2,\ldots,N-1$$

where A_k and B_k are real. The magnitude R_k is

$$R_k = +\sqrt{A_k^2 + B_k^2}$$

and the phase is

$$\theta_k = \tan^{-1}\left(\frac{B_k}{A_k}\right)$$

PROBLEMS FOR ARTICLE 9.1

1. Suppose the time series $x_0, x_1, \ldots, x_{N-1}$ are samples from a zero mean stationary real process x_n. Show that the frequency series $X_0, X_1, \ldots, X_{N-1}$ represents a complex random process with zero mean.

9.2 The periodogram

As we have seen in the foregoing Article, the finite Fourier transform of a time series gives a frequency series, where each frequency component X_k occurs at one of the harmonic frequencies $\omega_k = 2\pi k/N$. On the other hand, we may take the Fourier transform of the time series to obtain a frequency function; that is

$$X(\omega) = \sum_{n=0}^{N-1} x_n e^{-i\omega n} \qquad (1)$$

The frequency function $X(\omega)$ is periodic, with period 2π, so we can concern ourselves only with one period, say from 0 to 2π. The inverse Fourier transform is

$$x_n = \frac{1}{2\pi} \int_0^{2\pi} X(\omega) e^{i\omega n} d\omega. \qquad (2)$$

Let us now make the following important observation: The frequency series X_k, $k=0,1,\ldots,N-1$, may be obtained from the frequency function $X(\omega)$ by the equation

$$X_k = X(\omega_k) \quad \text{where} \quad \omega_k = \frac{2\pi k}{N}$$

That is, the frequency components X_k are simply the values of the frequency function $X(\omega)$ at the harmonic frequencies ω_k.

The periodogram $I(\omega)$ is defined as

$$I(\omega) = \frac{1}{N} |X(\omega)|^2 \qquad (3)$$

Equation (3) is called the periodogram even though it is a function of frequency rather than period. The reason is that historically the original concept of such a function was a function of period. Of special interest are the harmonic frequencies. The periodogram at the harmonic frequencies $\omega_k = 2\pi k/N$ gives the periodogram series

$$I_k = \frac{1}{N} |X(\omega_k)|^2 = \frac{1}{N} |X_k|^2, \quad k=0,1,2,\ldots,N-1 \qquad (4)$$

That is, the periodogram series I_k can be obtained from the frequency series X_k by simply squaring the magnitude of each X_k and dividing by N. Bessel's equality becomes

$$\text{Energy} = \sum_{n=0}^{N-1} |x_n|^2 = \sum_{k=0}^{N-1} I_k.$$

In practice, one does not usually compute the Fourier transform $X(\omega)$ and the periodogram $I(\omega)$, but instead computes the finite Fourier transform sequence X_k and the corresponding periodogram sequence I_k, where $k=0,1,2,\ldots,N-1$.

Chapter 9. Spectral estimation

9.3 Specialization for real-valued signals

In this chapter up to this point we have made no restrictions on the signal as to whether it is real-valued or complex-valued. However, often we deal with real-valued signals, so it is worthwhile to specialize our formulas for such a case. Therefore, we now assume the time series x_n is real-valued for $n=0,1,2,\ldots,N-1$. We now want to find an expression for X_{N-j}. First, we write

$$\omega_{N-j}n = 2\pi(N-j)n/N = n2\pi - (2\pi jn/N) = n2\pi - \omega_j n$$

from which it follows that

$$X_{N-j} = \sum_{n=0}^{N-1} x_n e^{-i\omega_{N-j}n} = \sum_{n=0}^{N-1} x_n e^{i\omega_j n} \qquad (1)$$

Because the x_n are all real-valued, we see that the right-hand side of equation (1) is X_j^*. Thus we have the important relationship

$$X_{N-j} = X_j^*$$

which holds whenever the time series x_n is real. As a result the frequency series

$$X_0, X_1, X_2, \ldots, X_N$$

can be written as

$$X_0, X_1, X_2, \ldots, X_{\frac{N}{2}-1}, X_{\frac{N}{2}}, X_{\frac{N}{2}-1}^*, \ldots, X_2^*, X_1^*$$

where the number N is even, and as

$$X_0, X_1, X_2, \ldots X_{\frac{N-1}{2}}, X_{\frac{N-1}{2}}^*, \ldots, X_2^*, X_1^*$$

when the number N is odd.

We recall that the Nyquist frequency is π, which represents the highest frequency about which one can find meaningful information in a set of data. In case N is even we see that the harmonic frequency corresponding to N/2 is the Nyquist frequency; that is

$$\omega_{N/2} = \frac{2\pi(N/2)}{N} = \pi \qquad \text{(N=even number)}$$

On the other hand when N is odd, there is no harmonic frequency corresponding to the Nyquist frequency; however, the harmonic frequencies corresponding to (N-1)/2 and (N+1)/2 enclose the Nyquist frequency; that is,

$$\omega_{\frac{N-1}{2}} = \frac{N-1}{N}\pi < \pi < \omega_{\frac{N+1}{2}} = \frac{N+1}{N}\pi$$

Let us now look at the frequency series in the case when N is even. If we break it down into its real and imaginary parts, where $X_k = A_k + iB_k$, we have two series

Real: $A_0, A_1, A_2, \cdots, A_{\frac{N}{2}-1}, A_{\frac{N}{2}}, A_{\frac{N}{2}-1}, \cdots, A_2, A_1$

Imaginary: $B_0, B_1, B_2, \cdots, B_{\frac{N}{2}-1}, B_{\frac{N}{2}}, -B_{\frac{N}{2}-1}, \cdots, -B_2, -B_1$

↑
Nyquist frequency π occurs here

We see that all terms to the right of the Nyquist frequency are found to the left of the Nyquist frequency. In order to avoid duplication, it is conventional to not write any terms to the right of the Nyquist frequency. Also we observe that B_0 and $B_{N/2}$ are each equal to zero; that is,

$$B_0 = \text{Im} X_0 = \sum_{n=0}^{N-1} x_n \sin \omega_0 n = 0$$

since $\omega_0 = 0$, and

$$B_{N/2} = \text{Im} X_{N/2} = \sum_{n=0}^{N-1} x_n \sin \omega_{N/2} n = \sum_{n=0}^{N-1} x_n \sin \pi n = 0$$

In summary, when the number N is even we can write the frequency series as

Real: $A_0, A_1, A_2, \cdots, A_{\frac{N}{2}-1}, A_{N/2}$

Imaginary: $0, B_1, B_2, \cdots, B_{\frac{N}{2}-1}, 0$

which is

$X_0, X_1, X_2, \cdots, X_{\frac{N}{2}-1}, X_{\frac{N}{2}}$

where X_0 and $X_{N/2}$ are real. Note that there are N real observations in the time series $x_0, x_1, \cdots, x_{N-1}$; also there are N real quantities in the above frequency series, namely, $\frac{N}{2} + 1$ real parts A_k and $\frac{N}{2} - 1$ imaginary parts B_k.

Let us now look at the frequency series when N is odd. If we break it down into its real and imaginary parts, where $X_k = A_k + iB_k$, we have two series

Real: $A_0, A_1, A_2, \cdots, A_{\frac{N-1}{2}}, A_{\frac{N-1}{2}}, \cdots, A_2, A_1$

Imaginary: $B_0, B_1, B_2, \cdots, B_{\frac{N-1}{2}}, -B_{\frac{N-1}{2}}, \cdots, -B_2, -B_1$

↑
Nyquist frequency π occurs between these terms

Chapter 9. Spectral estimation

Again we throw away all terms to the right of the Nyquist frequency, as they represent needless duplication. As before, we see that $B_0 = 0$. In summary, when the number N is odd we can write the frequency series as

Real: $A_0, A_1, A_2, \cdots, A_{\frac{N-1}{2}}$

Imaginary: $0, B_1, B_2, \cdots, B_{\frac{N-1}{2}}$

which is

$$X_0, X_1, X_2, \cdots, X_{\frac{N-1}{2}}$$

where X_0 is real. We note that there are N real quantities in the above frequency series, namely $\frac{N-1}{2} + 1$ real parts A_k and $\frac{N-1}{2}$ imaginary parts B_k.

We may summarize as follows. Given the real time series x_n made up of N observations (n=0,1,$\cdots$,N-1) we may compute the corresponding frequency series $X_k = A_k + iB_k$, where

$$A_k = \sum_{n=0}^{N-1} x_n \cos \frac{2\pi kn}{N}$$

$$B_k = \sum_{n=0}^{N-1} x_n \sin \frac{2\pi kn}{N}$$

In case N is even, we compute A_k for k=0,1,2,$\cdots$,N/2 and B_k for k=1,2,$\cdots$, $\frac{N}{2}-1$, which gives the frequency series

$$X_0 = A_0, X_1 = A_1 + iB_1, X_2 = A_2 + iB_2, \ldots, X_{\frac{N}{2}-1} = A_{\frac{N}{2}-1} + iB_{\frac{N}{2}-1}, X_{\frac{N}{2}} = A_{\frac{N}{2}}$$

In case N is odd, we compute A_k for k=0,1,2,$\cdots$,$\frac{N-1}{2}$ and B_k for k=1,2,$\cdots$, $\frac{N-1}{2}$, which gives the frequency series

$$X_0 = A_0, \; X_1 = A_1 + iB_1, \; X_2 = A_2 + iB_2, \cdots, \; X_{\frac{N-1}{2}} = A_{\frac{N-1}{2}} + iB_{\frac{N-1}{2}}.$$

However if we use the fast Fourier transformation, we generally would compute the entire frequency series

$$X_0, X_1, X_2, \cdots, X_{N-1}$$

despite the duplication to the right of the Nyquist frequency.

9.4 White noise sample

In order to gain insight about the periodogram, it is useful to study the properties of the periodogram computed from a sample of N observations of white noise. We assume for the purposes of this Article that the time series is ε_n, n=0,1,2,...,N-1, which is a sample sequence of a real, white, zero-mean process; that is, we assume

$$E[\varepsilon_n] = 0$$

$$E[\varepsilon_m \varepsilon_n] = \begin{cases} \sigma^2 & \text{when } m=n \\ 0 & \text{when } m \neq n \end{cases}$$

throughout this Article. The first of the above equations expresses the zero-mean property; the second, the white (or uncorrelated) property.

Let us now look at the frequency series $\mathcal{E}_k$, k=0,1,2,...,N-1. We see that

$$E[\mathcal{E}_k] = E[\sum_{n=0}^{N-1} \varepsilon_n e^{-i\omega_k n}] = \sum_{n=0}^{\infty} E[\varepsilon_n] e^{-i\omega_k n} = 0$$

because of the zero-mean property of the white noise. We also see that

$$E[\mathcal{E}_j \mathcal{E}_k] = E[\sum_{m=0}^{N-1} \varepsilon_m e^{-i\omega_j m} \sum_{n=0}^{N-1} \varepsilon_n e^{-i\omega_k n}]$$

$$= \sum_{m=0}^{N-1} \sum_{n=0}^{N-1} E[\varepsilon_m \varepsilon_n] e^{-i(\omega_j m + \omega_k n)} \tag{1}$$

$$= \sum_{n=0}^{N-1} \sigma^2 e^{-i(\omega_j + \omega_k)n}$$

The last summation in equation (1) is zero, unless $\omega_j = \omega_k = 0$ or unless $\omega_j = \omega_k = \pi$, in which case the summation is equal to $N\sigma^2$. Thus we have

$$E[\mathcal{E}_j \mathcal{E}_k] = \begin{cases} N\sigma^2 & j=k=0, \; j=k=\frac{N}{2} \text{ (for even N)} \\ 0 & \text{otherwise} \end{cases} \tag{2}$$

If we write $\mathcal{E}_j$ as $\mathcal{E}_j = A_j + iB_j$ and let j=k (but not equal to 0 or N/2), equation (2) gives

$$E[\mathcal{E}_j^2] = E[(A_j^2 - B_j^2) + i(2A_j B_j)] = 0, \quad j \neq 0, \; j \neq \frac{\pi}{2}$$

Thus

$$E[A_j^2] = E[B_j^2]$$

and

$$E[A_j B_j] = 0$$

Chapter 9. Spectral estimation

Hence the real and imaginary parts of ε_j have the same variance and are uncorrelated. It is not difficult to verify that this common variance is $\frac{N\sigma^2}{2}$ (See Problem 1).

In a similar way, we find that

$$E[\varepsilon_j \varepsilon_k^*] = \sigma^2 \sum_{n=0}^{N-1} e^{-i(\omega_j - \omega_k)n} = \begin{cases} N\sigma^2 & j=k \\ 0 & j \neq k \end{cases}$$

Thus when $j \neq k$ we have

$$E[(A_j + iB_j)(A_k + iB_k)] = E[A_j A_k - B_j B_k] + iE[A_j B_k + B_j A_k]$$

$$E[(A_j + iB_j)(A_k - iB_k)] = E[A_j A_k - B_j B_k] + iE[-A_j B_k + B_j A_k]$$

From these equations it follows that

$$E[A_j A_k] = 0, \quad E[A_j B_k] = 0$$

$$E[B_j B_k] = 0, \quad E[B_j, A_k] = 0$$

Thus A_j, A_k, B_j, B_k are mutually uncorrelated (when $j \neq k$).

In conclusion, given that the time series is a real, white, zero-mean process, the corresponding frequency series written in the form

$$A_0, A_1, B_1, A_2, B_2, \cdots, A_{\frac{N}{2}-1}, B_{\frac{N}{2}-1}, A_{N/2} \qquad \text{(when N is even)}$$

or

$$A_0, A_1, B_1, A_2, B_2, \cdots, A_{\frac{N-1}{2}}, B_{\frac{N-1}{2}} \qquad \text{(when N is odd)}$$

is a real, white, zero-mean process. From a statistical point of view, therefore, the white-noise time series and the corresponding white-noise frequency series have the same properties. This behavior is as we would expect, as each series can be obtained from the other by Fourier transformation.

PROBLEMS FOR ARTICLE 9.4

1. Verify that the real and imaginary parts of ε_j have the same variance, that is,

$$E(A_j^2) = E(B_j^2) = \frac{N\sigma^2}{2}$$

9.5 The Gaussian and chi-square distributions

We now want to make the assumption that the random variables $\varepsilon_0, \varepsilon_1, \varepsilon_2, \ldots, \varepsilon_{N-1}$ each have the same Gaussian (or normal) distributions. Because uncorrelated Gaussian variables are statistically independent, it follows that each observation in the white-noise time series $\varepsilon_0, \varepsilon_1, \varepsilon_2, \ldots, \varepsilon_{N-1}$ is statistically independent. Because linear combinations of Gaussian variables are also Gaussian, it follows each element in the corresponding frequency series $(A_0, A_1, B_1, A_2, B_2, \cdots, A_{N/2})$ when N is even or $(A_0, A_1, B_1, A_2, B_2, \ldots, B_{\frac{N-1}{2}})$ when N is even is also Gaussian and independent. The mean and variance of each element in the time series are respectively 0 and σ^2. The mean and variance of each element in the frequency series, except A_0 and except $A_{N/2}$, are 0 and $\frac{N\sigma^2}{2}$. The mean and variance of each of A_0 and $A_{N/2}$ are 0 and $N\sigma^2$.

Chi-square (χ^2_ν) is defined as the sum of square of ν independent Gaussian variables each with zero mean and unit variance. The number ν is called the degrees of freedom. In our case, the variable ε_n/σ would be a Gaussian variable with zero mean and unit standard deviation. Then, for example, the variable ε_1^2/σ^2 would have a chi-square distribution with one degree of freedom, the variable $(\varepsilon_1^2+\varepsilon_2^2)/\sigma^2$ would have a chi-square with two degrees of freedom, the variable $(\varepsilon_1^2+\varepsilon_2^2+\varepsilon_3^2)/\sigma^2$ would have a chi-square distribution with three degrees of freedom, and so on. An obvious deduction from the definition is that the sum of two independent chi-squares, say $\chi^2_{\nu_1}$ and $\chi^2_{\nu_2}$ with ν_1 and ν_2 degrees of freedom respectively, is in turn distributed as chi-square with $\nu_1 + \nu_2$ degrees of freedom; that is,

$$\chi^2_{\nu_1+\nu_2} = \chi^2_{\nu_1} + \chi^2_{\nu_2}.$$

For example, $(\varepsilon_1^2+\varepsilon_2^2+\varepsilon_3^2)/\sigma^2$ and $(\varepsilon_4^2+\varepsilon_5^2)/\sigma^2$ are χ^2_3 and χ^2_2 respectively; the sum $(\varepsilon_1^2+\varepsilon_2^2+\varepsilon_3^2+\varepsilon_4^2+\varepsilon_5^2)/\sigma^2$ is χ^2_5.

The expected value of $\chi^2_1 = \varepsilon_1^2/\sigma^2$ is

$$E(\chi^2_1) = E\left(\frac{\varepsilon_1^2}{\sigma^2}\right) = \frac{1}{\sigma^2}E(\varepsilon_1^2) = \frac{\sigma^2}{\sigma^2} = 1$$

The mean of $\chi^2_3 = (\varepsilon_1^2+\varepsilon_2^2+\varepsilon_3^2)/\sigma^2$ is

$$E(\chi^2_3) = E[(\varepsilon_1^2+\varepsilon_2^2+\varepsilon_3^2)/\sigma^2] = \frac{1}{\sigma^2}[E(\varepsilon_1^2)+E(\varepsilon_2^2)+E(\varepsilon_3^2)] = \frac{3\sigma^2}{\sigma^2} = 3$$

Thus we see that the mean of χ^2_ν is equal to its degrees of freedom; that is

$$E(\chi^2_\nu) = \nu$$

The variance of χ^2_1 is

Chapter 9. Spectral estimation

$$\text{var}(X_1^2) = \text{var}(\frac{\varepsilon_1^2}{\sigma^2}) = E[\frac{\varepsilon_1^4}{\sigma^4}] - [E(\frac{\varepsilon_1^2}{\sigma^2})]^2$$

$$= \frac{1}{\sigma^4}[E(\varepsilon_1^4) - (E\varepsilon_1^2)^2]$$

But for a Gaussian variable, we have

$$E(\varepsilon_1^4) = 3(E\ \varepsilon_1^2)^2 = 3\sigma^4$$

Thus

$$\text{var}(X_1^2) = \frac{1}{\sigma^4}[3\sigma^4 - \sigma^4] = 2$$

Since the variance of the sum of ν independent variables is equal to the sum of their variances, we have

$$\text{var}(X_\nu^2) = \text{var}(\frac{\varepsilon_1^2}{\sigma^2} + \frac{\varepsilon_2^2}{\sigma^2} + \cdots + \frac{\varepsilon_\nu^2}{\sigma^2})$$

$$= 2 + 2 + \cdots + 2 = 2\nu$$

That is, the variance of X_ν^2 is equal to twice its degrees of freedom.

The probability density functions for $X_1^2, X_2^2, X_4^2,$ and X_8^2 are shown in Figure 9-1. Note that the probability density for X_2^2 is exponential.

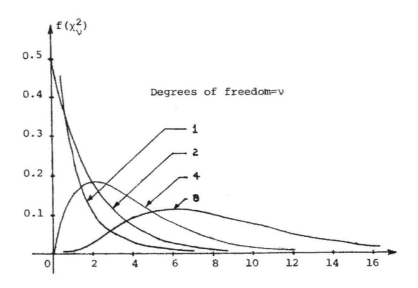

FIGURE 9-1

Probability density functions for χ_ν^2 variables.

9.6 Distribution of the periodogram for a white Gaussian process

Under the assumption of a Gaussian white noise time series, the frequency series is also Gaussian and white. The periodogram series is defined as

$$\mathcal{L}_k = \frac{|\mathcal{E}_k|^2}{N} = \frac{A_k^2 + B_k^2}{N} \qquad k=0,1,2,\ldots,N-1$$

Specializing for real valued signals the periodogram series is

$$(\mathcal{L}_0, \mathcal{L}_1, \mathcal{L}_2, \ldots \mathcal{L}_{N/2})$$

$$= \left(\frac{A_0^2}{N}, \frac{A_1^2+B_1^2}{N}, \frac{A_2^2+B_2^2}{N}, \ldots, \frac{A_{N/2-1}^2 + B_{N/2-1}^2}{N}, \frac{B_{N/2}^2}{N} \right)$$

when N is even, or

$$(\mathcal{L}_0, \mathcal{L}_1, \mathcal{L}_2, \ldots \mathcal{L}_{\frac{N-1}{2}})$$

$$= \left(\frac{A_0^2}{N}, \frac{A_1^2+B_1^2}{N}, \frac{A_2^2+B_2^2}{N}, \ldots, \frac{A_{\frac{N-1}{2}}^2 + B_{\frac{N-1}{2}}^2}{N} \right)$$

when N is odd. Since each A_k and B_k for $k \neq 0$ and $k \neq \frac{N}{2}$ (for N even) is an independent Gaussian variable with zero mean and variance $\frac{N\sigma^2}{2}$, it follows that

$$\frac{2\mathcal{L}_k}{\sigma^2} = \frac{A_k^2 + B_k^2}{\frac{N\sigma^2}{2}} = \chi_2^2 \qquad (k \neq 0, k \neq \frac{N}{2} \text{ when N is even})$$

Since the mean of χ_2^2 is 2 and the variance is 4 we have

$$E\left(\frac{2\mathcal{L}_k}{\sigma^2}\right) = 2$$

which is

$$E(\mathcal{L}_k) = \sigma^2$$

and

$$\text{var}\left(\frac{2\mathcal{L}_k}{\sigma^2}\right) = 4$$

or

$$\frac{4}{\sigma^4} \text{var}(\mathcal{L}_k) = 4$$

Chapter 9. Spectral estimation

which is

$$\text{var}(d_k) = \sigma^4$$

In case $k=0$ or $k=N/2$ (for N even) we know that A_0 and $A_{N/2}$ are each Gaussian with zero mean and variance $N\sigma^2$. It follows that

$$\frac{d_0}{\sigma^2} = \frac{A_0^2}{N\sigma^2} = \chi_1^2 \quad , \quad \frac{d_{N/2}}{\sigma^2} = \frac{A_{N/2}^2}{N\sigma^2} = \chi_1^2 \qquad \text{(when N is even)}$$

Since the mean of χ_1^2 is 1 and the variance is 2 we have

$$E(d_0) = \sigma^2 \quad , \quad E(d_{N/2}) = \sigma^2 \qquad \text{(when N is even)}$$

and

$$\text{var}(d_0) = 2\sigma^4 \quad , \quad \text{var}(d_{N/2}) = 2\sigma^4 \qquad \text{(when N is even)}$$

In summary, for N even the periodogram sequence is

$$(d_0, d_1, d_2, \cdots, d_{\frac{N}{2}-1}, d_{N/2})$$

with mean

$$(\sigma^2, \sigma^2, \sigma^2, \cdots, \sigma^2, \sigma^2)$$

and variance

$$(2\sigma^4, \sigma^4, \sigma^4, \cdots, \sigma^4, 2\sigma^4)$$

and is distributed as

$$(\sigma^2 \chi_1^2, \frac{\sigma^2}{2}\chi_2^2, \frac{\sigma^2}{2}\chi_2^2, \cdots, \frac{\sigma^2}{2}\chi_2^2, \sigma^2 \chi_1^2)$$

For N odd, the periodogram sequence is

$$(d_0, d_1, d_2, \cdots, d_{\frac{N-1}{2}})$$

with mean

$$(\sigma^2, \sigma^2, \sigma^2, \cdots, \sigma^2)$$

and variance

$$(2\sigma^4, \sigma^4, \sigma^4, \cdots, \sigma^4)$$

and is distributed as

$$(\sigma^2 x_1^2, \frac{\sigma^2}{2} x_2^2, \frac{\sigma^2}{2} x_2^2, \cdots, \frac{\sigma^2}{2} x_2^2)$$

The periodogram values $\mathcal{J}_j$ and $\mathcal{J}_k$ being functions of independent variables are independent ($j \neq k$).

The white Gaussian process ε_n has the flat spectral density given by

$$\Phi(\omega) = \sum_{n=-\infty}^{\infty} \phi_n e^{-i\omega n} = \phi_o = \sigma^2 \qquad (0 \leq \omega \leq 2\pi)$$

since

$$\phi_o = E(\varepsilon_n^2) = \sigma^2$$

We are interested in estimating the spectral density in the range $0 \leq \omega \leq \pi$ where π is the Nyquist frequency. From the above we know that the periodogram sequence over this same range has mean

$$(\sigma^2, \sigma^2, \sigma^2, \cdots, \sigma^2)$$

Since the spectral density is a constant function, the best procedure is to include all the elements of the periodogram series in an average to estimate σ^2. In the case of N even, we would compute the average

$$\overline{\mathcal{J}} = \frac{1}{N}(\mathcal{J}_0 + \mathcal{J}_1 + \mathcal{J}_2 + \cdots + \mathcal{J}_{N-1}) = \frac{1}{N} \sum_{k=0}^{N-1} \mathcal{J}_k$$

which by Bessel's equality is

$$\overline{\mathcal{J}} = \frac{1}{N} \sum_{n=0}^{N-1} \varepsilon_n^2$$

This expression shows that $\overline{\mathcal{J}}$ is the classic estimate of the variance σ^2 in the case of known mean $\mu=0$. Because the time series is real-valued, $\mathcal{J}_{N-k} = \mathcal{J}_k$ so the average is

$$\overline{\mathcal{J}} = \frac{1}{N}(\mathcal{J}_0 + 2\mathcal{J}_1 + 2\mathcal{J}_2 + \cdots + 2\mathcal{J}_{\frac{N}{2}-1} + \mathcal{J}_{\frac{N}{2}})$$

when N is even, and

$$\overline{\mathcal{J}} = \frac{1}{N}(\mathcal{J}_0 + 2\mathcal{J}_1 + 2\mathcal{J}_2 + \cdots + 2\mathcal{J}_{\frac{N-1}{2}})$$

when N is odd.

Chapter 9. Spectral estimation

9.7 Distribution of the periodogram for a Gaussian process

Let x_n be a Gaussian process with spectral density $\Phi(\omega)$. We know that x_n can be expressed as a moving summation

$$x_n = \sum_{j=-\infty}^{\infty} c_j \varepsilon_{n-j}$$

where ε_n is a Gaussian white noise process with zero mean and variance $\sigma^2 = 1$. The Fourier transform of a sample $(x_0, x_1, x_2, \cdots, x_{N-1})$ satisfies

$$X(\omega) \doteq C(\omega)\mathcal{E}(\omega)$$

where

$$\mathcal{E}(\omega) = \sum_{n=0}^{N-1} \varepsilon_n e^{-i\omega n}$$

and

$$C(\omega) = \sum_{j=-\infty}^{\infty} c_j e^{-i\omega j}$$

The function $C(\omega)$ satisfies $\Phi(\omega) = |C(\omega)|^2$. The difference between $X(\omega)$ and $C(\omega)\mathcal{E}(\omega)$ is due to end effects. That is, the segment $(x_0, x_1, x_2, \cdots, x_{N-1})$ can be obtained only approximately by filtering the segment $(\varepsilon_0, \varepsilon_1, \varepsilon_2, \cdots, \varepsilon_{N-1})$ with a linear system because of transient effects at the beginning and end of the time interval. However, if the sample length is long compared with the effective duration of the filter impulse response, this approximation is valid.

Using the above approximation, the periodogram is given by

$$\frac{1}{N}|X(\omega)|^2 \doteq |C(\omega)|^2 \frac{1}{N}|\mathcal{E}(\omega)|^2$$

which is

$$I(\omega) \doteq \Phi(\omega)\mathcal{J}(\omega) \tag{1}$$

Here $I(\omega)$ is the periodogram of the sample $(x_0, x_1, \cdots, x_{N-1})$, and $\mathcal{J}(\omega)$ is the periodogram of the white noise sample $(\varepsilon_0, \varepsilon_1, \cdots, \varepsilon_{N-1})$. At the harmonic frequencies $\omega_k = 2\pi k/N$ we have

$$I(\omega_k) \doteq \Phi(\omega_k)\mathcal{J}(\omega_k), \qquad k=0,1,2,\cdots,N-1$$

which we write as

$$I_k \doteq \Phi_k \mathcal{J}_k \qquad k=0,1,2,\cdots,N-1 \tag{2}$$

In equation (2), all the statistical variation occurs in I_k and $\mathcal{J}_k$, and Φ_k is an (unknown) constant. Thus, except for the scale factor Φ_k, the distribution of I_k is the same as the distribution of $\mathcal{J}_k$. Furthermore, we know the distribution of $\mathcal{J}_k$ from the last Article, namely $\mathcal{J}_0$ and $\mathcal{J}_{N/2}$

(for the case of even N) are distributed as χ_1^2 and the other I_k are distributed as $\chi_2^2/2$, because the σ^2 of the last Article is set equal to one here. All these periodogram values are mutually independent. As a result the periodogram I_k is distributed as a multiple of chi-square, namely I_0 and $I_{N/2}$ (for the case of even N) are distributed as $\Phi_0 \chi_1^2$ and $\Phi_{N/2} \chi_1^2$ respectively, and the other I_k are distributed as $\Phi_k \chi_2^2/2$. In particular,

$$E(I_0) = \Phi_0, \quad E(I_{N/2}) = \Phi_{N/2}, \quad E(I_k) = \Phi_k$$

$$\text{var}(I_0) = 2\Phi_0^2, \text{var}(I_{n/2}) = 2\Phi_{N/2}^2, \text{var}(I_k) = \Phi_k^2 \qquad (k \neq 0, k \neq \tfrac{N}{2})$$

An example of spectral estimation by smoothing the periodogram

We assume that the spectral density is a smooth, slowly-varying continuous function of ω. For large N, the frequency increment $\Delta\omega = 2\pi/N$ is small, and we can assume that $\Phi(\omega)$ is effectively constant over a range. Specifically, let us consider the range made up of three adjacent harmonic frequencies ω_{k-1}, ω_k, ω_{k+1}. Thus we assume

$$\Phi_k = \Phi(\omega_k) \doteq \Phi(\omega_{k-1}) \doteq \Phi(\omega_{k+1})$$

As a result I_{k-1}, I_k, I_{k+1} are each independently distributed as $\Phi_k \chi_2^2/2$, or in other words $2I_{k-1}/\Phi_k$, $2I_k/\Phi_k$, $2I_{k+1}/\Phi_k$ are each independently distributed as χ_2^2. Their sum

$$2(I_{k-1} + I_k + I_{k+1})/\Phi_k$$

is distributed as χ_6^2. Its mean is

$$E[2(I_{k-1} + I_k + I_{k+1})/\Phi_k] = E(\chi_6^2) = 6$$

so

$$E[0.333\, I_{k-1} + 0.333\, I_k + 0.333\, I_{k+1}] = \Phi_k$$

Thus, according to our approximations, the estimate

$$\tilde{\Phi}_k = \tfrac{1}{3}[I_{k-1} + I_k + I_{k+1}]$$

has the following properties. Its expected value is

$$E(\tilde{\Phi}_k) = \tfrac{1}{3}(\Phi_{k-1} + \Phi_k + \Phi_{k+1}),$$

which is equal to Φ_k only if the spectrum $\Phi(\omega)$ is linear over the interval. However, the bias will be unimportant if $\Phi(\omega)$ is a reasonably smooth function at ω and N is much larger than the number of points 3 in the estimate.

Chapter 9. Spectral estimation

The variance of the estimate is

$$\operatorname{var} \tilde{\Phi}_k \doteq \left(\frac{1}{3}\right)^2 3 \operatorname{var} I_k = \frac{1}{3} \Phi_k^2$$

Let us summarize. The periodogram value I_k provides an approximate unbiased estimate of the spectral density (i.e. $E(I_k) = \Phi_k$), but the variance of this estimate is equal to the square of the spectral density (i.e. $\operatorname{var} I_k = \Phi_k^2$). However, if we average three adjacent values of the periodogram series, that is, if we form the estimate

$$\tilde{\Phi}_k = \frac{I_{k-1} + I_k + I_{k+1}}{3}$$

the estimate is still approximately unbiased, but it has only 1/3 of the variance of the previous estimate. This example illustrates the principle of estimating the spectral density by smoothing the periodogram.

Confidence limits may be obtained as follows. The quantity $2(I_{k-1} + I_k + I_{k+1})/\Phi_k$ is distributed as χ_6^2. That is, the quantity $6\tilde{\Phi}_k/\Phi_k$ is distributed as χ_6^2. Thus

$$P(\chi_6^2(0.975) \leq \frac{6\tilde{\Phi}_k}{\Phi_k} \leq \chi_6^2(0.025)) = 0.95$$

so a 95 percent confidence interval is given by

$$\frac{6\tilde{\Phi}_k}{\chi_6^2(0.025)} \leq \Phi_k \leq \frac{6\tilde{\Phi}_k}{\chi_6^2(0.975)}$$

where $\chi_6^2(0.975) = 1.24$ is the 97.5% point, and $\chi_6^2(0.025)$ is the 2.5% point, of the chi-square distribution with 6 degrees of freedom. See Table 9-1. Often spectral densities are plotted on a logarithmic scale. In such a case we write the above inequality as

$$\log \tilde{\Phi}_k + \log \left(\frac{6}{\chi_6^2(0.975)}\right) \leq \log \Phi_k + \log \frac{6}{\chi_6^2(0.025)}$$

In the above discussion we have assumed that the frequency point ω_k at which the estimate is made is not $\omega_0 = 0$ or $\omega_{N/2} = \pi$ (in case N is even). In order to estimate $\Phi(\omega)$ at $\omega = 0$ or $\omega = \pi$, the formula for the estimate has to be modified by treating the periodogram as being symmetric about 0 and π.

In this Article we have illustrated an estimate which averages three consecutive values of the periodogram series. Generally, one may use an estimate which is an average of m consecutive values. The positive integer m has to be chosen so as to balance bias against the variance. The bias represents the discrepancy between the expected value of the estimate

$$E(\tilde{\Phi}_k) = \frac{1}{m} \sum_j \Phi_j \qquad \text{(where j runs over m points centered at or near k)}$$

and the value of the spectral density Φ_k. The larger m, the greater the bias. Since neighboring values in the periodogram series are uncorrelated, it is clear that the variance will be var $\tilde{\Phi}_k = \Phi_k^2/m$. Thus, the larger m, the smaller the variance. For example, a large value of m would mean a small variance, but a large bias in that interesting features of $\Phi(\omega)$ such as peaks would be smoothed out in $E(\tilde{\Phi}_k)$ and thus lost. On the other hand, a small value of m would mean that features of the spectral density $\Phi(\omega)$ are preserved, but the scatter of the estimate due to a large variance would seriously affect its reliability. In summary, a large value of m may show the large peaks in $\Phi(\omega)$ but the estimated curve may be too smooth to show the small peaks. A small value of m may show many peaks, great and small, but the estimated curve may be too rough to indicate which of the large number of peaks may be spurious.

Probability of a larger value

ν	.995	.990	.975	.950	.050	.025	.010	.005
1	---	---	---	.004	3.84	5.02	6.63	7.88
2	.01	.02	.05	.10	5.99	7.38	9.21	10.60
3	.07	.11	.22	.35	7.81	9.35	11.34	12.84
4	.21	.30	.48	.71	9.49	11.14	13.28	14.86
5	.41	.55	.83	1.15	11.07	12.83	15.09	16.75
6	.68	.87	1.24	1.64	12.59	14.45	16.81	18.55
7	.99	1.24	1.69	2.17	14.07	16.01	18.48	20.28
8	1.34	1.65	2.18	2.73	15.51	17.53	20.09	21.96
9	1.73	2.09	2.70	3.33	16.92	19.02	21.67	23.59
10	2.16	2.56	3.25	3.94	18.31	20.48	23.21	25.19
11	2.60	3.05	3.82	4.57	19.68	21.92	24.72	26.76
12	3.07	3.57	4.40	5.23	21.03	23.34	26.22	28.30
13	3.57	4.11	5.01	5.89	22.36	24.74	27.69	29.82
14	4.07	4.66	5.63	6.57	23.68	26.12	29.14	31.32
15	4.60	5.23	6.26	7.26	25.00	27.49	30.58	32.80
16	5.14	5.81	6.91	7.96	26.30	28.85	32.00	34.27
17	5.70	6.41	7.56	8.67	27.59	30.19	33.41	35.72
18	6.26	7.01	8.23	9.39	28.87	31.53	34.81	37.16
19	6.84	7.63	8.91	10.12	30.14	32.85	36.19	38.58
20	7.43	8.26	9.59	10.85	31.41	34.17	37.57	40.00
21	8.03	8.90	10.28	11.59	32.67	35.48	38.93	41.40
22	8.64	9.54	10.98	12.34	33.92	36.78	40.29	42.80
23	9.26	10.20	11.69	13.09	35.17	38.08	41.64	44.18
24	9.89	10.86	12.40	13.85	36.42	39.36	42.98	45.56
25	10.52	11.52	13.12	14.61	37.65	40.65	44.31	46.93
26	11.16	12.20	13.84	15.38	38.89	41.92	45.64	48.29
27	11.81	12.88	14.57	16.15	40.11	43.19	46.96	49.64
28	12.46	13.56	15.31	16.93	41.34	44.46	48.28	50.99
29	13.12	14.26	16.05	17.71	42.56	45.72	49.59	52.34
30	13.79	14.95	16.79	18.49	43.77	46.98	50.89	53.67
40	20.71	22.16	24.43	26.51	55.76	59.34	63.69	66.77
50	27.99	29.71	32.36	34.76	67.50	71.42	76.15	79.49
60	35.53	37.48	40.48	43.19	79.08	83.30	88.38	91.95
70	43.28	45.44	48.76	51.74	90.53	95.02	100.43	104.22
80	51.17	53.54	57.15	60.39	101.88	106.63	112.33	116.32
90	59.20	61.75	65.65	69.13	113.14	118.14	124.12	128.30
100	67.33	70.06	74.22	77.93	124.34	129.56	135.81	140.17

Table 9-1. Percentage Points of the Chi-square Distribution

Chapter 9. Spectral estimation

9.8 An example of spectral estimation by transforming the autocorrelation

First let us show that the periodogram $I(\omega)$ and the sample autocorrelation

$$r_n = \frac{1}{N} \sum_{j=0}^{N-1-|n|} x_{j+n} x_j$$

are finite Fourier transforms of each other. The periodogram may be written as

$$I(\omega) = \frac{1}{N} |X(\omega)|^2 = \frac{1}{N} \sum_{k=0}^{N-1} x_k e^{-i\omega k} \sum_{j=0}^{N-1} x_j e^{i\omega j}$$

$$= \frac{1}{N} \sum_{k=0}^{N-1} \sum_{j=0}^{N-1} x_k x_j e^{-i\omega(k-j)}$$

$$= \frac{1}{N} \sum_{n=-N+1}^{N-1} e^{-i\omega n} \sum_{j=0}^{N-1-|n|} x_{j+n} x_j$$

$$= \sum_{n=-N+1}^{N-1} r_n e^{-i\omega n}$$

Since $r_{-n} = r_n$ this last expression becomes

$$I(\omega) = r_0 + 2 \sum_{n=1}^{N-1} r_n \cos \omega n$$

A well-known type of procedure for estimating the spectral density consists of taking the Fourier transform of a truncated and weighted sample autocorrelation. As we have just seen the periodogram is the finite Fourier transform of the complete and unweighted sample autocorrelation. Because the precision of the sample autocorrelation r_n decreases as n increases, the method gives less weight to the values of r_n as n increases, and actually cuts off (or truncates) all values of r_n for n greater than some value M. We write such an estimate as

$$\tilde{\phi}(\omega) = r_0 w_0 + 2 \sum_{n=1}^{M} r_n w_n \cos \omega n$$

where the weights $w_0, w_1, w_2, \cdots, w_M$ are called the lag window, and M is called the truncation point (M<N).

A lag window in popular use is the cosine-squared window given by

$$w_n = \cos^2 \frac{\pi n}{2M} = 0.5(1 + \cos \frac{\pi n}{M}) \, , \, n=0,1,2,\ldots,M$$

These weights are used in the above formula for $\tilde{\phi}(\omega)$ to give the cosine-squared estimate.

An alternative way for computing the cosine-squared estimate $\tilde{\phi}(\omega)$ is as follows. The estimate is calculated in two steps. First, a truncated unweighted cosine transform of the sample autocorrelation is computed to give

$$\hat{\Phi}(\omega) = r_o + 2 \sum_{n=1}^{M} r_n \cos \omega n$$

That is, $\hat{\Phi}(\omega)$ is a truncated estimate with lag window equal to unity. In practice, the estimates are computed at the discrete frequencies $\omega_k = 2\pi k/2M = \pi k/M$; that is, we compute

$$\hat{\Phi}_n = \hat{\Phi}(\omega_n) = r_o + \sum_{n=1}^{M} r_n \cos \frac{\pi k n}{M}$$

The series of these estimates are then smoothed by the weights 0.25, 0.50, 0.25 to give the required estimates

$$\tilde{\Phi}_n = 0.25 \hat{\Phi}_{n-1} + 0.50 \hat{\Phi}_n + 0.25 \hat{\Phi}_{n+1} \quad \text{for } n=1,2,\ldots,M-1$$

At zero frequency $\omega_o=0$ and at the Nyquist frequency $\omega_M=\pi$, corresponding respectively to n=o and n=M , the required estimates are

$$\tilde{\Phi}_o = 0.50 \hat{\Phi}_o + 0.50 \hat{\Phi}_1$$

$$\tilde{\Phi}_M = 0.50 \hat{\Phi}_{M-1} + 0.50 \hat{\Phi}_M$$

The cosine-squared window and its Fourier transform

$$W(\omega) = \sum_{n=-M}^{M} w_n e^{-i\omega n} = \sum_{n=-M}^{M} \cos^2 \frac{\pi n}{2M} \cos \omega n$$

are shown in Figure 9-2.

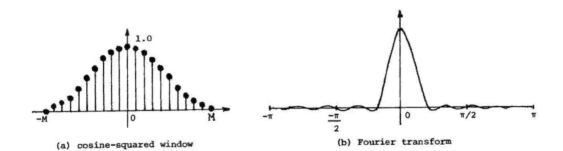

(a) cosine-squared window

(b) Fourier transform

Figure 9-2

The cosine-squared window and its Fourier transform. Graphs are for M=10.

Because its Fourier transform does have negative ordinates, it is possible for this window to give negative estimates of the spectral density. As a result other lag windows often are used which have the property of non-negative Fourier transforms.

Chapter 10. Seismic deconvolution

10.1 Exploration for oil and natural gas

The earth is a giant thermodynamic engine fueled by the sun and by massive internal reservoirs of thermal energy and constrained by the force of gravity. The outer layers of the earth are continually driven in a slow-motion turmoil. If a motion-picture film were made of the earth, with one exposure every one hundred years from the time of origin until now, and if we could look at selected portions of this film run through a projector at the speed we consider normal for movies, then we would see that the surface of the earth is not constant at all but in fact is changing all the time. On a human time scale, mountains appear eternal, but viewed over the long course of geologic time they are transient events marking some phase of geologic history. In one place or another, rocks in the earth's crust have been constantly upthrust and eroded. The weathered materials made up of gravel, sand and silt are carried to the seas and deposited in extensive sedimentary sheets. The shells of marine animals also formed sedimentary layers. The final result was that as time passed the accumulated deposits hardened into layers of rock, mainly sandstone, shale, and limestone. The separate layers were on top of each other much like a stack of cards. In turn these layers have been subjected to massive undulating upwarpings and downwarpings, often of several hundred miles in wavelength and several miles in vertical amplitude. Faulting, erosion and new sedimentation gave further structural properties to the sedimentary layers.

Extensive marine life existed in the shallow seas where these sedimentary deposits were being formed. Oil and gas are formed from ancient animal life in the sea, such as the one-celled plankton. Such microscopic marine life when it died would settle to the bottom and would remain there with billions of its parrs in those places where there was not enough air to oxidize the organic remains. In turn, this organic material would be buried in the sediments and would represent the first step in the formation of oil. No one knows the chemical transition to the final composition of petroleum except that time is an important factor. The sedimentary beds in which this oil is formed must be porous in order for oil to have room to collect within the rock. In addition, the oil-bearing formation must be permeable, in that oil must be able to move from place to place within the rock in which it occurs. When porosity and permeability are not present, certain oil-like material may still be found, as in the so-called oil shale formations in the Rocky Mountains. However, porosity and permeability are necessary factors for the commercial production of oil and gas.

Still another factor is necessary for oil and gas production. There must be a trap to prevent the oil and gas from escaping. One key factor for the trapping of oil and gas is the alternating deposition of permeable and impermeable rock types. For example, a highly porous and permeable

Chapter 10. Seismic deconvolution

sandstone layer may be sandwiched between two impermeable shale beds. In the course of burial and compaction, the salt water, oil and gas are concentrated in the permeable rock layers where they are free to migrate large distances laterally but are prevented from escaping upward by impervious beds. In any case, the oil and gas are going to rise to the highest part of the formation where it must be stopped or else be lost. Sometimes a slope reversal (or anticline) forms a trap that holds the oil in place. Sometimes the earth has slipped, sliding a face of impervious rock across the rising column of oil-bearing rock to hold the oil in place. Sometimes the oil bearing strata becomes narrower and narrower and pinches out forming a trap. Sometimes the trap is not made up of any structural feature, such as an anticline, fault, or pinch-out, but is formed by simply a change in the rock type within the bed that prevents further migration and loss of the oil: the so-called stratigraphic traps. See Figure 10-1.

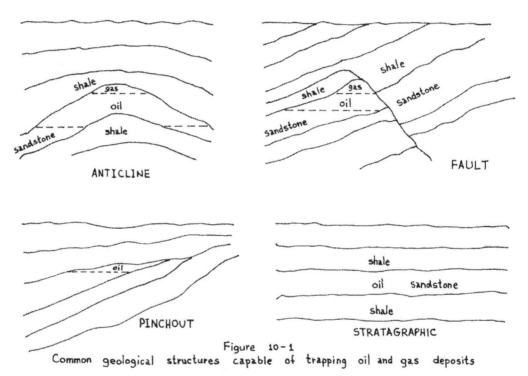

Figure 10-1
Common geological structures capable of trapping oil and gas deposits

Water, oil and gas segregate into layers in accord with their relative densities. In exploration, the objective is to locate the geologic traps in which oil and gas are likely to occur. The final test to establish the presence of oil and gas is the drilling of an oil well. Geologic and geophysical methods are used to find likely locations for successful oil wells. A wet well represents success; a dry well, failure. Geologists and geophysicists cannot cover up their mistakes, but despite good and accurate work, they are still at the mercy of nature. Geophysical methods may locate an excellent geologic structure, but devoid of oil. Because geophysical methods can only detect structure but not the actual presence of oil, a geophysicist is always faced with the workings of chance. As we will see, these workings of chance extend beyond the presence or absence of oil in any given structure. Indeed, they extend to the whole process of nature which formed these geologic formations over the eons of time. The geophysicist in his work must consider the whole moving picture of the crustal formation, as we have described it, as a random process. The rock formations in which oil and gas are found represent the outcome or realizations of this random process.

Geophysical methods are used extensively in the exploration for oil and gas. These techniques exploit the diagnostic capabilities of practically all the observable physical properties of the earth. To locate the deposits of oil, the geophysicist must look for traps that lie beneath the surface. The most successful method is the seismic method. This method exploits the elastic properties of rocks. A man-made energy source such as an explosion is located on or close to the surface. This source excites elastic waves in the rocks (seismic waves) which in various forms propagate through the subsurface rock layers. Some of these waves penetrate to depths of thousands of feet where they are reflected from various interfaces. A portion of these reflected waves return to the surface where they are recorded in the form of seismic traces (or time series) on a seismogram. The time-series data can then be analyzed and interpreted so as to yield valuable information as to the subsurface rock formations.

In order to obtain a feeling for the seismic process, we may describe it by saying that the rock layers are partially transparent to seismic waves several hundred feet in length. The seismic method can be described as an approach in which the subsurface is illuminated by seismic wave radiation from a surface source. The nature of the geophysicists' problem can be illustrated by the following analogy. We imagine that the earth's crust is a stack of glass plates of various thicknesses and bent out of shape. Each plate is of a different color, each has irregular surfaces, and some have traps of various sizes and shapes. Now we shine a light into the stack from the surface and we analyze the returning rays to determine the color and thickness of each plate, the details of the interfaces between the plates, and the locations and shapes of the traps. Returning now to the real earth, we may say that a geophysicist must be able to locate the position and determine the size of hydrocarbon (oil and gas) traps in a heterogeneous, multilayered medium which is partially translucent to seismic waves. Petroleum traps of commercial value may have a horizontal extent of only a few hundred acres and be as much as four miles below the surface of the earth. These deep oil fields as a rule have no expression of their structure on the surface, which could aid in their location.

The basic principles of reflection seismology are illustrated in Figure 10-2. The source S of seismic energy is placed at the surface. Downward-traveling seismic waves are reflected from the boundaries of rock layers, the so-called interfaces. All possible multiple reflections between different interfaces occur. Some of the total energy

Chapter 10. Seismic deconvolution

finally reaches the surface in the form of upgoing waves which are recorded by a surface receiver R.

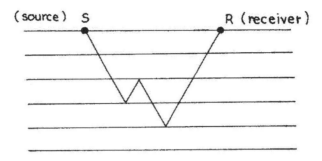

Figure 10-2

One of the many possible paths of seismic waves.

Seismic prospecting can be conducted either on land or at sea. On land the source may be an explosive charge from 1 to 100 pounds of dynamite in shot holes drilled from 10 to 500 feet below the surface. In other cases, the source may be a surface impactor device making use of a propane-oxygen explosion, or by a heavy weight that can be dropped from a specially equipped truck. These methods give an impulsive source signal, that is, one of high energy concentrated in a short time duration. At the other extreme, is the continuous-wave source signal produced by a surface vibrator. Such a signal has low energy over a long time duration; an example is the chirp signal which has constant amplitude over a six-second time duration. The chirp signal is frequency modulated, with frequency changing continuously from say 20 hertz at the beginning of the signal to 60 hertz at the end. At sea, the source device is towed from a ship at a depth of 20 to 50 feet in the water. The device may generate either impulsive or chirp signals. Impulsive source signals result from devices that give the sudden release of compressed air, that detonate a propane-oxygen mixture, or that set off an electric discharge. A chirp source signal can be formed by underwater transducers driven by programmed hydraulic power packs.

In seismic prospecting for oil and gas, the principal frequency range of interest is from 0 to 100 hertz. Unlike radio waves, seismic waves have a velocity which is very much dependent upon the medium. Velocity of seismic wave transmission through sedimentary rocks varies between 5000 and 20000 feet per second. Thus for a frequency of 25 hertz and a velocity of 10000 feet per second, the seismic wave would have a wavelength of 400 feet.

The reflection of a seismic wave occurs at an interface where there is a change in the acoustic impedance. The acoustic impedance is defined as the product of the velocity and the density of the rock. Often the rock layers have well-defined interfaces that offer a good impedance contrast. The roughness of the interfaces may not exceed a few feet, so to a seismic wave several hundred feet in length, such an interface appears to have a smoothness equivalent to that of a high-grade optical reflecting surface for light. The interfaces act as a series of reflecting surfaces, each of which partially transmits and partially reflects the seismic energy, where the reflection process represents specular partial reflection instead of diffuse scattering as in many radar applications. For example, in side-looking radars, the returned energy is for the most part back-scattered from many separate objects, so that the returned signals have more or less random phase relationships. In reflection seismic work, the returned energy is predominantly reflected energy from continuous slowly-varying interfaces, so the returned signals have highly coherent phase relationships.

The returned energy is detected by highly sensitive transducers or seismometers called geophones on land and hydrophones at sea. On land or at sea, these transducers are distributed in linear arrays, the output of each group of transducers being combined electronically to form one channel. (See Article 1.5). At sea, the transducers are placed in a marine cable or streamer which is a neutrally buoyant oil-filled plastic sleeve. A 24 channel marine cable consists of 24 groups. Each group may contain 30 transducers distributed with tapered spacing over a 200 foot length. These groups are then placed at equal intervals in a towed streamer cable that may be 9000 feet long. Towing speeds are 5 knots or more, and seismic source repetition rates can be as much as 10 shots per minute. The signals received by each channel are transmitted aboard ship by wires; these signals are amplified, sampled at intervals such as 0.002 or 0.004 seconds, digitized, and recorded on digital magnetic tape. The output of each channel represents a seismic trace.

Let us now look at the seismic method from a "data" point of view. Let us think of the unit of data as the signal received by one transducer as the result of one shot. Then, for example, 30 units of data would be received by 10 transducers as the result of three shots. We now want to consider the amount of received data per unit of length along a seismic profile. For example, about half a million miles of seismic lines are run in the United States each year. The number of units of data per line mile represents the intensity of the seismic prospecting. Let us take 1950 as the reference year, and so set our unit of intensity equal to one for that year. Figure 10-3 shows how this intensity has increased over the years. As we see, exploration intensity has increased by a factor of 2000 since 1950. In other words, we are using 2000 times as many received signals in each mile of seismic exploration than we used in 1950.

Chapter 10. Seismic deconvolution 341

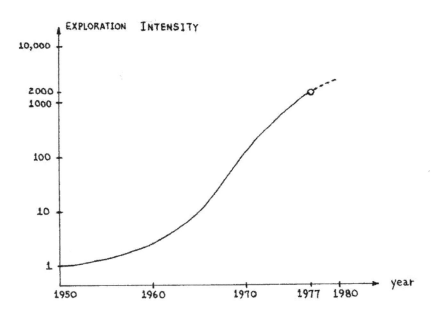

Figure 10-3

The intensity of seismic prospecting since the year 1950.

PROBLEMS FOR ARTICLE 10.1

1. Electromagnetic waves travel at the velocity of light ($c=3 \times 10^8$ meters/sec.). Thus, the wavelength of an electromagnetic wave of frequency $f = 10^{10}$ Hz is $\lambda = c/f = 0.03 m = 3$ cm. Compare this to the wavelength of a seismic wave with a propagation velocity of 9000 m/sec and a frequency of 30 Hz.

2. A seismic signal is passed through an ideal low-pass filter which has a bandwidth of 125 Hz. If 15 seconds of this signal is to be stored in a digital computer with a capability of 16 bits/sample, how many bits of information are required to faithfully reproduce the original seismic event?

10.2 Sedimentary model of the earth's crust

The ability to handle the increasing quantity of data in seismic prospecting is related to the expanding use of statistical models in geophysics. Let us now give an example of such a model. To a first approximation, this model is based on the following assumptions: (1) The layer interfaces are parallel, and the seismic waves are plane compressional waves travelling in an up-direction or down-direction normal to the interfaces. As a result, the model becomes one with one-spatial dimension, namely depth. (2) The layers are perfectly elastic so there are no energy losses due to absorption within the layers.

The section of earth crust of interest is represented by a layered system of N sedimentary layers of finite thickness sandwiched in between the basement rock and the air. The term <u>sedimentary system</u> refers to the N layers of finite thickness and will not include the air and basement rock. There are N+1 horizontal interfaces. The lowest interface is denoted by index N and represents the top of layer N+1, that is, the top of the basement. The highest interface is denoted by index 0 and represents the top of layer 1, that is, the surface of the ground or the water as the case may be. Generally, we may say that interface n is the top of layer n+1, where the integer n runs from 0 through N. See Figure 10-4.

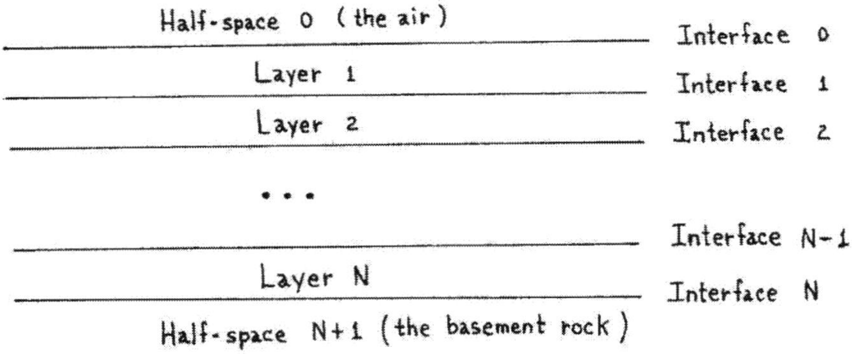

```
_____
         Half-space  0  (the air)              Interface  0
_____
              Layer  1                         Interface  1
_____
              Layer  2                         Interface  2
_____
                  . . .
                                               Interface  N-1
_____
              Layer  N                         Interface  N
_____
         Half-space  N+1  (the basement rock)
```

Figure 10-4

An N-layered sedimentary system.

For convenience, we suppose that the amplitudes of the waves are measured in units that represent the square root of energy. For example, in electric terms the amplitudes would be measured in units of (voltage-current)$^{1/2}$. Thus the square of the amplitude is in units of energy.

Chapter 10. Seismic deconvolution

If a downgoing unit spike is incident on the top of interface n, then the reflection coefficient ϵ_n is equal to the resulting upgoing spike reflected from the top of interface n, and the transmission coefficient τ_n is equal to the resulting downgoing spike transmitted through interface n. That is, the incident pulse of amplitude one is converted into a reflected pulse of amplitude ϵ_n and a transmitted pulse of amplitude τ_n. Because no energy is lost, the energy of the incident pulse must equal the sum of the energies of the reflected and transmitted pulses:

$$1 = \epsilon_n^2 + \tau_n^2$$

Solving this equation for τ_n we have

$$\tau_n = \sqrt{1-\epsilon_n^2}$$

where by convention the positive square root is taken.

If an upgoing unit spike is incident on the bottom of interface n, then the reflection coefficient ϵ_n' is equal to the resulting downgoing spike reflected from the bottom of interface n, and the transmission coefficient τ_n' is equal to the resulting upgoing spike transmitted through interface n. The reflection coefficient ϵ_n' is the negative of the reflection coefficient ϵ_n, but the transmission coefficient τ_n' is the same as τ_n:

$$\epsilon_n' = -\epsilon_n, \quad \tau_n' = \tau_n = \sqrt{1-\epsilon_n^2}$$

These quantities are shown in Figure 10-5.

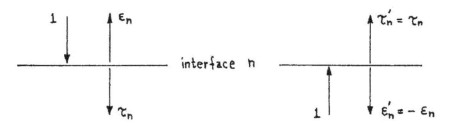

Figure 10-5

A schematic diagram illustrating the convention of reflection and transmission coefficients at an interface.

For computational reasons, it is convenient to add hypothetical (i.e. mathematical, not geological) interfaces where necessary, so as to make the two-way travel time in each layer equal to the same quantity, which we shall define as one time unit. Of course, the reflection coefficients are zero and the transmission coefficients are one for any such hypothetical interfaces that are added. We let z represent the unit delay operator.

If one attempts to apply Newtonian mechanical laws to ultra-highspeed charged particles, then an insurmountable contradiction is encountered. That is, the simple addition of velocities does not apply in electrodynamics, and instead, one should use the Einstein addition formula for combining velocities which guarantees that the resulting velocity will never exceed the velocity of light.

Likewise in combining reflection coefficients from a system of layers it turns out that the counterpart of the Einstein addition formula has to be used which guarantees that the resulting reflectivity cannot exceed unity in magnitude. Let us now derive this counterpart of the Einstein addition formula.

Let us now consider a sedimentary subsystem denoted by (n+1,N) made up of the bottom N-n layers with reflection coefficients $\varepsilon_{n+1}, \varepsilon_{n+2}, \cdots, \varepsilon_N$. Let us also consider another sedimentary subsystem denoted by (n,N) made up of the bottom N-n+1 layers with the same reflection coefficients $\varepsilon_{n+1}, \varepsilon_{n+2}, \cdots, \varepsilon_N$ plus the additional reflection coefficient ε_n. In order for these reflection coefficients to be the same, layer n+1 of the second system must be of the same material as the half-space n+1 of the first system, and all of the layers below must be identical in the two systems. See Figure 10-6.

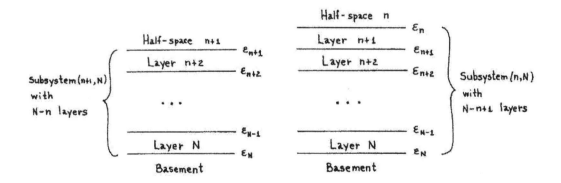

Figure 10-6

The decomposition of a sedimentary system into two sedimentary systems; subsystem (n+1, N) and subsystem (n, N).

Chapter 10. Seismic deconvolution

Because we always let the input be a unit downgoing spike at time zero incident at the topmost interface of a sedimentary subsystem, we can simply refer to the output wave train reflected up into the upper half-space as the <u>reflection response</u> R and the output wave train transmitted down into the basement as the <u>transmission response</u> T. Figure 10-7 shows the responses for sybsystem (n+1,N) and Figure 10-8 for sybsystem (n,N).

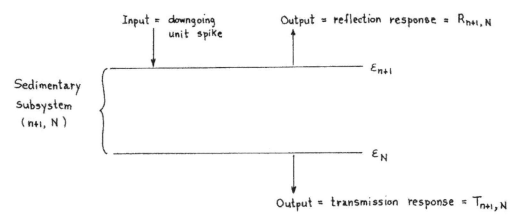

Figure 10-7

The reflection and transmission responses for sedimentary subsystem (n+1, N).

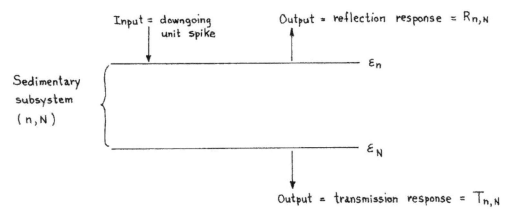

Figure 10-8

The reflection and transmission responses for sedimentary subsystem (n,N).

We now wish to combine the reflection response $R_{n+1,N}$ of subsystem $(n+1,N)$ with the reflection coefficient ϵ_n in such a way so as to give the reflection response $R_{n,N}$ of subsystem (n,N). If we refer to Figure 10-9, we see that the reflection response $R_{n,N}$ is made up of an infinite series of components, namely:

(1) the spike ϵ_n resulting from the reflection upward of the source spike from the nth interface,

(2) the spike train $\tau_n R_{n+1,N} \tau_n'$ resulting from the transmission downward of the source spike through the nth interface, reflection upward from the subsystem $(n+1,N)$, and transmission upward through the nth interface,

(3) the spike train $\tau_n R_{n+1,N} \epsilon_n' R_{n+1,N} \tau_n'$ resulting from the transmission downward of the source spike through the nth interface, reflection upward from subsystem $(n+1,N)$, reflection downward from the nth interface, reflection upward from subsystem $(n+1,N)$, and transmission upward through the nth interface,

and so on. The spike (1) above occurs at the time of the source spike, the spike train (2) above occurs at a delay of one time unit (i.e. at a delay of the two-way travel time through the nth layer), the spike train (3) above occurs at a delay of two time units, and so on. Summing all these contributions, we have

$$R_{n,N} = \epsilon_n + \tau_n R_{n+1,N} \tau_n' z + \tau_n R_{n+1,N} \epsilon_n' R_{n+1,N} \tau_n' z^2 + \cdots$$

This expression may be factored as

$$R_{n,N} = \epsilon_n + \tau_n R_{n+1,N} \tau_n' z \left[1 + \epsilon_n' R_{n+1,N} z + (\epsilon_n' R_{n+1,N} z)^2 + \cdots \right]$$

which, if we sum the geometric series in brackets, becomes

$$R_{n,N} = \epsilon_n + \frac{\tau_n R_{n+1,N} \tau_n' z}{1 - \epsilon_n' R_{n+1,N} z}$$

Using the relationships given earlier between the reflection and transmission coefficients, this expression becomes

$$R_{n,N} = \frac{\epsilon_n + R_{n+1,N} z}{1 + \epsilon_n R_{n+1,N} z} \tag{1}$$

Chapter 10. Seismic deconvolution 347

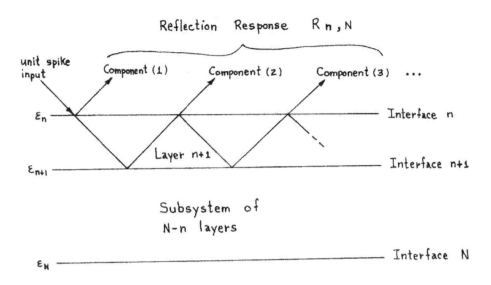

Figure 10-9

Schematic make-up of the reflection response $R_{n,N}$

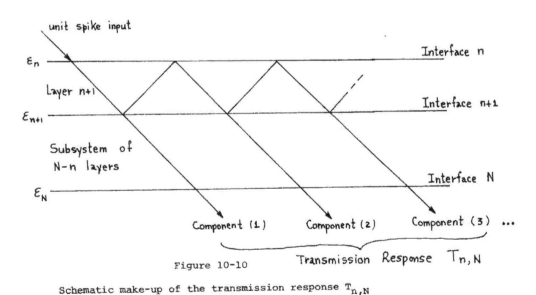

Figure 10-10

Schematic make-up of the transmission response $T_{n,N}$

This equation for combining ε_n and $R_{n+1,N}$ to form $R_{n,N}$ is of the same mathematical form as the Einstein addition formula in the theory of relativity to combine two velocities to give resulting velocity, and hence represents the required counterpart of the Einstein addition formula in the case of layered media.

In a similar manner, the transmission response $T_{n,N}$ of subsystem (n,N) can be obtained in terms of the reflection coefficient ε_n and the transmission coefficient τ_n of the nth interface and the reflection response $R_{n+1,N}$ and the transmission response $T_{n+1,N}$ of subsystem (n+1,N). If we refer to Figure 10-10, we see that the transmission response $T_{n,N}$ is made up of an infinite series of components, namely

(1) the spike train $\tau_n T_{n+1,N}$

(2) the spike train $\tau_n R_{n+1,N} \varepsilon_n^\frown T_{n+1,N}$,

(3) the spike train $\tau_n R_{n+1,N} \varepsilon_n^\frown R_{n+1,N} \varepsilon_n^\frown T_{n+1,N}$,

and so on. We choose the time origin of the transmission response as the time of its first break (i.e. at its first non-zero amplitude). Its first break occurs at a delay of N/2 (i.e. the one-way travel time) from the time of the surface input spike. With reference to the time origin of the transmission response, the spike train (1) occurs with no delay, spike train (2) occurs with a delay of one time unit, spike train (3) occurs with a delay of two time units, and so on. Summing all these contributions, we have

$$T_{n,N} = \tau_n T_{n+1,N} + \tau_n R_{n+1,N} \varepsilon_n^\frown T_{n+1,N} z + \tau_n R_{n+1,N} \varepsilon_n^\frown R_{n+1,N} \varepsilon_n^\frown T_{n+1,N} z^2 + \cdots$$

$$= \tau_n T_{n+1,N} [1 + R_{n+1,N} \varepsilon_n^\frown z + (R_{n+1,N} \varepsilon_n^\frown z)^2 + \cdots].$$

Summing the geometric series, we have

$$T_{n,N} = \frac{\tau_n T_{n+1,N}}{1 + \varepsilon_n R_{n+1,N} z} \qquad (2)$$

We note that the final expressions for $R_{n,N}$ and $T_{n,N}$ each have the same denominator.

We now wish to define a sequence of polynomials $E_{N,N}, E_{N-1,N}, \cdots, E_{0,N}$ which we call the feedforward polynomials and a sequence of polynomials $A_{N,N}, A_{N-1,N}, \cdots, A_{0,N}$ which we call the feedback polynomials. In the case of no layers (i.e. just half-spaces N+1 and N separated by interface N), the reflection and transmission responses are

$$R_{N,N} = \varepsilon_N \;, \quad T_{N,N} = \tau_N$$

Chapter 10. Seismic deconvolution

These responses may be expressed in terms of polynomials $E_{N,N}$ and $A_{N,N}$ each of zero degree as

$$R_{N,N} = \frac{E_{N,N}}{A_{N,N}} \;,\quad T_{N,N} = \frac{\tau_N}{A_{N,N}}$$

where the polynomials satisfy

$$E_{N,N} = \varepsilon_N \;,\quad A_{N,N} = 1.$$

Let us suppose that in the case of subsystem $(n+1,N)$ the reflection and transmission responses may be expressed in terms of polynomials $E_{n+1,N}$ and $A_{n+1,N}$ each of degree $N-n-1$ as

$$R_{n+1,N} = \frac{E_{n+1,N}}{A_{n+1,N}} \;,\quad T_{n+1,N} = \frac{\tau_{n+1}\tau_{n+2}\cdots\tau_N}{A_{n+1,N}}$$

where the polynomials satisfy

$$E_{n+1,N}(0) = \varepsilon_{n+1} \;,\quad A_{n+1,N}(0) = 1.$$

Using the Einstein addition formula we have

$$R_{n,N} = \frac{\varepsilon_n + \dfrac{E_{n+1,N}}{A_{n+1,N}} z}{1 + \varepsilon_n \dfrac{E_{n+1,N}}{A_{n+1,N}} z}$$

which is

$$R_{n,N} = \frac{\varepsilon_n A_{n+1,N} + E_{n+1,N} z}{A_{n+1,N} + \varepsilon_n E_{n+1,N} z}$$

Let us define the feedforward polynomial $E_{n,N}$ of degree $N-n$ and the feedback polynomial $A_{n,N}$ of degree $N-n$ by the <u>recursion formulas</u>

$$\begin{aligned} E_{n,N} &= \varepsilon_n A_{n+1,N} + E_{n+1,N} z \\ A_{n,N} &= A_{n+1,N} + \varepsilon_n E_{n+1,N} z \end{aligned} \qquad (3)$$

From these recursion formulas we see that the polynomials satisfy

$$E_{n,N}(0) = \varepsilon_n \;,\quad A_{n,N}(0) = 1$$

The reflection response $R_{n,N}$ is given by the ratio

$$R_{n,N} = \frac{E_{n,N}}{A_{n,N}} \tag{4}$$

Similarly, the transmission response is

$$T_{n,N} = \frac{\tau_n T_{n+1,N}}{1 + \epsilon_n R_{n+1,N} z} = \frac{\tau_n \tau_{n+1} \cdots \tau_N / A_{n+1,N}}{1 + \epsilon_n \frac{E_{n+1,N}}{A_{n+1,N}} z}$$

which is

$$T_{n,N} = \frac{\tau_n \tau_{n+1} \cdots \tau_N}{A_{n+1,N} + \epsilon_n E_{n+1,N} z} = \frac{\tau_n \tau_{n+1} \cdots \tau_N}{A_{n,N}} \tag{5}$$

Because $T_{n,N}$ is the z-transform of a stable one-sided time function, it follows that the polynomial $A_{n,N}$ is minimum-delay. Because the inverse of a minimum-delay function is also minimum-delay, it follows that $T_{n,N}$ itself is minimum-delay.

The reflection response of the entire sedimentary section $(0,N)$ is

$$R_{0,N} = \frac{E_{0,N}}{A_{0,N}} \tag{6}$$

and the transmission response is

$$T_{0,N} = \frac{\tau_0 \tau_1 \cdots \tau_N}{A_{0,N}} \tag{7}$$

Explicit formulas for the feedforward and feedback polynomials can be given in terms of the reflection coefficients. Using the recursion formulas, we obtain

$$E_{N,N} = \epsilon_N$$

$$A_{N,N} = 1$$

$$E_{N-1,N} = \epsilon_{N-1} + \epsilon_N z$$

$$A_{N-1,N} = 1 + \epsilon_{N-1} \epsilon_N z$$

$$E_{N-2,N} = \epsilon_{N-2} + (\epsilon_{N-1} + \epsilon_{N-2}\epsilon_{N-1}\epsilon_N)z + \epsilon_N z^2$$

$$A_{N-2,N} = 1 + (\epsilon_{N-1}\epsilon_N + \epsilon_{N-2}\epsilon_{N-1})z + \epsilon_{N-2}\epsilon_N z^2$$

Chapter 10. Seismic deconvolution

$$E_{N-3,N} = \varepsilon_{N-3} + (\varepsilon_{N-2} + \varepsilon_{N-3}\varepsilon_{N-2}\varepsilon_{N-1} + \varepsilon_{N-3}\varepsilon_{N-1}\varepsilon_N)z$$
$$+ (\varepsilon_{N-1} + \varepsilon_{N-3}\varepsilon_{N-2}\varepsilon_N + \varepsilon_{N-2}\varepsilon_{N-1}\varepsilon_N)z^2 + \varepsilon_N z^3$$

$$A_{N-3,N} = 1 + (\varepsilon_{N-1}\varepsilon_N + \varepsilon_{N-2}\varepsilon_{N-1} + \varepsilon_{N-3}\varepsilon_{N-2})z$$
$$+ (\varepsilon_{N-2}\varepsilon_N + \varepsilon_{N-3}\varepsilon_{N-1} + \varepsilon_{N-3}\varepsilon_{N-2}\varepsilon_{N-1}\varepsilon_N)z^2 + \varepsilon_{N-3}\varepsilon_N z^3$$

This process can be continued to obtain higher-degree polynomials. However, at this point we can make an interesting observation. In many practical situations, the reflection coefficients ε_i are of the order of magnitude such that $|\varepsilon_i| < 0.1$. The products of reflection coefficients involving three or more coefficients are small in relationship to single coefficients or to products involving only two coefficients. We are led to the idea of neglecting such higher order terms in the expressions for the polynomials. By so doing, we obtain the following approximations

$$E_{N,N} = \varepsilon_N$$
$$A_{N,N} = 1$$

$$E_{N-1,N} = \varepsilon_{N-1} + \varepsilon_N z$$
$$A_{N-1,N} = 1 + \varepsilon_{N-1}\varepsilon_N z$$

$$E_{N-2,N} = \varepsilon_{N-2} + \varepsilon_{N-1}z + \varepsilon_N z^2$$
$$A_{N-2,N} = 1 + (\varepsilon_{N-1}\varepsilon_N + \varepsilon_{N-2}\varepsilon_{N-1})z + \varepsilon_{N-2}\varepsilon_N z^2$$

$$E_{N-3,N} = \varepsilon_{N-3} + \varepsilon_{N-2}z + \varepsilon_{N-1}z^2 + \varepsilon_N z^3$$
$$A_{N-3,N} = 1 + (\varepsilon_{N-1}\varepsilon_N + \varepsilon_{N-2}\varepsilon_{N-1} + \varepsilon_{N-3}\varepsilon_{N-2})z$$
$$+ (\varepsilon_{N-2}\varepsilon_N + \varepsilon_{N-3}\varepsilon_{N-1})z^2 + \varepsilon_{N-3}\varepsilon_N z^3$$

We observe two things. First we observe that the coefficients of the feedforward polynomial, say $E_{N-3,N}$, are simply the reflection coefficients $\varepsilon_{N-3}, \varepsilon_{N-2}, \varepsilon_{N-1}, \varepsilon_N$ of the subsystem. Secondly, we observe that the coefficients of the feedback polynomial, say $A_{N-3,N}$, are simply unity for the constant term and the serial correlations of the reflection coefficients for the other terms. Let us denote the serial correlations by γ_j. For the subsystem (N-3,N) we have the reflection coefficients $\varepsilon_{N-3}, \varepsilon_{N-2}, \varepsilon_{N-1}, \varepsilon_N$ with serial correlations

$$\gamma_1 = \varepsilon_{N-1}\varepsilon_N + \varepsilon_{N-2}\varepsilon_{N-1} + \varepsilon_{N-3}\varepsilon_{N-2}$$
$$\gamma_2 = \varepsilon_{N-2}\varepsilon_N + \varepsilon_{N-3}\varepsilon_{N-1}$$
$$\gamma_3 = \varepsilon_{N-3}\varepsilon_N$$

Thus the feedback polynomial for the subsystem $(N-3,N)$ is

$$A_{N-3,N} = 1 + \gamma_1 z + \gamma_2 z^2 + \gamma_3 z^3$$

For the entire sedimentary system $(0,N)$ with reflection coefficients $\varepsilon_0, \varepsilon_1, \varepsilon_2, \ldots, \varepsilon_N$ the feedforward polynomial (to the stated approximation) is

$$E_{0,N} = \varepsilon_0 + \varepsilon_1 z + \varepsilon_2 z^2 + \cdots + \varepsilon_N z^N$$

and the feedback polynomial (to the stated approximation) is

$$A_{0,N} = 1 + \gamma_1 z + \gamma_2 z^2 + \cdots + \gamma_N z^N$$

where the serial correlations are given by

$$\gamma_1 = \varepsilon_0 \varepsilon_1 + \varepsilon_1 \varepsilon_2 + \varepsilon_2 \varepsilon_3 + \cdots + \varepsilon_{N-1} \varepsilon_N$$

$$\gamma_2 = \varepsilon_0 \varepsilon_2 + \varepsilon_1 \varepsilon_3 + \varepsilon_2 \varepsilon_4 + \cdots + \varepsilon_{N-2} \varepsilon_N$$

$$\cdots$$

$$\gamma_N = \varepsilon_0 \varepsilon_N$$

As a result the reflection response for the entire layered system $(0,N)$ is

$$R_{0,N} = \frac{E_{0,N}}{A_{0,N}} = \frac{\varepsilon_0 + \varepsilon_1 z + \varepsilon_2 z^2 + \cdots + \varepsilon_N z^N}{1 + \gamma_1 z + \gamma_2 z^2 + \cdots + \gamma_N z^N} \qquad (8)$$

and the transmission response is

$$T_{0,N} = \frac{\tau_0 \tau_1 \cdots \tau_N}{A_{0,N}} = \frac{\tau_0 \tau_1 \cdots \tau_N}{1 + \gamma_1 z + \gamma_2 z^2 + \cdots + \gamma_N z^N} \qquad (9)$$

(both to the stated approximation).

Let us now look at this transmission response. The direct pulse travels from the surface to the basement. The direct pulse starts as a unit spike at the surface and is multiplied by a transmission coefficient τ_i for each interface through which it passes, so the direct pulse emerges into the basement with amplitude $\tau_0 \tau_1 \tau_2 \cdots \tau_N$. The denominator $A_{0,N}$ is minimum-delay and its inverse, defined as

$$B_{0,N} = \frac{1}{A_{0,N}}$$

Chapter 10. Seismic deconvolution

may be regarded as representing the reverberation of the entire system. The function $B_{0,N}$ is a power series with coefficients b_k; that is,

$$B_{0,N}(z) = \sum_{k=0}^{\infty} b_k z^k$$

The coefficients b_k for $k=0,1,2,...$ make up the reverberation wavelet. Thus the transmission response $T_{0,N}$ is equal to the reverberation weighted by the constant $\tau_0 \tau_1 \tau_2 \cdots \tau_N$; that is,

$$T_{0,N} = \tau_0 \tau_1 \cdots \tau_N \, B_{0,N}$$

Next let us consider the reflection response. The reflection response can be written as

$$R_{0,N} = E_{0,N} B_{0,N}$$

If we let h_k denote the coefficients of $R_{0,N}$ then the above equation gives

$$h_k = \sum_{j=0}^{N} \epsilon_j b_{k-j} \qquad k=0,1,2,...$$

which states that the reflection response coefficients are equal to the convolution of the reflection coefficients with the reverberation coefficients.

PROBLEMS FOR ARTICLE 10.2

1. Under the condition that the reflection coefficients are less than 0.1, that is $|\epsilon_n| < 0.1$,

    (a) Write down an expression for the impulse response h_n of a sedimentary system in terms of the reflection coefficients ϵ_n and the reverberation sequence b_n.

    (b) The reverberation polynomial $B_{0,N}(z)$ is minimum-delay as expected, since the sedimentary system is stable. Is there any reason why the feedforward polynomial $E_{0,N}(z)$ should be minimum-delay?

2. The sedimentary model discussed in this Article is an ARMA system. Determine whether or not the system is invertible.

3. Assume that the serial correlations $\gamma_1, \gamma_2, ..., \gamma_{N-1}$ of the sedimentary system are all zero. What are the corresponding poles of such a system?

10.3 Random reflection model

Each method of deconvolution is based upon a model of the geophysical structure, and the success of the method depends upon how well the conditions imposed by the model are met in practice. Let us now describe the random reflection model. In this model the seismic trace due to a spike source is given as the convolution

$$h_k = \sum_{j=0}^{N} \varepsilon_j b_{k-j}$$

This equation was derived in the last Article under the hypothesis of the sedimentary model. As we have seen the reverberation wavelet b_k is minimum-delay. The further hypothesis made for the random reflection model is that a segment of the reflection coefficient sequence represents an uncorrelated sequence. Let this segment be $\varepsilon_M, \varepsilon_{M+1}, \cdots, \varepsilon_{M+J}$. Then the corresponding segment of the seismic trace, namely, $h_M, h_{M+1}, \cdots, h_{M+J}$ represents the time series to be analyzed. This model has two characteristic features, namely:

(1) the statistical feature that the primary events ε_k are represented by a random uncorrelated series, and

(2) the deterministic feature that the reverberations b_k attached to the primary events have the same minimum-delay wavelet shape.

The observational data is in the form of the observed segment of a seismic trace recorded at the surface. If we compute the autocorrelation of this segment, the contribution from the random reflection series is averaged out (i.e. destroyed), and we are left with the autocorrelation of the reverberatory wavelet. We can then compute the prediction-error operator from this autocorrelation by solving a system of normal equations. Because the reverberatory wavelet is minimum-delay, this prediction-error operator is the operator that compresses the reverberatory wavelet to a spike, and hence is the required deconvolution operator. Thus the method of predictive deconvolution for this model consists of computing the prediction-error operator from the autocorrelation of the seismic trace, and then convolving the operator with the trace to yield the random-reflection series as the deconvolved trace. This deconvolved trace gives the required primary events which describe the deep subsurface structure.

Computation steps for seismic deconvolution

Let us now summarize the computational steps required for seismic deconvolution. These steps can be readily programmed for a digital computer. For more details, the reader is referred to the Appendix.

The sampled values of the received seismic trace are donoted by x_i. The subscript i denotes the discrete time index; for example, if the sampling were at 4 ms intervals then the trace reading x_2 would follow the reading x_1 by 4 ms in seismic time, etc.

Chapter 10. Seismic deconvolution

The *first step* is to compute the autocorrelation function of that portion of the sampled trace within a specified time gate. The autocorrelation coefficients ϕ_j are computed from the sampled trace by means of the formula

$$\phi_j = \Sigma x_{i+j} x_i$$

where the summation runs over all the time indices i within the time gate. Because $\phi_{-j} = \phi_j$ the autocorrelation coefficients need only be computed for nonnegative values of the time-shift index j.

Often it is useful to weight the autocorrelation by some set of tapered weighting factors w_j in order to obtain the weighted autocorrelation

$$r_j = w_j \phi_j.$$

A typical set of weighting factors would be the triangular weighting factors given by

$$w_j = \begin{cases} 1 - \frac{|j|}{N} & \text{for } |j| = 0,1,2,3,\cdots,N \\ 0 & \text{for } |j| = N+1, N+2, \ldots \end{cases}$$

Here N represents the time index at which the autocorrelation is truncated; the value of the parameter N must be specified.

The *second step* is to compute the coefficients of the prediction-error operator. According to the method of least squares the prediction operator is determined by minimizing the mean-square prediction error:

$$v = E(e_k^2)$$

where the prediction error is given by

$$e_k = a_0 x_k + a_1 x_{k-1} + \cdots + a_m x_{k-m} \quad, \text{ where } a_0 = 1.$$

The minimization leads to the set of simultaneous linear equations called the *normal equations*, which involve the autocorrelation coefficients that we have just computed as the knowns, and the prediction operator coefficients as the unknowns. The normal equations are

$$a_0 r_0 + a_1 r_1 + \cdots + a_m r_m = v$$
$$a_0 r_1 + a_1 r_0 + \cdots + a_m r_{m-1} = 0$$
$$a_0 r_m + a_1 r_{m-1} + \cdots + a_m r_0 = 0$$

These equations may be solved by an efficient recursive procedure called the Toeplitz recursion. Using this procedure the machine time required to solve the normal equations for a digital filter with m coefficients is proportional to m^2, as compared to m^3 for the conventional methods of solving simultaneous equations. Another advantage of using this recursive method is that it requires computer storage space proportional to m, rather than m^2 as in the case of the conventional methods.

A simplified treatment of the Toeplitz recursion (the general and auxiliary recursions) may be found in the Appendix.

It is the prediction-error operator that is the required inverse operator for deconvolving the seismic trace x_i. Accordingly the *third step* is to convolve the prediction-error operator with the seismic trace x_i; this computation is carried out according to the discrete convolution formula:

$$e_i = x_i + a_1 x_{i-1} + a_2 x_{i-2} + \cdots + a_m x_{i-m}$$

The result e_i is the prediction-error series which represents the deconvolved (but uncleaned) seismic trace.

Note: The "deconvolution" of the trace is accomplished by "convolving" the trace with the "inverse" operator, i.e. with the prediction-error operator.

The prediction-error operator is the least-squares inverse of the (minimum-delay) waveform b_t, and the prediction-error series represents the random spike series ε_t (i.e. the series designating the strengths and arrival times of the deep reflections).

All of the above, of course, holds within the limitations of statistical errors imposed by noise, computational approximation, and the finiteness of the data, and within the limitations of specification errors imposed by the model. The success of the method of seismic deconvolution, as we have discussed, depends largely upon the validity of the basic hypotheses as to the minimum-delay nature of the waveform b_t and the random nature of the spikes series ε_t. The beauty of the deconvolution method is that the only data required in order to perform the deconvolution is the received seismic trace.

In order to clean up the prediction-error series, we can apply a post-filtering operation to it. This post-filter can be some type of digital band-pass filter or a digital shaping filter. Instead of applying the post-filter to the prediction-error series, we can instead first cascade the prediction-error filter with the post-filter, and apply the cascaded filter to the received seismic trace. The final output will be the same in either case, namely the cleaned-up deconvolved seismic trace without reverberations.

PROBLEMS FOR ARTICLE 10.3

1. Show that the prediction-error operator is basically a noise-whitening filter.

2. Show that the autocorrelation of the seismic trace is equivalent to the autocorrelation of the reverberation wavelet to within a scale factor. Does this scale factor affect the solution of the normal equations associated with the prediction-error operator? Explain.

Chapter 10. Seismic deconvolution

10.4 Conclusions

Now that many successful digital seismic data processing methods have been developed it is appropriate at this time to look at some of the basic ideas of seismic deconvolution. In this chapter we have concentrated our attention on the fundamental concepts involved. It is possible to process seismic data successfully without knowledge of many of these underlying geophysical and mathematical concepts. However, if one is interested in getting the most useful information out of seismic data at a reasonable cost, if one is interested in extreme accuracy in the time domain, if one is concerned about the difference between a satisfactory deconvolution method and a better than satisfactory deconvolution method, then basic concepts become important and are worth learning about.

Inverse filtering or deconvolution has proved to be an effective way to increase the resolving power of the seismograph.

With the advent of the so-called "digital revolution" in exploration seismology in the early 1960's, much work has been done in this area, and further developments are still taking place.

In this chapter we have reviewed the method of deconvolution in terms of the basic concepts involved in relationship to the sedimentary earth model.

There are two basic approaches to seismology, namely the deterministic approach and the statistical approach. The deterministic approach is concerned with the building of mathematical and physical models of the layered earth in order to better understand seismic wave propagation. These models involve no random elements; they are completely deterministic. The statistical approach is concerned with the building of seismic models involving random components. For example, in the statistical model which we discussed, the depths and reflectivities of the deep reflecting horizons are considered to have a random distribution. A major justification for using the statistical approach in seismology is due to the fact that large amounts of data must be processed; any data in large enough quantities takes on a statistical character even if each individual piece of data is of a deterministic nature.

The model required for the application of seismic deconvolution is a statistical model. This model depends upon two basic hypotheses, namely, (1) the statistical hypothesis that the strengths and arrival times of the information-bearing events on a seismic trace can be represented as a random spike series, and (2) the deterministic hypothesis that the basic waveform associated with each of these events is minimum-phase. There are various ways of checking a model to see if it conforms with the physical situation This model has been studied carefully in the laboratory and been used in one form or another in virtually every oil exploration venture since the mid 1960's. The success of the usage of this model is attested to by the great volume of oil and gas discovered since that time. Each time an oil well is drilled and the sedimentary layers are revealed, the results of deconvolving seismic records by means of this model are put to the ultimate test. The model is meeting that test today as it has in the past. However, as long as our civilization is dependent upon oil and gas, improvements and refinements are always in demand.

Chapter 11. Speech deconvolution

11.1 Speech production

   Each method of deconvolution is based upon a model of the physical phenomenon, and the success of the method depends upon how well the conditions imposed by the model are met in practice. The word convolution means folding. Convolution represents the filtering operation performed by a physical system on the input in order to produce the output. The word deconvolution means unfolding. Deconvolution represents the inverse filtering operator performed on the previous output in order to regain the previous input. The important concepts are physical system, model and method. In this chapter the physical system is the human vocal tract which acts on the input at the glottis in order to produce speech at the lips. A model is a simplification of the physical system. A good model is one that retains the essential characteristics of the physical system for the purposes at hand. A method is a series of mathematical operations to be performed on the physical data to produce certain desired results. The logic of the method is based upon the model. In general, the better the model, the better the results. In comparing deconvolution methods, we must always be careful to be specific about what model is used.
   The prediction of future values from past observations has always been a major goal of time series analysis. However, in certain applications of time series analysis, it is not the predicted values but the prediction error that is of interest. In these cases, the prediction-error operator is the required deconvolution operator and the resulting prediction errors make up the deconvolved time series. In this chapter we consider the production of speech by the human vocal tract, the deconvolution of the speech signal, and the relationship of the vocal tract parameters to the deconvolution operator.
   Speech sounds are produced as the result of the excitation of the vocal tract. The vocal tract runs from the glottis in the throat to the lips. In order to produce a voiced sound, the vocal tract is excited by a series of nearly periodic pulses generated by the vocal cords. In order to produce an unvoiced sound, the vocal tract is excited by turbulent air which has the characteristics of white random noise. Each sound is the result of an appropriate excitation driving the vocal tract which has the appropriate shape for that sound. Different sounds are produced by varying the type of excitation and by varying the shape of the vocal tract by moving the tongue, velum, jaw, and lips. A simple model of the vocal tract is that of a time-varying linear filter. In practice the variations with time of the type of excitation and of the shape of the vocal tract can be accurately approximated by a succession of stationary segments. That is, the time series that represents the speech waveform can be cut up into a sequence of segments, where each segment can be treated as the result of passing a fixed excitation into a fixed vocal tract shape. Each segment represents an output which is equal to the convolution of the excitation and the impulse response of the vocal-tract shape. The problem of deconvolution is one of taking an observed

Chapter 11. Speech deconvolution

output segment of speech, and decomposing it into its excitation and its vocal-tract impulse response. The excitation can be characterized by a few numbers of parameters, namely the r.m.s. value of the excitation, a binary voiced-unvoiced parameter, and in the case of voiced sound, the pitch period. In other words, as it will turn out, the entire excitation waveform can be thrown away, and only certain of its rough features needs to be saved, because any excitation waveform of the same type and r.m.s. value will produce the same sound for a given vocal tract shape. That is, in producing a sound, the shaping is done by the vocal tract, and the air coming up from the lungs only has to be controlled as to its rough features. Thus one result of the deconvolution of a speech segment is the set of excitation parameters. The other result of the deconvolution is the set of parameters comprising the impulse response of the vocal tract shape. In practice as few as twelve parameters can be used to characterize the vocal tract shape. Thus the result of the deconvolution of the speech segment can be as few as 15 parameters, namely three excitation parameters and 12 vocal tract parameters. If each speech segment had 150 observations, then the result of deconvolution would replace these 150 observations by 15 parameters, a reduction of 10 to 1. In fact, a reduction of 50 to 1 seems to be a goal in speech analysis that is within reach.

Finally, the results of the deconvolution of speech can be evaluated by reconvolution. The excitation is generated as follows. The selection between a pulse sequence and a white-noise sequence is made by the voiced-unvoiced parameter. In the case of a voiced sound, a pulse train is generated with pitch period and r.m.s. value as given by the respective parameters. In the case of unvoiced sound, a white noise sequence is generated with r.m.s. value as given by the r.m.s. parameter. This constructed excitation function, which agrees with this actual excitation function resulting from the deconvolution only in regard to the rough features as given by the excitation parameters, is then convolved with the vocal-tract impulse response. The result is the reconvolved segment of speech. This convolution process is called reconvolution because a reconstructed excitation function is used instead of the original one. By attaching together all of the reconvolved segments, we obtain a reconvolved speech signal which can be compared to the original speech signal. It turns out that in listening tests, the quality of the reconvolved speech is very close to that of the original speech for a wide range of spoken text and a wide range of speakers, both male and female.

PROBLEMS FOR ARTICLE 11.1

1. Discuss and compare the propagation velocities and frequencies encountered in speech, seismic, and electromagnetic wave propagation.

11.2 Acoustic tube model

Thus the basic problem of speech analysis is one of deconvolution of each sound segment to separate its excitation function from its vocal tract shape. In order to solve this problem it is first necessary to obtain a good working model of the vocal tract. The model is based on an approximation to the vocal tract made up of a set of interconnected sections. Such a model is called an acoustic tube model. We assume that each section is cylindrical in shape, the sections are piled on top of each other, and each section has the same height. The cross-sectional area of each section varies according to the sound being uttered. For any given sound let the cross-sectional area of the nth section be denoted by S_n, where n runs from 1 to N. Let section 1 be the one closest to the glottis, and let section N be the one closest to the lips. For the purposes of description, we speak of the glottis as being at the left, and the lips as being at the right, of the horizontally lying tube made up of the N sections.

The acoustic tube can support travelling wave-motion from the glottis to the lips, which we call forward waves, and also travelling wave motion from the lips to the glottis, which we call backward waves. At each interface between two adjacent sections of the acoustic tube, a travelling wave will be partially reflected and partially transmitted, the division of energy between the reflected and transmitted being governed by the reflection coefficient associated with that interface. If S_n is the cross-sectional area of section n and S_{n+1} is the cross-sectional area of section n+1, then from physical considerations it can be shown that the reflection coefficient at the interface between sections n and n+1 is given by

$$\varepsilon_n = \frac{S_n - S_{n+1}}{S_n + S_{n+1}} \tag{1}$$

The interpretation of this reflection coefficient is as follows. Let us use the convention that all wave motion is measured in physical units that are equal to or proportional to the square-root of energy. Thus the square of the amplitude of a wave is in terms of energy. If a forward impulse of amplitude one is incident on the given interface, then a reflected impulse and a transmitted impulse are produced. The reflected impulse has amplitude ε_n and the transmitted impulse has amplitude τ_n. By the law of the conservation of energy the input energy 1^2 is equal to the output energy, namely the sum of the reflected energy ε_n^2 and the transmitted energy τ_n^2. Thus

$$1 = \varepsilon_n^2 + \tau_n^2$$

Solving for τ_n we have

$$\tau_n = \sqrt{1 - c_n^2}$$

Chapter 11. Speech deconvolution

The constant τ_n is called the (square-root energy) transmission coefficient. In the above example we considered a forward impulse. If instead we consider a backward impulse striking the same interface, the reflection coefficient becomes $-c_n$ and the transmission coefficient remains the same, namely $\tau_n = \sqrt{1-c_n^2}$.

Let us now consider the operation of the acoustic tube model. The source is the excitation function. The excitation function represents the forward waveform that enters at the left interface of section 1, namely at the glottis. This source gives rise to forward and backward wave motion in each section, due to the reflections and transmissions at each interface. In other words the vocal tract represents a reverberating system with the full array of multiple reflections. The velocity of sound waves is constant, and it is convenient to choose each section of the same length. Choose the length such that it takes exactly one-half time unit for a wave to travel from one side of the section to the other. In other words, the finer we choose the section length the smaller the time unit, and the grosser we choose the section length the larger the time unit.

At this point it is apparent that our acoustic tube model is mathematically the same as the sedimentary model given in the previous chapter, except that the acoustic model is on its side with forward and backward wave motion and the seismic model is standing up with downgoing and upgoing wave motion. As we have seen the seismogram represents the reflection response of the model to an impulsive source. On the other hand, human speech represents the transmission response of the model to the excitation function as source. Thus if we let $X(z)$ be the Laplace z-transform of the speech waveform, and let $S(z)$ be the Laplace z-transform of the excitation function, then

$$X(z) = T_{0,N} S(z) \qquad (2)$$

where the system transmission response is

$$T_{0,N} = \frac{\tau_0 \tau_1 \tau_2 \cdots \tau_N}{A_{0,N}} \qquad (3)$$

This result can be written in autoregressive form as

$$A_{0,N} X(z) = \tau_0 \tau_1 \tau_2 \cdots \tau_N\, S(z) \qquad (4)$$

which in the time-domain is

$$a_0 x_k + a_1 x_{k-1} + \cdots + a_N x_{k-N} = c\, s_k$$

where we have defined the constant c as $c = \tau_0 \tau_1 \tau_2 \cdots \tau_N$.

11.3 Conclusions

Speech represents the spoken word, whereas text represents the written word. When we read, we convert text to speech. When we write, we convert speech to text. However, there is an intermediate point between speech and text. This intermediate point is characterized by numbers, which we call parameters. Let us define speech analysis as the conversion of speech to the parameters, and define speech synthesis as the conversion of the parameters to speech. In this chapter we have given the methods that make speech analysis and synthesis possible with the digital computer technology available today.

Let us further define text analysis as the conversion of text to the parameters as required for speech synthesis. Also we define text synthesis as the conversion of the parameters as generated by speech analysis to text. Text analysis and text synthesis are not yet perfected but may be within the next few years. A combination of text analysis and speech synthesis would result in an automatic reading machine for which the input is printed text and the output is speech. A combination of speech analysis and text synthesis would result in an automatic writing machine for which the input is speech and the output is printed text.

At the present time both speech analysis and speech synthesis can be implemented by use of a digital computer. An application of speech analysis is an automatic speech recognition system. For example, an airplane pilot could speak into such a system and the result would be some desired action based on the recognition of his speech. Another application of speech analysis would be one of speaker identification or verification. An application of both speech analysis and synthesis would be secure voice transmission; that is, the sender's speech would be analyzed into its parameters, the parameters would be transmitted, and the receiver would synthesize the speech from the parameters. Another application of speech analysis and synthesis is the data-rate compression of speech. If speech is transmitted simply by sampling and digitizing, the data-rate required is 100,000 bits per second of speech. The parameters, however, can represent a reduction of about 50 to 1 so that by transmitting the parameters instead the data-rate required would only be 2000 bits per second of speech. A third application of speech analysis and synthesis would be speech retrieval systems. In this application the results of the analysis of speech are stored on a computer. A person could telephone the computer, and the computer would synthesize the stored parameters into speech which the person would hear on the telephone in answer to his questions.

Chapter 11. Speech deconvolution

DECONVOLUTION OF TIME SERIES
AS APPLIED TO SPEECH

ENDERS A. ROBINSON
Lincoln, Massachusetts

The vocal tract shape and the excitation function that drives the vocal tract can be obtained from the human speech signal by deconvolution. The speech-producing acoustic tube model of the vocal tract is a deep-source model. If the corresponding surface-source model is constructed, then the sound waves in this model are the physical embodiments of the recursive method of solving the normal equations for the deconvolution operator.

1. INTRODUCTION

Human speech is produced as the result of passing air from the lungs through the vocal tract. The vocal tract is a non-uniform acoustic tube that extends from the glottis to the lips. Each sound produced at the lips is the resultant of two factors, namely (1) the type of wave motion used to excite the vocal tract and (2) the shape of the vocal tract. For example, in order to produce a voiced sound, the excitation function is a series of periodic pulses generated by the vocal cords. In order to produce an unvoiced sound, the excitation function is white random noise generated by turbulent air. These are the two main types of excitation functions that are inputs into the vocal tract at the glottis. The various sounds that are outputs from the vocal tract at the lips are produced by changing the shape of the vocal tract by moving the lips, jaw, tongue, and velum.

A particular sound at the lips represents a segment of a stationary time series that is produced by a given type of excitation function and a given shape of the vocal tract. More specifically, a particular sound is equal to the convolution of its excitation function with the impulse response function of the vocal tract shape. We can make this statement because the vocal tract acts like a linear filter in producing speech.

The problem of deconvolution is one of decomposing the observed output sound into its excitation function and its vocal-tract impulse response. As it turns out, the actual shape of the excitation function is not important, so only the gross features of the excitation function need to be saved, such as (1) its r.m.s. amplitude, (2) knowledge of whether it is a pulse train (in case of a voiced sound) or whether it is random (in case of an unvoiced sound) and (3) the period of the pulses (in case of a voiced sound). That is, the excitation function can be characterized by three parameters, namely (1) r.m.s. value, (2) a binary voiced-unvoiced parameter, and (3) in case of a voiced sound, the pitch period. It also turns out that the vocal-tract impulse response can be characterized by as few as 12 numbers. Thus the result of the deconvolution of a particular sound can be as few as 15 parameters, namely 3 excitation parameters and 12 vocal-tract parameters. Since the sound in question would be represented by a time series of several hundreds or thousands of observations, and since deconvolution would replace these observations by 15 parameters characterizing that sound, this approach results in a considerable reduction of the data. In fact, a reduction of 50 to 1 seems to be a goal in speech analysis that is within reach. Another goal is the identification of the parameters representing a sound with the phonetic symbol for that sound, so that an automatic typewriter could be constructed that would type out printed text from the spoken word.

Finally the results of the deconvolution of speech can be evaluated by reconvolution. For each sound an excitation function is generated from its parameters. This excitation function is convolved with the vocal-tract impulse response function to produce the output time-series segment for that sound. This convolution process is called reconvolution because we are not using the original excitation function but a reconstructed one which agrees with the original in its gross features only. The result of this process is the reconvolved sound. By attaching together all these reconvolved sound segments, we obtain the reconvolved speech signal which can be compared to the original speech signal. Experimental listening tests with various auditors establish that the quality of the reconvolved speech is very close to that of the original speech for a wide range of spoken messages and for many different speakers both male and female.

X-Ray techniques have been used as a direct method of determining the vocal tract shape. Wakita (1973) gave a mathematical method for extracting the vocal-tract shape by showing the relationship of the acoustic tube model to the recursive method given in Robinson (1967) for solving the normal equations. In this paper we show that the vocal tract shape and the excitation function can be obtained from the speech signal by deconvolution. We make use of a constructive proof that relates the speech-producing acoustic tube model, which is a deep-source model, to the corresponding surface-source acoustic tube model. In this way we can physically construct the recursive method for solving the normal equations from the acoustic properties of the system, and can physically obtain the autocorrelation, the prediction error operators, and the reflection coefficients in terms of the model.

Because of the limitation of space, we have been forced to make some of our derivations in this paper quite brief. For background material on the model and the polynomial manipulations, the reader is referred to Robinson (1967, Chapter 3).

Chapter 11. Speech deconvolution

DECONVOLUTION OF TIME SERIES AS APPLIED TO SPEECH

2. ACOUSTIC TUBE MODEL

The acoustic tube model is an approximation to the vocal tract consisting of a set of interconnected cylindrical sections piled on top of each other. See Figure 1. Each section may have a different cross-sectional area but has the same height. The cross-sectional areas vary according to the sound being uttered. For any given sound let the cross-sectional area of the nth section be denoted by S_n, where n runs from 1 to N. We let section 1 be the closest to the lips, and let section N be the one closest to the glottis. For the purposes of description, we speak of the lips as being at the top, and the glottis as being at the bottom, of the vertically standing tube made up of the N sections.

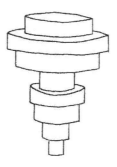

Fig. 1

The acoustic tube can support travelling wave-motion from the glottis to the lips, which we call upgoing waves, and also travelling wave-motion from the lips to the glottis, which we call downgoing waves. At each interface between two adjacent sections of the acoustic tube, a travelling wave will be partially reflected and partially transmitted, the division of energy between the reflected and transmitted portions being governed by the reflection coefficient associated with that interface. Let n denote the interface between sections n and n+1, and let c_n denote the refelction coefficient of this interface. The interpretation of this reflection coefficient is as follows. Let us use the convention that all wave motion is measured in physical units that are proportional to the square-root of energy. Thus the square of the amplitude of a wave is in terms of energy. If a downgoing impulse of unit amplitude is incident on the given interface, then a reflected impulse and a transmitted impulse are produced. See Figure 2.

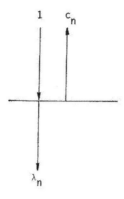

Fig. 2

The reflected impulse has implitude c_n and the transmitted impulse has amplitude λ_n. By the law of the conservation of energy, the input energy is equal to the output energy, namely the sum of the reflected energy and the transmitted energy, that is

$$1^2 = c_n^2 + \lambda_n^2 .$$

Solving for λ_n we have

$$\lambda_n = \sqrt{1 - c_n^2}$$

The constant λ_n is called the (square-root energy) transmission coefficient. In the above example we considered a downgoing impulse. If instead we consider an upgoing impulse striking the same interface, the reflection coefficient becomes $-c_n$ and the transmission coefficient remains the same. See Figure 3.

Let us now consider the operation of the acoustic tube model in producing speech. The source is the excitation function which represents an upgoing waveform that enters at the lower interface N, namely at the glottis. As a result, speech production represents a deep-source acoustic tube model. This deep source gives rise to upgoing and downgoing wave motion in each section, due to the reflections and transmissions at each interface. In other words, the excited vocal tract represents a reverberating system. When we reach interface 0 (namely, the lips) we meet a *boundary condition*, because the lips are connected to the open air which has infinite cross-sectional area. As a result there is perfect reflection at the lips. If we assume that our wave motion is related to pressure, then

DECONVOLUTION OF TIME SERIES AS APPLIED TO SPEECH   451

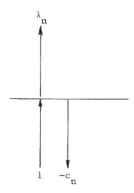

Fig. 3

the pressure must vanish at the lips, so at the lips the downgoing wave in section 1 is the negative of the upgoing wave in section 1.

The velocity of sound waves is constant, and it is convenient to choose the common height of each section such that it takes exactly one-half discrete time unit for a wave to travel from one face of the section to the other. We introduce the unit delay operator z. The delay operator z is defined as that operator which delays a time variable by one time unit. It follows that $z^{\frac{1}{2}}$ is the operator that delays a time variable by one-half time unit, namely the one-way travel time through a section.

For the deep-source model let $x_n(t)$ and $y_n(t)$ be the downgoing and upgoing waves respectively at the top of section n, and let $x'_n(t)$ and $y'_n(t)$ be the corresponding waves at the bottom of section n. See Figure 4.

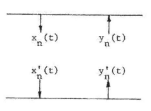

Fig. 4

Then we have

$$\begin{bmatrix} x_n'(t) \\ y_n'(t) \end{bmatrix} = \begin{bmatrix} z^{\frac{1}{2}} & 0 \\ 0 & z^{-\frac{1}{2}} \end{bmatrix} \begin{bmatrix} x_n(t) \\ y_n(t) \end{bmatrix}$$

Here and throughout, the variable t is the discrete time variable.

The waves at interface n are shown in Figure 5. They can be related as follows. See Figure 6. The wave $y_n'(t)$ is made up of a part due to the reflection of $x_n'(t)$ and a part due to the transmission of $y_{n+1}(t)$, that is,

$$y_n'(t) = c_n x_n'(t) + \lambda_n y_{n+1}(t).$$

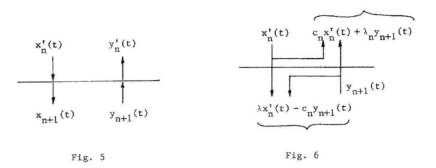

Fig. 5 Fig. 6

The wave $x_{n+1}(t)$ is made up of a part due to the reflection of $y_{n+1}(t)$ and a part due to the transmission of $x_n'(t)$, that is

$$x_{n+1}(t) = - c_n y_{n+1}(t) + \lambda_n x_n'(t).$$

If we solve these two equations for the unprimed quantities we obtain

$$\begin{bmatrix} x_{n+1}(t) \\ y_{n+1}(t) \end{bmatrix} = \frac{1}{\lambda_n} \begin{bmatrix} 1 & -c_n \\ -c_n & 1 \end{bmatrix} \begin{bmatrix} x_n'(t) \\ y_n'(t) \end{bmatrix}$$

Combining this matrix equation with the previous matrix equation, we obtain the *scattering equation*:

$$\begin{bmatrix} x_{n+1}(t) \\ y_{n+1}(t) \end{bmatrix} = \frac{z^{-\frac{1}{2}}}{\lambda_n} \begin{bmatrix} z & -c_n \\ -c_n z & 1 \end{bmatrix} \begin{bmatrix} x_n(t) \\ y_n(t) \end{bmatrix}$$

The z-transform of the scattering equation is

$$\begin{bmatrix} X_{n+1}(z) \\ Y_{n+1}(z) \end{bmatrix} = \frac{z^{-\frac{1}{2}}}{\lambda_n} \begin{bmatrix} z & -c_n \\ -c_n z & 1 \end{bmatrix} \begin{bmatrix} X_n(z) \\ Y_n(z) \end{bmatrix}$$

The z-transform is defined as

$$X_n(z) = \Sigma\, x_n(t) z^t$$

where the summation is over all discrete t values. That is, the z-transform of a time sequence denoted by a lower case letter is denoted by the corresponding capital letter. For simplicity, we often drop the argument z, so $X_n(z)$ would be simply X_n. A bar over a z-transform indicates that each z in the z-transform has been replaced by z^{-1}, that is $\bar{X}_n = X_n(z^{-1})$.

If we assume that the time sequence $x_n(t)$ has finite energy, then the quantity $X_n \bar{X}_n$ represents the energy spectrum of the time sequence $x_n(t)$; that is, $X_n \bar{X}_n$ is the z-transform of the autocorrelation of $x_n(t)$. From the scattering equation we obtain

$$X_{n+1} \bar{X}_{n+1} - Y_{n+1} \bar{Y}_{n+1} = X_n \bar{X}_n - Y_n \bar{Y}_n$$

which says that the net downgoing energy in section n+1 is equal to the net downgoing energy in section n. A recursive application of this result shows that the net downgoing energy in any two sections is the same, provided of course that there are no energy sources or sinks between the two sections in question.

The polynomials P_n and Q_n are defined as

$$\begin{bmatrix} P_n^R & Q_n^R \\ Q_n & P_n \end{bmatrix} = \begin{bmatrix} z & -c_n \\ -c_n z & 1 \end{bmatrix} \begin{bmatrix} z & -c_{n-1} \\ -c_{n-1} z & 1 \end{bmatrix} \cdots \begin{bmatrix} z & -c_1 \\ -c_1 z & 1 \end{bmatrix}$$

where the polynomial P^R is the reverse of P_n and Q_n^R is the reverse of Q_n, that is

$$P_n^R = z^n \bar{P}_n, \qquad Q_n^R = z^n Q_n$$

We also define $\sigma_n = \lambda_n \lambda_{n-1} \cdots \lambda_1$ and $A_n = P_n - Q_n$. We note that in the polynomial A_n the coefficient of z^0 is one and the coefficient of z^n is c_n. The recursive use of the scattering equation gives

$$\begin{bmatrix} X_{n+1} \\ Y_{n+1} \end{bmatrix} = \frac{z^{-n/2}}{\sigma_n} \begin{bmatrix} P_n^R & Q_n^R \\ Q_n & P_n \end{bmatrix} \begin{bmatrix} X_1 \\ Y_1 \end{bmatrix}$$

3. DEEP SOURCE MODEL

We are interested in the impulse response of the acoustic tube in the case of speech, that is, in the case of a deep source. If we let the upgoing wave at the glottis be a unit impulse, that is, if we let $Y_{N+1} = 1$, and if we impose the boundary condition of perfect reflection $Y_1 = -X_1$ at the lips (see Figure 7), we obtain

$$\begin{bmatrix} X_{N+1} \\ 1 \end{bmatrix} = \frac{z^{-N/2}}{\sigma_N} \begin{bmatrix} P_N^R & Q_N^R \\ Q_N & P_N \end{bmatrix} \begin{bmatrix} X_1 \\ -X_1 \end{bmatrix}$$

which gives

$$1 = -\frac{z^{-N/2}}{\sigma_N} (P_N - Q_N) X_1 .$$

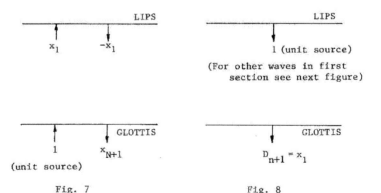

Fig. 7   Fig. 8

Chapter 11. Speech deconvolution

DECONVOLUTION OF TIME SERIES AS APPLIED TO SPEECH

Thus the impulse response of the vocal tract is

$$X_1 = -\frac{\sigma_N z^{N/2}}{P_N - Q_N} = -\frac{\sigma_N z^{N/2}}{A_N}$$

4. SURFACE-SOURCE MODEL

Speech is produced by an acoustic tube subject to a deep source. Let us now consider the same acoustic tube but subject to a surface source. More specifically, we want to find the downgoing response D_{N+1} at the glottis subject to a downgoing unit impulsive source at the lips. See Figure 8. In the previous section we have found the vocal-tract impulse response, namely the upgoing response X_1 at the lips subject to an upgoing unit impulse source at the glottis. The physical principle of reciprocity states that if we interchange source and receiver we observe the same waveform. Thus the above two responses are the same, i.e. $D_{N+1} = X_1$. We note that no energy is reflected back from the glottis in this surface-source model, so the upgoing waveform at the glottis is zero, i.e. $U_{N+1} = 0$. The net downgoing energy in the glottis is therefore

$$D_{N+1} \bar{D}_{N+1} - U_{N+1} \bar{U}_{N+1} = D_{N+1} \bar{D}_{N+1} = X_1 \bar{X}_1.$$

Let us now look at the first section of the surface-source model (i.e. the section at the lips). The downgoing impulsive source can be represented by the Kronecker delta function δ_t at the top of the first section. This source gives rise to an upgoing wave in the first section as a result of internal reflections from interfaces below; we denote this upcoming wave by $-r_1, -r_2, -r_3, \ldots$ where the subscript represents the time of occurrence. Because the top interface (i.e. the lips) is a perfect reflector, this upgoing wave is reflected at the lips back into the downgoing wave $r_1, r_2, r_3, \ldots$ Thus the entire downgoing wave in section 1 is made up of the downgoing impulse δ_t and the reflected wave $r_1, r_2, r_3, \ldots$; that is $\delta_t + r_t$. The z-transform of this downgoing wave is

$$D_1 = 1 + R$$

The upgoing wave in section 1 is $-r_t$ with z-transform

$$U_1 = -R$$

See Figure 9.

The net downgoing energy in section 1 is

$$D_1 \bar{D}_1 - U_1 \bar{U}_1 = (1+R)(1+\bar{R}) - R\bar{R} = 1 + R + \bar{R}$$

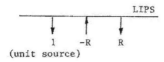

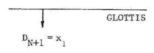

Fig. 9

which is equal to the net downgoing energy in the glottis, that is

$$X_1 \bar{X}_1 = 1 + R + \bar{R}$$

Thus we see that $1 + R + \bar{R}$ is the z-transform of the autocorrelation of $x_1(t)$. That is, the autocorrelation of the impulse response function $x_1(t)$ of the vocal tract for speech is

$$\ldots, r_2, r_1, 1, r_1, r_2, \ldots$$

where 1 is the autocorrelation coefficient for lag 0, r_1 for lag -1 and also for lag 1, and so on.

5. NORMAL EQUATIONS

In the surface source model let $d_{n+1}(t)$ and $u_{n+1}(t)$ denote the downgoing and upgoing waves respectively at the top of section n+1, and let their respective z-transforms be D_{n+1} and U_{n+1}. Then the scattering equation gives

$$\begin{bmatrix} D_{n+1} \\ U_{n+1} \end{bmatrix} = \frac{z^{-n/2}}{\sigma_n} \begin{bmatrix} P_n^R & Q_n^R \\ Q_n & P_n \end{bmatrix} \begin{bmatrix} 1 + R \\ -R \end{bmatrix}$$

In this equation we first solve for D_{n+1} and U_{n+1}, from which we find that

$$\bar{D}_{n+1} - U_{n+1} = \frac{z^{-n/2}}{\sigma_n} A_n (1 + R + \bar{R})$$

which is

$$A_n (1 + R + \bar{R}) = z^{n/2} \sigma_n (\bar{D}_{n+1} - U_{n+1}).$$

The function D_{n+1} is the z-transform of the downgoing wave at the top of section n+1 in the surface source model. This downgoing wave is made up of the direct pulse $d_{n+1}(\frac{n}{2})$ together with succeeding pulses $d_{n+1}(\frac{n}{2}+1)$, $d_{n+1}(\frac{n}{2}+2)$, ... Because the direct pulse is the result of transmissions through the first n interfaces, the direct pulse is equal to the product of the first n transmission coefficients, i.e.

$$d_{n+1}(\tfrac{n}{2}) = \lambda_1 \lambda_2 \ldots \lambda_n = \sigma_n$$

and the time of the direct pulse is n/2. Thus

$$D_n = \sigma_n z^{n/2} + \text{terms in higher powers of } z.$$

The function U_{n+1} is the z-transform of the upgoing wave at the top of section n+1. The first pulse in the upgoing wave is the reflection of the direct downgoing pulse at interface n+1. Thus the magnitude of this pulse is $\sigma_n c_{n+1}$; that is, the magnitude is equal to the magnitude of the direct downgoing pulse times the reflection coefficient. Because one time unit elapses for the round trip in section n+1, the first pulse of the upgoing wave occurs at one time unit later than the first pulse of the downgoing wave in section n+1; that is, the first upgoing pulse at the top of section n+1 occurs at $\frac{n}{2} + 1$. Thus

$$U_{n+1} = \sigma_n c_{n+1} z^{\frac{n}{2}+1} + \text{terms in higher powers of } z.$$

We therefore have

$$A_n(1 + R + \bar{R}) = \sigma_n (\text{terms in negative powers of } z + \sigma_n - \sigma_n c_{n+1} z^{n+1} - \text{terms in higher powers of } z)$$

We note that the powers of z from 1 to n are missing on the right-hand side of the above equation; it is this fact that allows us to extract the normal equations. More specifically, let us now equate coefficients on each side of this equation for the powers of z from 0 to n+1. We obtain

$$a_{n0} r_0 + a_{n1} r_1 + \ldots + a_{nn} r_n = \sigma_n^2$$
$$a_{n0} r_1 + a_{n1} r_0 + \ldots + a_{nn} r_{n-1} = 0$$
$$\ldots$$
$$a_{n0} r_n + a_{n1} r_{n-1} + \ldots + a_{nn} r_0 = 0$$
$$a_{n0} r_{n+1} + a_{n1} r_n + \ldots + a_{nn} r_1 = -c_{n+1} \sigma_n^2$$

where $a_{no}, a_{n1}, \ldots, a_{nn}$ are the coefficients of A_n.

We note that $r_o \equiv 1$ and $a_{no} \equiv 1$.

Let us now look at these equations. The time function r_t is the autocorrelation of the vocal-tract impulse response function $x_1(t)$ for speech. Thus the first n+1 of these equations are the normal equations for the prediction-error operator $a_{no}, a_{n1}, \ldots, a_{nn}$. The last of these equations allows us to find c_{n+1}, and we shall make use of this fact in the next section.

By the definition of P_n and Q_n we have

$$\begin{bmatrix} P^R_{n+1} & Q^R_{n+1} \\ Q_{n+1} & P_{n+1} \end{bmatrix} = \begin{bmatrix} z & -c_{n+1} \\ -c_{n+1}z & 1 \end{bmatrix} \begin{bmatrix} P^R_n & Q^R_n \\ Q_n & P_n \end{bmatrix}$$

which gives the recursions

$$P_{n+1} = P_n - c_{n+1} \, z \, Q^R_n$$

$$Q_{n+1} = Q_n - c_{n+1} \, z \, P^R_n$$

Because $A_n = P_n - Q_n$ we can subtract the above two equations to obtain the *polynomial recursion*

$$A_{n+1} = A_n + c_{n+1} \, z \, A^R_n$$

where $A^R_n = P^R_n - Q^R_n = z^n \bar{A}$. Thus if we know A_n and c_{n+1} we can compute the polynomial A_{n+1}.

6. DECONVOLUTION OF SPEECH

As we have seen, each sound in speech is produced by the convolution of excitation function with vocal-tract impulse response function. In case the excitation function is white noise, it follows that the autocorrelation of the vocal-tract impulse response function can be approximated by the autocorrelation of the sound signal. In case the excitation function is a periodic pulse sequence, the autocorrelation of the vocal-tract impulse response function also can be derived approximately from knowledge of the autocorrelation of the sound signal. Thus the first step in the deconvolution of a sound signal measured at the lips is to compute its autocorrelation which is then used to approximate the autocorrelation

$$\ldots, r_2, r_1, 1, r_1, r_2, \ldots \quad \text{(where } r_o \equiv 1\text{)}$$

of the impulse-response function of the vocal tract.

The next step is to compute the sequence of prediction error operators and reflection coefficients for n=1 to N. Initially, we have

$$a_{oo} = 1$$
$$\sigma_o^2 = a_{oo} r_o = 1 .$$

Then given the prediction error operator $a_{no}, \ldots, a_{nn}$ and σ_n^2 we compute the reflection coefficient

$$c_{n+1} = -(a_{no} r_{n+1} + a_{n1} r_n + \ldots + a_{nn} r_1) / \sigma_n^2 ,$$

the variance

$$\sigma_{n+1}^2 = \lambda_{n+1}^2 \sigma_n^2 = (1 - c_{n+1}^2) \sigma_n^2$$

and the new prediction error operator by the polynomial recursion

$$a_{n+1,o} = a_{no} = 1$$
$$a_{n+1,1} = a_{n1} + c_{n+1} a_{nn}$$
$$\ldots$$
$$a_{n+1,n} = a_{nn} + c_{n+1} a_{n1}$$
$$a_{n+1,n+1} = c_{n+1} a_{no} = c_{n+1}$$

Using this recursive algorithm we can compute the reflection coefficients $c_1, c_2, \ldots, c_N$ of the vocal tract. These reflection coefficients are related to the cross-sectional areas $S_1, S_2, \ldots, S_N$ of the vocal tract by the equation

$$c_n = \frac{S_n - S_{n+1}}{S_n + S_{n+1}}$$

Solving this equation for S_{n+1} we have

$$S_{n+1} = \frac{1 - c_n}{1 + c_n} S_n$$

Thus given the cross-sectional area S_1 at the lips we can compute in a stepwise fashion the areas of all the sections from the lips to the glottis. Thus the deconvolution process has given us the shape of the vocal tract.

The final prediction error operator $a_{N0}, a_{N1}, \ldots, a_{NN}$ is the required deconvolution operator. This statement follows from the fact that the impulse response function of the vocal tract, as we have seen, is

$$X_1 = -\frac{\sigma_N z^{N/2}}{A_N}$$

If E is the z-transform of the excitation function then the z-transform of the sound signal at the lips is $X_1 E$. The z-transform of the deconvolution operator is A_N. The z-transform of the deconvolved sound signal is

$$A_N X_1 E = -\sigma_N z^{N/2} E$$

Since σ_N represents a scale factor and $z^{N/2}$ represents a delay (both of which we know), the deconvolution has yielded E. That is, the deconvolution of the sound signal yields the excitation function.

7. CONCLUSION

The deconvolution of a sound produced in speech yields the reflection coefficients, or equivalently the cross-sectional areas, which make up the numerical parameters necessary to characterize the vocal tract shape for that sound. The deconvolution also yields the excitation function which drives the vocal tract for that sound. In order to establish the results, we have made use of an acoustic tube model with a source at the lips, as this model physically gives us the autocorrelation of the vocal tract impulse response, the normal equations for the prediction error operators, and the reflection coefficients.

REFERENCES

[1] ROBINSON, ENDERS A. (1967). *Multichannel Time Series Analysis with Digital Computer Programs*. Holden-Day Publishing Co., San Francisco.

[2] WAKITA, HISASHI (1973). Direct estimation of the vocal tract shape by inverse filtering of acoustic speech waveforms. *IEEE Transactions on Audio and Electroacoustics*, AU-21, 417-427.

Appendix A

The Toeplitz recursion

The solution of the least squares optimum filtering problem involves solving a set of simultaneous equations called the *normal equations*. In general, there will be one equation for each coefficient in the filter. The requirements for computer time and computer storage space for solving these equations by use of a standard simultaneous equations routine is prohibitive, except in the case of a small number of filter coefficients. The Toeplitz recursion gives a more efficient scheme for arriving at the desired filter coefficients.

This scheme makes use of the special form of the autocorrelation matrix ϕ, called the Toeplitz form. This form can be written as

$$\phi = \begin{bmatrix} \phi_0 & \phi_1 & \phi_2 & \cdots & \phi_M \\ \phi_1 & \phi_0 & \phi_1 & \cdots & \phi_{M-1} \\ \phi_2 & \phi_1 & \phi_0 & \cdots & \phi_{M-2} \\ \vdots & & & & \vdots \\ \phi_M & \phi_{M-1} & \phi_{M-2} & \cdots & \phi_0 \end{bmatrix}$$

All terms along each diagonal are the same. Thus, given the entries in the top row of ϕ, the matrix ϕ is fully specified.

The Toeplitz recursion involves initially finding a filter of length one, using this filter to find a filter of length two, and so on, until the desired length filter is reached. The principal advantages of using the recursive techniques are time and space savings. The standard solution of simultaneous equations requires time proportional to m^3 and space proportional to m^2. The recursive technique reduces these requirements to m^2 and m for time and space respectively. An important side benefit for using this scheme is that we can compute the mean-square error at each step of the process. This allows us to formulate a criterion for determining the length of the filter. As the filter becomes longer, the mean-square error will decrease and then level off at some filter length M.

The Toeplitz recursion is a classic recursion occurring in the theory of polynomials orthogonal on the unit circle. The scheme given here includes a recursive formula for the mean-square error as well as for the filter coefficients.

The normal equations for a scalar process are

$$\sum_{k=0}^{M} h_k \phi_{j-k} = g_j \quad (j = 0,1,2,\ldots,M)$$

where the h_k are the filter coefficients, the ϕ_{j-k} are the autocorrelation coefficients, and the g_j are the cross-correlation coefficients. Associated with the normal equations are the normal equations for the unit-step prediction-error operator a_k:

$$\sum_{k=0}^{M} a_k \phi_{j-k} = \begin{cases} v, & \text{when } j = 0 \\ 0, & \text{when } j = 1, 2, \ldots, M \end{cases}$$

where $a_0 \equiv 1$ and v is the mean-square error or *prediction-error variance*.

The hindsight operator is one which "predicts" past values of a time series from future values. For the scalar case, the unit-step hindsight-error operator b_k is just the reverse of the unit-step prediction-error operator since ϕ is symmetric; that is,

$$\begin{bmatrix} b_0 \\ b_1 \\ \cdot \\ \cdot \\ \cdot \\ b_M \end{bmatrix} = \begin{bmatrix} a_M \\ a_{M-1} \\ \cdot \\ \cdot \\ \cdot \\ a_0 \end{bmatrix}$$

The scheme for extending the unit-step prediction-error operator $\underline{a} = (a_0, a_1, \ldots, a_M)$ to the new unit-step prediction-error operator $a'_0, a'_1, \ldots, a'_{M+1}$ involving one more coefficients is first to extend $\underline{a}$ by adding a zero to the right end of $\underline{a}$:

$$\begin{bmatrix} \phi_0 & \cdots & \phi_{M+1} \\ & \cdots & \\ \phi_{M+1} & \cdots & \phi_0 \end{bmatrix} \begin{bmatrix} a_0 \\ a_1 \\ \cdots \\ a_M \\ 0 \end{bmatrix} = \begin{bmatrix} v \\ 0 \\ \cdots \\ 0 \\ d \end{bmatrix}$$

The quantity d is called the discrepancy, defined as the dot product

$$d = \phi_{M+1} a_0 + \phi_M a_1 + \cdots + \phi_1 a_M$$

If the discrepancy is zero, then the extended prediction-error operator is the correct one. Generally, the discrepancy will not be zero, so the next step is to modify the coefficients of the extended operator so as to cancel out the discrepancy. We do this by adding a weighted version of the extended hindsight-error operator to the extended prediction-error operator. Thus, we obtain

Appendix A

$$\begin{bmatrix} \phi_0 & \cdots & \phi_{M+1} \\ & & \\ & \cdots & \\ & & \\ \phi_{M+1} & \cdots & \phi_0 \end{bmatrix} \begin{bmatrix} a_0 \\ a_1-ca_M \\ \cdots \\ a_M-ca_0 \\ -ca_0 \end{bmatrix} = \begin{bmatrix} v-cd \\ 0 \\ \cdots \\ 0 \\ d-cv \end{bmatrix}$$

The quantity $d-cv$ is set equal to zero in order to determine the value of c:

$$c = \frac{d}{v}$$

That is, c is equal to the ratio of the discrepancy d to the prediction-error variance v. The new operator is thus

$$\begin{bmatrix} a_0' \\ a_1' \\ \cdot \\ \cdot \\ a_M' \\ a_{M+1}' \end{bmatrix} = \begin{bmatrix} a_0 \\ a_1-ca_M \\ \cdot \\ \cdot \\ a_M-ca_1 \\ -ca_0 \end{bmatrix} = \begin{bmatrix} 1 \\ a_1-ca_M \\ \cdot \\ \cdot \\ a_M-ca_1 \\ -c \end{bmatrix}$$

and the new prediction-error variance is

$$v' = v-cd = v-c(cv) = v(1-c^2)$$

We now use the new prediction-error operator to extend the length of the filter $\underline{h} = (h_0, h_1, \ldots, h_M)$. As before, we make a first approximation to $\underline{h}'$ by adding a zero to the right end of $\underline{h}$:

$$\begin{bmatrix} \phi_0 & \cdots & \phi_{M+1} \\ & & \\ & \cdots & \\ & & \\ \phi_{M+1} & \cdots & \phi_0 \end{bmatrix} \begin{bmatrix} h_0 \\ h_1 \\ \cdots \\ h_M \\ 0 \end{bmatrix} = \begin{bmatrix} g_0 \\ g_1 \\ \cdot \\ \cdot \\ g_M \\ q \end{bmatrix}$$

where q is defined as the dot product

$$q = \phi_{M+1}h_0 + \phi_M h_1 + \cdots + \phi_1 h_M$$

If we weight and add the new hindsight-error operator to the above extended filter we get

$$\begin{bmatrix} \phi_0 & \cdots & \phi_{M+1} \\ & \cdots & \\ & \cdots & \\ \phi_{M+1} & \cdots & \phi_0 \end{bmatrix} \begin{bmatrix} h_0 - s\, a'_{M+1} \\ h_1 - s\, a'_M \\ \cdots \\ h_M - s\, a'_1 \\ -s\, a'_0 \end{bmatrix} = \begin{bmatrix} g_0 \\ g_1 \\ \cdots \\ g_M \\ q - sv' \end{bmatrix}$$

Now we choose the constant s such that

$$q - sv' = g_{M+1}$$

That is, if we define s as

$$s = \frac{q - g_{M+1}}{v'}$$

then the new filter is

$$\begin{bmatrix} h'_0 \\ h'_1 \\ \cdot \\ \cdot \\ \cdot \\ h'_M \\ h'_{M+1} \end{bmatrix} = \begin{bmatrix} h_0 - s\, a'_{M+1} \\ h_1 - s\, a'_M \\ \cdot \\ \cdot \\ \cdot \\ h_M - s\, a'_1 \\ -s\, a'_0 \end{bmatrix} = \begin{bmatrix} h_0 - s\, a'_{M+1} \\ h_1 - s\, a'_M \\ \cdot \\ \cdot \\ \cdot \\ h_M - s\, a'_1 \\ -s \end{bmatrix}$$

In summary, the Toeplitz recursion consists of two parts, namely, the *general Toeplitz recursion* which solves for the filter coefficients $h_0, h_1, \ldots, h_M$ associated with the normal equations

$$\sum_{k=0}^{M} h_k \phi_{j-k} = g_j \quad (j = 0, 1, 2, \ldots, M)$$

and the *auxillary Toeplitz recursion* which solves for the prediction-error operator $a_0, a_1, a_2, \ldots, a_M$ associated with the normal equations

$$\sum_{k=0}^{M} a_k \phi_{j-k} = \begin{cases} v, & j = 0 \\ 0, & j = 1, 2, \ldots, M \end{cases}$$

where $a_0 = 1$ and v = the corresponding mean-square error or prediction-error variance. Thus, the solution of the general least-squares filtering problem and the solution of the prediction-error operator go hand in hand.

Appendix A

BIBLIOGRAPHY

DIGITAL SIGNAL PROCESSING

Oppenheim, Alan V. and Ronald W. Schafer. *Digital Signal Processing*, Prentice-Hall, Englewood Cliffs, N.J., 1975.

Rabiner, L. R. and B. Gold. *Theory and Applications of Digital Signal Processing*. Prentice-Hall, Englewood Cliffs, N.J., 1975.

Robinson, Enders A. *Statistical Communication and Detection, with Special Reference to Digital Data Processing of Radar and Seismic Signals*, Charles Griffin and Co., London, and Hafner, N.Y., 1967.

FOURIER TRANSFORMATION

Bogert, B. P. et al. *Special Issue on Fast Fourier Transform and Its Application to Digital Filtering and Spectral Analysis*. IEEE Transactions on Audio and Electroacoustics, Vol. AU-15, June 1967.

Brigham, E. O. *The Fast Fourier Transform*. Prentice-Hall, Englewood Cliffs, N.J., 1974.

Cooley, J. W. et al. *Special Issue on Fast Fourier Transform*. IEEE Transactions on Audio and Electroacoustics, Vol. AU-17, June 1969.

Dym, H. and H. P. McKean, *Fourier Series and Integrals*, Academic Press, N.Y., 295 pp. 1972.

Winograd, S., On Computing the Discrete Fourier Transform. *Proc. Nat. Acad. Sci.* USA, Vol 73, pp. 1005-1006, 1976.

SPECTRAL ANALYSIS

Båth, Markus. *Spectral Analysis in Geophysics*. Elsevier, Amsterdam, 563 pp. 1974.

Bloomfield, Peter. *Fourier Analysis of Time Series, An Introduction*, John Wiley, N.Y., 258 pp., 1976.

Jenkins, G. M. and D. G. Watts. *Spectral Analysis and Its Applications*, Holden-Day, San Francisco, 541 pp., 1968.

Jones, R. H. Multivariate Maximum Entropy Spectral Analysis, *Proceedings of the Symposium on Applied Time Series Analysis*, Academic Press, N.Y., 1978.

Nuttall, A. H., Multivariate Linear Predictive Spectral Analysis Employing Forward and Backward Averaging: A Generalization of Burg's Method, *Naval Underwater Systems Center Technical Report 5501*, 1976.

TIME SERIES ANALYSIS

Box, G.E.P. and G. M. Jenkins. *Time Series Analysis, Forecasting and Control*. Holden-Day, San Francisco, 550 pp., 1976.

Findley, David F., *Applied Time Series Analysis*, Academic Press, N.Y., 345 pp., 1978.

Parzen, E. *Stochastic Processes*. Holden-Day, San Francisco, 335 pp., 1962.

Parzen, E. *Time Series Analysis Papers*, Holden-Day, San Francisco, 580 pp. 1967.

Robinson, Enders A. *Multichannel Time Series Analysis with Digital Computer Programs*, Holden-Day, San Francisco, 322 pp., 1967.

Rozanov, Yu. A. *Stationary Random Processes*, Holden-Day, San Francisco, 216 pp., 1967.

GEOPHYSICS

Båth, Markus. *Mathematical Aspects of Seismology*, Elsevier, Amsterdam, 415 pp., 1968.

Chen, C. H., *Computer-Aided Sysmic Analysis and Discrimination*, Elsevier, Amsterdam, 175 pp., 1978.

Claerbout, Jon F., *Fundamentals of Geophysical Data Processing*, McGraw-Hill, N.Y., 274 pp., 1976.

Dobrin, M. B. *Introduction to Geophysical Prospecting*, McGraw-Hill, N.Y., 1976.

Robinson, Enders A. and S. Treitel. *The Robinson-Treitel Reader Compiled as a Service to the Industry*, Seismograph Service Company, Tulsa, Oklahoma, Third Edition, 402 pp., 1973.

Silvia, Manuel T. and Enders A. Robinson. *Deconvolution of Geophysical Time Series in the Exploration for Oil and Natural Gas*, Elsevier, Amsterdam, 250 pp., 1979.

SPEECH

Markel, J. D. and A. H. Gray. *Linear Prediction of Speech*, Springer-Verlag, Berlin, 288 pp., 1976.

FUNCTIONS OF A COMPLEX VARIABLE

Levinson, Norman and Ray Redheffer. *Complex Variables*, Holden-Day, San Francisco, 428 pp., 1970.

Knopp, K., *Theory of Functions*, Parts I and II, Dover, N.Y., 146 pp and 150 pp, 1945 and 1947.

Answers to problems

CHAPTER V

Article 5.1

2. The plot is the function $|X(\omega)|\,|p|$, which is periodic with period $\omega = 5$.

3. When $\omega_s \geq W$. Pass $x'_p(t)$ through an ideal low-pass filter with bandwidth W.

4. $$\theta'_p(\omega) = \tan^{-1}\left(\frac{-\sum_{n=-\infty}^{\infty} A_n \sin\frac{n\omega_s p}{2}}{\sum_{n=-\infty}^{\infty} A_n \cos\frac{n\omega_s p}{2}} \right)$$

   where
   $$A_n = \frac{p}{T} \frac{\sin\frac{n\omega_s p}{2}}{\frac{n\omega_s p}{2}} X(\omega - n\omega_s)$$

5. (b) The energy in the continuous waveform is proportional to energy in the sample values.

Article 5.2

2. The minimum sampling rate is $\omega_s = 40$. No, for we can sample at any rate above the minimum.

3. $x(t)$ should be sampled at a rate $\omega_s \geq 40\pi$ rad/sec. By choosing $b = 2(2\pi 10)^2$, the filter bandwidth (defined at the -3 db point, that is, half-power point) is 10 Hz. Since this is not an *ideal* low-pass filter, we should expect some distortion in the recovered signal. However, by sampling at a very high rate we can minimize this distortion.

4. Assume that the output of the microphone is a bandlimited low-pass signal with a bandwidth of 10,000 Hz. (This is a typical spectrum for speech). Thus, the minimum sampling rate required is $\omega_s = 2\pi(20,000)$ rad/sec. The bandwidth of the filter should be about 10,000 Hz. For a 3 minute recording, 3.6×10^6 samples are required. These samples must be kept in order. If any of these samples are lost, one can expect some distortion in her song.

5. (a) $x(t) = \frac{15}{2} \cos(2\pi \cdot 500t) + \frac{5}{2} \cos(2\pi \cdot 1500t)$

    (b) 25/32

    (c) $\omega_s > 2\pi(5000)$ rad/sec. for no distortion

6. (a) $12\omega_o$ (b) $12\omega_o$

7. For $\omega_1 < \omega_o/2$, the signal $\cos\omega_1 t$ can be completely recovered.

CHAPTER VI

Article 6.1

2. (a) $H(\omega) = e^{-i(M\omega - \frac{\pi}{2})} \sum_{n=0}^{M-1} 2h_n \sin(M-n)\omega$

    where $M = \frac{N-1}{2}$

    (b) The phase-lag is a linear function of ω only over certain intervals and does not pass through the origin like the *true linear phase-lag* spectrum $\phi(\omega) = M\omega$. Further, there are discontinuities in the phase-lag spectrum. Hence, the phase-lag spectrum of an antisymmetric filter does not have a true linear phase relationship like the symmetric filters.

3. (a) $H(\omega) = 2^{N-1} \cos^{N-1} \frac{\omega}{2} e^{-i(\frac{N-1}{2})\omega}$

    (b) $|H(\omega)| = 256 \cos^8 \frac{\omega}{2}$; $\phi(\omega) = (\frac{N-1}{2})\omega$, $-\pi \leq \omega \leq \pi$

4. (a) $A(z) = z^{(N-1)}$ (all-pass system)

    (b) $\phi(\omega) = 19\omega$, $0 \leq \omega \leq \pi$ (c) zero

5. (a) $h_n = (0, 0.01, 0.08, 0.20, 0.25, 0.20, 0.08, 0.01, 0)$

    (b) $h_n = (0, 0.02, 0.08, 0.17, 0.25, 0.17, 0.08, 0.02, 0)$

Answers to problems

6. (a) $W(\omega) = \left\{ \dfrac{a\sin\dfrac{N\omega}{2}}{\sin\dfrac{\omega}{2}} + \dfrac{b}{2}\dfrac{\sin\dfrac{N}{2}(\omega-\alpha)}{\sin(\dfrac{\omega-\alpha}{2})} + \dfrac{b}{2}\dfrac{\sin\dfrac{N}{2}(\omega+\alpha)}{\sin(\dfrac{\omega+\alpha}{2})} \right\} e^{-iM\omega}$

where $\alpha = \dfrac{\pi}{M}$ and $M = \dfrac{N-1}{2}$

(b) For the Hanning window $a/b = 1$; for the Hamming window $a/b = 1.17$. In this case, the Hamming window has smaller side lobes than the Hanning window. This suggests that for $a/b > 1$ we achieve a side lobe reduction.

Article 6.2

1. (b) $|H(\omega)|^2 = \dfrac{\sum\limits_{k=0}^{N}\sum\limits_{m=0}^{k} g'_k (-1)^m \binom{k}{m} \sin\dfrac{2m\omega}{2}}{\sum\limits_{k=0}^{N}\sum\limits_{m=0}^{k} f'_k (-1)^m \binom{k}{m} \sin\dfrac{2m\omega}{2}}$

where $\binom{k}{m}$ are the binomial coefficients

2. (a) $a = \left[\sin^{2N}\dfrac{\omega_c}{2} \right]^{-1}$

(b) $|H(\pi - \omega_c)|^2 = \dfrac{1}{1 + \cot^{2N}\dfrac{\omega_c}{2}}$

(c) Under the condition $\dfrac{\omega_c}{2} \ll 1$, then

$\dfrac{1}{1 + \cot^{2N}\dfrac{\omega_c}{2}} \approx \left(\dfrac{\omega_c}{2}\right)^{2N}$

(d) $N = 4$

3. (a) $H(z) = \dfrac{\gamma(z+1)^N}{A(z)}$

Due to the Nth order zero at $z = -1$, the filter is not *strictly* minimum-delay and not invertible by definition.

(b) Let $\dfrac{1}{A(z)} = B(z) = \sum\limits_{k=0}^{\infty} b_k z^k$, then

$h_n = \gamma \sum\limits_{k=0}^{n} \binom{N}{k} b_{n-k}$, $n = 0, 1, 2, \ldots$

4. $\Delta\phi = N\pi$. No, for a minimum-delay filter we have $\phi(\pi) - \phi(-\pi) = 0$.

5. $N = 19$, $\omega_c = 0.8\pi$, $\omega_1 = 0.9\pi$

   The pole positions $z_k = x_k + iy_k$ are

   $$x_k = \frac{-8.472}{10.472 - 6.155\cos\frac{\pi}{19}k}, \quad k = 0,1,\ldots,18$$

   $$y_k = \frac{\sin\frac{\pi}{19}k}{1.701 - \cos\frac{\pi}{19}k}, \quad k = 0,1,\ldots,18$$

Article 6.3

1. $I_{min} = \sum_{n=-\infty}^{\infty} s_{n+\alpha}^2 - \sum_{k=0}^{M} h_k g_{k+\alpha}$. When $\alpha=0$ and $g_k=0$ for $k=0,1,\ldots,M$, then I_{min} is the total energy in the signal s_n.

2. For the input $x_n = (1, 0.5)$ we get the shaping filter $h_n = (0.952, 0.119)$. For the input $x_n = (0.5, 1)$ we get the shaping filter $h_n = (0.762, 0.095)$. The minimum-delay input yields the smallest mean-square error and provides a better approximation to s_n than the maximum-delay input.

3. $x_n \longrightarrow$ [spiking filter] $\longrightarrow s_n$ (desired output)

    Output of spiking filter is least-squares inverse. For $x_n = (0.5, 1)$, the desired signal could be the unit spike $s_n = (1, 0, 0)$. For this case, the least-squares inverse is $x_n^{-1} = (0.476, -0.190)$.

4. For the input $x_n = (1, 0.5)$ and $s_n = (1, 0, 0)$, we get the filter $h_n = (0.952, -0.381)$. For the input $x_n = (0.5, 1)$ and the same s_n, we get the filter $h_n = (0.476, -0.190)$. The minimum-delay input yields the smallest mean-square error and provides the best spiking result. For the desired signal $s_n = (0, 0, 1)$, the maximum-delay input provides the best spiking result.

CHAPTER VII

Article 7.1

1. $|H(\omega)| = [1 + 2a\cos\omega + a^2]^{1/2}$

2. $\phi(\omega) = \frac{1}{2\pi} P \int_{-\pi}^{\pi} \cot(\frac{\omega-\omega'}{2}) \log|H(\omega')| d\omega'$

Answers to problems

3. Let $F(\omega)$ be defined on $-\pi \leq \omega \leq \pi$, except possibly at any interior point ω_0, which is a singular point of $F(\omega)$. If

$$\int_{-\pi}^{\pi} F(\omega) d\omega \tag{1}$$

does not exist, but

$$\lim_{\varepsilon \to 0} [\int_{-\pi}^{\omega_0-\varepsilon} F(\omega) d\omega + \int_{\omega_0+\varepsilon}^{\pi} F(\omega) d\omega]$$

does exist, we call this the *Cauchy principal value* of the integral (1) and write it as

$$P \int_{-\pi}^{\pi} F(\omega) d\omega = \lim_{\varepsilon \to 0} [\int_{-\pi}^{\omega_0-\varepsilon} F(\omega) d\omega + \int_{\omega_0+\varepsilon}^{\pi} F(\omega) d\omega]$$

Article 7.2

1. $\phi(\omega) = \log\alpha \sin\omega$
2. $H_{min}(z) = 1+az$

3. (a)
$$f_n = \begin{cases} 0 & , \quad n=0,1,3,5,7,9,\ldots \\ \dfrac{(-1)^n 2^{2n-1} B_{2n}}{n(2n)!} & , \quad n=2,4,6,8,\ldots \end{cases}$$

where B_n are the *Bernoulli numbers*, that is $B_0=1$, $B_1=-\tfrac{1}{2}$, $B_2=1/6$, $B_4=-1/30$, ...

(b) $G(\omega) = \sum_{n=0}^{\infty} f_n \cos n\omega$, $\phi(\omega) = \sum_{n=0}^{\infty} f_n \sin n\omega$

Article 7.3

1. (a) 0   (b) $(-1)^{n+1} \dfrac{a^n}{n}$, $n>0$ (c) δ_{n-1}

2. $\log\alpha \, \delta_{n-1}$

3. (a) false   (b) false   (c) true   (d) false

CHAPTER VIII

Article 8.1

1. (a) $\mu = 0$, $v = 1/12$

   (b) $\phi(\omega) = 1/12$, $-\pi \leq \omega \leq \pi$

2. (a) μ_x (b) $\sigma_y^2 = \frac{1-\alpha}{1-\alpha}\sigma_x^2$

3. (a) $\phi_k = \frac{A^2}{2}\cos\omega k$; yes

   (b) $E(x_n x_{n+k}) = \frac{1}{2}[\cos k\omega - \cos(2n\omega + 2\theta + k\omega)]E(A^2)$, where $E(A^2)$ is determined from the distribution of A. In this case, $E(x_n x_{n+k})$ is not a function of k only and the process is not stationary.

Article 8.2

1. (a) $\phi_\ell = \sum_{k=1}^{\infty} a_k \phi_{\ell-k}$, $\ell = 1,2,3,\ldots$

   (b) The prediction error is a white noise process with variance

   $\phi_0 - \sum_{k=1}^{\infty} a_k \phi_k$.

   (c) $\phi_\ell = \sum_{k=1}^{N} a_k \phi_{\ell-k}$, $\ell = 1,2,\ldots,N$

   In this case, the prediction error ε_n is correlated.

CHAPTER X

Article 10.1

1. 300 m   2. minimum sampling frequency=250 Hz; at least 60,000 words x 16 bits/word

Article 10.2

1. (a) $h_n = \varepsilon_n * b_n$

   (b) The reflection coefficients are a function of the geologic layering and vary from location to location. $E_{0,N}(z)$ has no reason to be minimum-delay.

2. Since $E_{0,N}(z)$ is not necessarily minimum-delay, the system is not necessarily invertible.

Answers to problems

3. The N roots of $z^N \varepsilon_o \varepsilon_N + 1 = 0$, which are equally spaced on a circle of radius $1/|\varepsilon_o \varepsilon_N|$.

Article 10.3

2. The scale factor does not affect the solution of the normal equations.

Subject index

SUBJECT INDEX

Acoustic tube model, 360
  see also speech deconvolution, 358
Advance, 67
Aliasing, 239
  see also sampling, 232-239
All-pass systems, 210, 284, 290
  dispersive system, 212
  pure-advance system, 210
  pure-delay system, 210
  trivial system, 210
Analog signals, 232
Analytic continuation, 35, 36, 37
Analytic functions, 31
Angular frequency, 65, 70, 105, 176, 177, 178
  phasor explanation, 69
  range for digital signals, 70
Aperiodic signals, 75, 76
Arrays, 21-28, 29, 30
  amplitude pattern of, 21
  beamwidth of, 29
  definition of, 21
  phase pattern of, 21
  progressive phasing of, 28
  shading of, 29, 30
  tapered arrays, 29
Autocorrelation function, 156, 303, 310, 333
  of deterministic signals, 156
  of random processes, 303, 310, 333
  properties of, 303, 304
  relation to spectral estimation, 333
  see also serial correlation, 156
Autorecursive filter, 85, 163
  transfer function of, 164
  see also autoregressive filter
Autoregressive-moving average filter, 85, 86, 100, 114, 154, 163
  difference equation of, 85, 163
  invertibility of, 154
  schematic diagram of, 85
  transfer function of, 163
Average power, 74
Band-limited signals, 236, 240
  bandpass, 236
Bandpass filter, 182

Bartlett window, 251, 252, 253
Bessel's equality, 317
Binomial coefficients, 56
Binomial expansion, 43, 55
Binomial window, 251, 252, 253
Bit reversal, 229
Box-car window, 251, 252, 253
Butterfly operation, 230
Canonical representation, 210, 214, 290
Cauchy-Goursat theorem, 31
Cauchy-Hadamard theorem, 32, 101
Cauchy's integral formula, 31
Cauchy principal value, 281, 315
Cauchy-Riemann equations, 31
Causal filters and Taylor series, 99-120
Causal moving summation process, 303
Causal signal, 72
Causal system, 83, 84, 294, 295
  definition of, 83
  example of, 84
Chi-square distribution, 324, 332
Circle of convergence, 32
Complex conjugate, 3
Complex numbers, 1-18
  absolute value of, 4
  argument of, 8
  definition of, 2
  imaginary part of, 3
  nth root of, 11
  polar form of, 7, 8, 18
  properties of, 2-6
  real part of, 2
  rectangular form of, 7
  vector representation of, 13-16
Complex plane, 7-13
Complex variables, 1-48
  analytic functions, 31
  complex functions, 30
Confidence limits, 331
Conjugate Fourier series, 279
Contour integration, 31, 41, 45, 46
  Cauchy-Goursat theorem, 31
  Cauchy's integral formula, 31
  inverse Laplace z-transform, 133

residue theorem, 46
Convolution, 89-93
  associative property, 93
  commutative property, 90
  definition of, 90
  distributive property, 92
Covariance, 301
Cross-correlation coefficient, 271, 312
Cross-correlation function, 310
Cumulative energy, 77, 156, 157
  of a wavelet, 77
  minimum-delay, 156, 157
Cumulative distribution function, 304
  see also spectral distribution function, 304
Cut-off frequency, 255
Decimation-in-time, 229
Deconvolution, 94, 336, 358
  seismic, 336
  speech, 358
Degree of freedom, 324
Delay, 67
Delay operator, 58
  see also unit-delay operator, 58
Delaying difference operator, 55
DeMoivre's formula, 11
Deterministic signal, 76
Difference equations, 58-63
  definition of, 58
  examples of, 59, 60, 61
  general solution of, 62
Difference table, 50, 51, 53
Digital signals, 49, 66, 170, 198, 199
  classification of, 70, 71, 72
  definition of, 66
  frequency domain representation of, 170
  symmetry of, 198, 199
Divided difference, 54
  of order n, 54
Echo removal, 298
Eigenfunction, 111
Eigenvalue, 111
Energy, 72, 185, 186, 192, 317
  of a sequence, 72
  Parseval's equality, 192
  Riesz-Fischer theorem, 185, 186
  total energy, 72

Energy signal, 73
Energy spectrum, 192
Energy transfer function, 192
Ensemble, 300
Ergodic process, 303
Essential singularity, 44
Euler's formula, 18, 25
Even symmetry, 26, 198
  in real signals, 198
  of amplitude pattern, 26
Exponential function, 287
Exponential sequence, 75, 76, 109, 110
  complex, 109, 110
  real, 75, 76
Extrapolation, 51
Fast Fourier transform, 224-230
  bit reversal, 229
  butterfly operation, 230
  merging, 229
  shuffling procedure, 226, 229
Feedback coefficients, 85
Feedback polynomial, 348, 349, 350
Feedforward coefficients, 85
Feedforward polynomial, 348, 349, 350
Fibonacci numbers, 40
Filter, 85, 176, 177, 181, 182, 244
  bandpass, 182
  highpass, 181
  lowpass, 181
  moving-average, 244
  recursive, 85
  simple differentiating, 177
  simple smoothing, 176
  transversal, 182
Finite differences, 49-56
Finite Fourier transform, 217-221, 316
  definition of, 220
  two dimensional, 221
Finite-length signal, 71
First backward difference, 55
First divided difference, 49
First forward difference, 52
Fourier series, 183-186, 218, 279
  coefficients of, 186
  conjugate, 279
  relation to finite Fourier

transform, 218
Riesz-Fischer theorem, 185, 186
Fourier transform, 170-199
   definition of, 172
   inverse, 188
   of real signals, 197-199
   properties of, 188-192
   relation to Fourier series, 183-186
Frequency response, 172, 174
   relation to impulse response, 174
Frequency spectrum, 172
Gain, 283
Gaussian distribution, 324
Geologic structure, 337
Geometric series, 34, 35
Hamming window, 251, 252, 254
Hanning window, 251, 252, 254
Harmonic analysis, 316
Harmonic frequencies, 218, 220, 316
Highpass filter, 181
Hilbert transform, 276-282, 290
   and minimum-delay, 290
   derivation of, 276-282
Homogeneous equation, 62
Impulse response, 89
Inner system, 210, 215
Interpolation, 49, 50
Inverse finite Fourier transform, 221, 316
Inverse Fourier transform, 88
Inverse Laplace z-transform, 144-151
   by contour integration, 148
   by long division, 144
   by partial fractions, 145
Inverse sequence, 295
Invertibility, 153-159
   definition of, 155
   relation to minimum-delay, 156
Irrational numbers, 1
Isolated singular point, 44
Isotropic sensor, 21
Kepstrum, 276, 292, 294-297
   definition of, 292
   properties of, 294-297
Lag, 23, 175, 314
   in relation to arrays, 23
   in relation to autocorrelation, 314
   phase-lag, 175

Laplace z-transform, 24, 124-140
   bilateral definition of, 127
   generating function, 124
   inverse of, 144-151
   properties of, 133-140
   relation to engineering z-transform, 124-127
   relation to linear arrays, 24
Last break, 71
Laurent series, 35, 40-47
   convergence of, 41, 42
   Laurent's theorem, 41
   uniqueness of, 43
Lead, 23
Least squares, 268-275, 310, 312
   design of MA filters, 268
   in prediction theory, 310
   shaping filter, 271
   smoothing, 310
   spiking filter, 273
   Toeplitz normal equations, 271, 312
Legendre polynomials, 40
Linear filter, 81
Linear operator, 81
Line array, 24, 25, 26
   uniformly weighted, 25, 26
Linear systems, 81, 82, 89
   definition of, 81
   examples of, 82
   impulse response of, 89
Log power spectrum, 298
Low-pass filter, 255
Low-pass signal, 236, 240
Maclaurin series, 33, 134
Magnitude spectrum, 175, 314
Maximum-delay, 156, 157, 201-207, 213
   definition of, 156
   in canonical representation, 213
   in comparison to minimum-delay, 201-207
Maximum-phase-lag, 180
Mean value, 301
Merging, 229
Minimum-advance, 159
Minimum-delay, 156-159, 213
   and invertibility, 156-159

Subject index

and minimum-phase-lay, 201-207
canocial representation, 213
definition of, 156
front-loaded property, 157
Minimum-phase-lay, 178, 180, 201-207
example of, 179-180
Mixed-delay, 158
Modulation, 138
Moving average, 83, 85, 103, 164, 244, 245, 247, 268
filters, 244, 245, 247, 268
systems, 85, 164
Moving summation process, 303
Neighborhood of a point, 31
Neper, 283
Newton's binomial expansion, 43, 55
Newton's divided difference formula, 49
Noncausal filters and Laurent series, 121, 122
Noncausal signal, 72
Noncausal system, 83, 84
Nonlinear system, 82
Nonminimum-delay system, 202
Nonrandom signal, 76
Normal equations, 355
see also least squares
Nyquist frequency, 105, 240, 319
see also sampling theorem
Odd symmetry, 26, 198
in real signals, 198
of phase pattern, 26
Oil exploration, 336
One-sided signals to the future, 70, 71
One-sided signals to the past, 70, 71
Ordinary difference equations, 52
Outer system, 207, 215
Paley-Wiener condition, 286, 289, 314
Parseval's equality, 192
Periodic convolution, 282
Periodic signal, 75
Periodogram, 318-322, 326, 329, 330
definition of, 318
distribution of, 326, 329
of white noise, 322
specialization for real signals, 319-321
smoothing of, 330

Phase-lag, 283
Phase-lag spectrum, 175
of MA filter, 117
Phasors, 17-20, 108
fixed, 18
in communication theory, 20
moving, 18
rotating, 20, 108
Poisson's conjugate kernel, 280
Poisson's kernel, 280
Pole, 44, 45
definition of, 44
simple, 45
Power series, 32
Power signal, 74
Power spectral density, 314
Power spectrum, 298
Prediction, 308, 310, 355, 356
error, 355, 356
filter, 308
least squares theory of, 310
Quasi-polynomial, 27
Radius of convergence, 32
Random digital signal, 76
Random processes, 300-303
ensemble, 300
moving summation process, 303
stationary, 301
Random reflection model, 354
Random variables, 300-303
covariance of, 301
mean of, 301
probability density function, 300
uncorrelated, 301
Rational numbers, 1
Real numbers, 1, 6
Receiving pattern, 24, 25
Recursion formula, 349
Recursive filters, 85, 163, 259-266
AR filters, 85
ARMA filters, 85
Butterworth, 261
design of, 259, 263, 264
polynomial, 260
Recursive relation, 58
Recursive systems, 163-166
AR and ARMA, 163, 164
classes of, 166

definition of, 163
Reflection coefficient, 343, 360
  in seismic deconvolution, 343
  in speech deconvolution, 360
Reflection response, 345, 347
Region of convergence, 32
Residue, 45
Residue theorem, 46
Resonant frequency, 182
Reverberation, 353, 354
Reverse-inverse sequence, 296
Reverse sequence, 295
Riesz-Fischer theorem, 185
Sampling, 232, 239
  as a pulse modulation process, 234
  band-limited signals, 236
  sampling frequency, 235
Sampling theorem, 239, 240
  aliasing, 239
  folding frequency, 240
  Nyquist frequency, 240
  Nyquist rate, 240
Sedimentary system, 342
Seismic deconvolution, 336, 338, 354, 355, 357
  computational steps for 354, 355
  geophysical methods, 338
  inverse filtering, 357
Serial correlation, 352
Serial correlation coefficient, 73, 156
Shaping filters, 271-273
  optimum shift, 273
Shift-invarient system, 83
Signal decomposition, 276
  even and odd parts, 276
Signal enhancement, 308, 309, 310
  least squares theory of, 310
  smoothing filter, 308
  with advance, 309
  with delay, 308
Singularities, 34
Singular point, 31
Sinusoidal sequence, 69, 106
Spectral density, 305, 314
  properties of, 314
  relation to spectral distribution function, 305

spectral factorization, 314
Spectral distribution function, 304
Spectral estimation, 316, 318, 333
  periodogram, 318
  transform of autocorrelation, 333
Spectral factorization, 314
Spectrum, 172, 175
  definition of, 172
  magnitude and phase-lag, 175
Speech deconvolution, 358, 360
  acoustic tube model, 360
Spiking filters, 273
  optimum lag, 273
Stability of a signal, 71, 72, 186
  definition of, 72
  relation to Fouier transform, 186
Stability of a system, 94, 95
  definition of, 94, 95
Symmetry, 198, 199, 244, 247
  in MA filters, 244
Taylor series, 30-37
  definition of, 33
  uniqueness of, 33
Taylor's theorem, 33
Time delay of an echo, 298
Time-invariant, 83
Time-varying system, 83
Toeplitz normal equations, 271, 363
  solution of, 363-366
  Toeplitz recursion, 363-366
Toeplitz recursion 363-366
  auzillary recursion, 366
  general recursion, 366
Transfer function, 99, 100, 101, 105
  definition of, 99
  of a causal system, 100
  sinusoidal steady-state interpretation, 105
  stability of, 101
Transmission coefficient, 343
Transmission response, 345, 347, 361
  in seismic, 345
  in speech, 361
Triangle inequality, 4, 15
  geometrical interpretation, 15
Two-sided signals, 70
Unit advance operator, 54
Unit circle, 13

Unit delay operator, 54, 58, 59, 167
Unit impulse, 66
Unit phasor, 27
Unit step function, 235
Unit step sequence, 69
Unit spike, 66
Wavelets, 76, 77
  examples of, 77
  properties of, 76
Weighting coefficients, 24
White noise process, 301, 302, 322
  periodogram of, 322
Windows, 248, 249, 250, 333
  in designing MA filters, 248, 249, 250
  in spectral estimation, 333
  well-known windows, 251

Made in the USA
Monee, IL
04 June 2022